English Word-Stress

English Word-Stress

Erik Fudge
Professor of Linguistics, University of Hull

London
GEORGE ALLEN & UNWIN
Boston   Sydney

George Allen & Unwin (Publishers) Ltd,
40 Museum Street, London WC1A 1LU, UK

George Allen & Unwin (Publishers) Ltd,
Park Lane, Hemel Hempstead, Herts HP2 4TE, UK

Allen & Unwin Inc.,
9 Winchester Terrace, Winchester, Mass. 01890, USA

George Allen & Unwin Australia Pty Ltd,
8 Napier Street, North Sydney, NSW 2060, Australia

First published in 1984.

British Library Cataloguing in Publication Data

Fudge, Erik
   English word-stress.
1. English language – Text-books for foreign speakers   2. English
language – Accents and accentuation
I. Title
428′.1   PE1128
ISBN 0–04–418004–7
ISBN 0–04–418005–5 Pbk

Library of Congress Cataloging in Publication Data

Fudge, Erik C.
   English word-stress.
Includes bibliographical references and index. 1. English language –
Accents and accentuation.
I. Title.
PE1139.F8 1984   421′.6   84–6258
ISBN 0–04–418004–7
ISBN 0–04–418005–5 (pbk.)

Set in 10 on 11 point Times by Bedford Typesetters Ltd,
and printed in Great Britain by Biddles Ltd, Guildford, Surrey

To twenty-four girls called Maria (and a few others besides)

Contents

Preface

There are those treatments of English stress which consist of little more than long lists of words with an indication of the stress-pattern of each, and there are those which demand familiarity with a sophisticated theoretical apparatus and in which the theoretical aspects assume primary importance. Extreme examples of both kinds are of little use to the foreign learner who wishes to grasp the essential basis of English stress so that he or she can go on to predict the stress-patterns of new words. A good treatment from this point of view must bridge the gap between the anecdotal and the abstract, the practical and the theoretical, the lists and the principles.

My own contribution[1] to the huge volume of discussion on English word-stress sparked off by Chomsky and Halle's *The Sound Pattern of English*[2] was uncompromisingly of the second kind, and it was therefore with the greatest trepidation that I agreed to give a lecture on the topic to a group of Portuguese teachers of English[3] in Hull in 1974. I was surprised and gratified by the keen interest they showed, and was persuaded to produce some notes for them giving an outline of the principles I had put forward.

This made the idea of 'bridging the gap' seem a distinct possibility; the present book is the fruit of my efforts to turn this possibility into reality. It is aimed primarily at helping the teacher of English as a foreign or second language to understand the basic pattern of English word-stress and to communicate this understanding to his or her students. Furthermore, sufficiently motivated students should be able to teach themselves from the book, using the exercises provided. I hope, too, that the full word lists will be of use as reference material to a wide range of readers. Finally, since the book spells out in detail the proposals I made in my theoretical article (see note 1), and in one or two respects goes beyond them and modifies them, I would expect it to be of interest to scholars and students in phonetics and in linguistics.

Sections 1.1 and 1.2 are indispensable to the understanding of the book, but those who have no interest in the historical development of the understanding of English stress can omit Sections 1.3–1.5 without ill effects. Section 2 is quite straightforward, and again is of basic importance in following the argument of the book. Sections 3–5 are more detailed, but should pose no complex problems for the reader. Section 6 may be more difficult, but the reader should persevere. If Section 7 proves too indigestible, little is lost in the way of understanding the stress-system proper; on the other hand, readers who cope successfully with the content of this section should be in a position to attempt the study of some of the original sources if they are interested: M. Halle and S. J. Keyser, *English Stress*,[4] and the second chapter of Chomsky and Halle's *The Sound Pattern of English* are suggested as good places to start. Other suggestions will be found under 'Further Reading' at the end of each section.

The list of acknowledgements must begin with recognition of my mother's invaluable contribution to the finished book. On a number of occasions I was able to spend a week in exclusive and messy occupation of her kitchen table, making uninterrupted progress out of reach of the everyday demands of home and office; I think it is true to say that, without this, the book would never have been completed. A number of people saw earlier drafts of certain chapters and made helpful comments; in alphabetical order these were: Constance Cullen, George Hewitt, Nigel Vincent and Paul Werth. I would dearly love to blame them for the shortcomings of the book, but realise I haven't a hope of getting away with it. I am also grateful to all the people who kept asking 'How's the book going?'; in addition to all the above-named, I would especially like to mention Michael Bowen, Laurie Brown, Rosie Brener, Ryan Carpenter, David Hatcher, Arthur Hunter, John McKenna and Terence Waight in this connection.

Then I would like to thank those who have played a part in the printing and publishing process, especially Allen & Unwin, mentioning in particular Keith Ashfield for his encouragement, and the anonymous readers, who made some very useful and constructive suggestions. Above all in this connection I am grateful to Val Hunter for her unfailing ability to turn the roughest of rough drafts into immaculate typescript in what seems like seconds. Try as I might, with that whole battery of the writer's evil devices which include scratchings out, carets, inserts, arrows, balloons and scribbled additions, I have never succeeded in undermining her.

Finally, the writing of a book never fails to cause the author's family a modicum of protracted suffering, and the present case is no exception; even when I was not away from home writing, there were many occasions when the only sign of my presence at home was a light in the study. I thank all my family for their patience, and especially my wife for her unfailing support and encouragement.

Erik Fudge
Winchester, December 1982
Deo gratias.

Notes: Preface

1 E. C. Fudge, 'English word-stress: an examination of some basic assumptions', in D. L. Goyvaerts and G. K. Pullum (eds), *Essays on the Sound Pattern of English* (Ghent: Story-Scientia, 1975), pp. 277–323.
2 N. Chomsky and M. Halle, *The Sound Pattern of English* (New York: Harper & Row, 1968).
3 It is to this group that this book is dedicated.
4 M. Halle and S. J. Keyser, *English Stress* (New York: Harper & Row, 1971).

Introduction

1.1 What Is Stress?

Stress means essentially that one phonological element is singled out within another, longer, phonological element. *Sentence-stress* involves the picking out of one *word* or *phrase* within a *sentence*; this word or phrase is usually given special emphasis of some kind in pronunciation. Which word the speaker picks out will depend on the situation in which he finds himself, and about which he wants to inform the hearer. Thus the string of words **John hasn't arrived** can be uttered in three ways:

(1) John hasn't **arrived**.
(2) John **hasn't** arrived.
(3) **John** hasn't arrived.

The first of these might be spoken in a context where it is known that John has set out to get here, but is not yet here; the second might be uttered as a correction to someone else's assertion that John has arrived; the third might be said if John was expected to be among the people who have arrived, but is not in fact among them.

Word-stress, on the other hand, essentially picks out one *syllable* within a *word*; in English, the syllable singled out in a given word is nearly always the same one, irrespective of the context: the word **arrived**, for example, is always **arRIVED**, never **ARrived**.[1] Sometimes the syllable is picked out from a stretch which is longer than a single word: in **the postman hasn't arrived**, the word **the** normally has no stress of its own at all, and it would make sense to say that the syllable **post** is picked out of the longer stretch **the postman** rather than out of just the single word **postman**. We shall refer to such longer stretches as *stress-groups*, although other terms are in current use.[2] Word-stress also differs from sentence-stress in that the stressed syllable of a word is not always given special prominence in pronunciation; if the word is not an important one in the sentence, it is quite likely that *none* of its syllables will be emphasised. For example, let us imagine that Edward's golf style is the topic of conversation, and that Edward has just been specifically mentioned; if someone utters sentence 4, the word **Edward** is likely to show few signs of emphasis, and in that case neither of its syllables will be more prominent than the other from the point of view of its physical properties.

(4)   But I've never actually **seen** Edward playing golf.

The place where we can be most sure[3] that prominence will show is on the syllable which bears word-stress within the word which bears sentence-stress; in the examples we have had so far, the syllables concerned are (1) -**rived**, (2) **has**-, (3) **John** and (4) **seen**. The term *nuclear syllable* is used to denote this syllable, and the stress on the nuclear syllable is often referred to as *nuclear stress*.

The signs of prominence (i.e. the physical properties which signal stressed syllables, and nuclear syllables in particular) vary somewhat from language to language. Certainly, various head or hand movements are likely to accompany prominence, and this takes place in just about all languages. However, the common assumption that a stressed syllable is simply said more loudly than other syllables in the word or sentence is not completely substantiated by research. A number of experimental studies[4] have indicated that when English-speaking listeners have to determine which syllables in an utterance actually bear stress they may pay at least as much attention to pitch changes or to increased duration as they do to differences of loudness.

For example, sentence 4 above, in the stated situation, might be uttered with the pitch-pattern and time characteristics represented in Figure 1.1. The nuclear syllable **seen** is not necessarily much (if at all) louder than the rest, but it carries a very noticeable pitch movement, and is longer than any two-syllable stretch in the utterance (until the very last syllables, which tend to be prolonged in any utterance). (Note that the two syllables of **Edward** differ from each other very little in pitch and duration in this context.) This noticeable inequality in the duration of syllables is the basis of English speech-rhythm, and that of

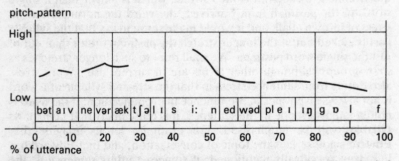

Figure 1.1   The lower half of the diagram shows the relative duration of the syllables of an utterance of sentence 4, while the upper part of the diagram indicates typical pitch movements associated with such an utterance.

a number of other languages, including German, Swedish, Persian and Mandarin Chinese.

This is in strong contrast to the rhythmic principle in languages like French, Hindi, Finnish, Cantonese and Vietnamese, in which syllables occur at approximately equal intervals of time; the rhythm of these languages is often called *syllable-timed*, for this reason. Speakers of such languages often experience particular difficulty in mastering the rhythm of the languages listed in the previous paragraph.[5] Moreover, the imposition of syllable-timed rhythm on English is probably far more detrimental to intelligibility than any distortion of vowel or consonant pronunciation, and so the effort to master the English rhythmic principle is well worth making.

To see what this principle is, we have only to look again at Figure 1.1; if we consider *stressed* syllables, we in fact find that they occur at approximately equal intervals of time.[6] Thus the beginnings of the syllables **ne-** of **never**, **ac-** of **actually**, and **seen** occur at approximately equal intervals of time. Furthermore, although the pitch evens out from **Edward** onwards, and the physical loudness of the utterance dies away over this stretch (a fact which is not shown in Figure 1.1, but which is true for most normal utterances of sentence 4 and similar sentences), yet the stressed syllables of the words after the nuclear syllable (**Ed-**, **play** and **golf**) still maintain a comparable rhythm. English, together with the other languages mentioned with it two paragraphs back, is therefore often called a *stress-timed* language, and is said to have *isochronous stress*. The lines marking the beginnings of stressed syllables in Figure 1.1 are almost like musical bar-lines from this point of view.

Stresses in a sentence which are not nuclear are usually referred to as *secondary stresses*; thus **ne-**, **ac-** and, on rhythmic grounds, **Ed-**, **play-** and **golf** in our sentence 4 have secondary sentence-stress. One respect in which word-stress is like sentence-stress is that secondary stress occurs at this level also. In the word **undenominational**, for example, the main word-stress falls on the syllable **-na-**, but other, less important, stresses fall on **un-** and **-no-**.

In some languages the place of main word-stress when a word is said in isolation may differ markedly from its place in that same word when it is part of a longer utterance. Thus the French word **charmante** is [ʃarˈmɑːt] in isolation (with final stress), but in a phrase like **une charmante petite maison** the first syllable of **charmante** is very likely to be stronger than the second.[7]

In English, however, in all cases other than those cited in note 1, the place of word-stress within the word remains constant. The best way of determining where stress will fall within a word is to hear a native speaker pronounce that word in isolation, as if it formed a one-word

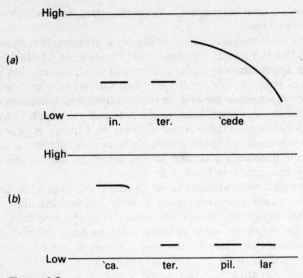

Figure 1.2

answer to a question. In this situation it forms a one-word sentence, and the nuclear stress is then bound to show up on one particular syllable, normally in terms of a falling pitch-pattern, cf. **seen** in Figure 1.1; for further examples see Figure 1.2. This is the basis for the use of the marking ' for the main stress in a word; its precise implication is that a fall occurs either *on* the syllable following it (as in case *a* of Figure 1.2) or *beginning from* the syllable following (as in case *b* of Figure 1.2).

Because English rhythm is stress-timed, a wrong stressing will lead to a wrong and misleading rhythm, even if the *principle* of stress-timing is correctly handled by the speaker. Comprehensibility depends on rhythm, and therefore the placing of stress within words can play a large part in determining how well a native English hearer will understand the foreign speaker. The problem is made much more complex by the fact that English is not a language in which stress is placed on a fixed syllable within every word (e.g. on the initial syllable as in Czech or Hungarian, or on the last but one as in Polish or Welsh). Historically, English is a blend of Germanic elements (typified basically by initial stress) and Romance elements (typified by stress on one of the last three syllables) and clearly such a blend is likely to be somewhat chaotic in its results.

There are, however, some clear and useful principles for deciding where stress falls in an English word, and this book is intended to give a full treatment of these principles, together with details of exceptions of many kinds. Our first need is for a viable notation, and this is dealt with in the next section.

1.2 The notation

The place of main word-stress in the word is indicated (as stated in 1.1 above) by placing the mark ' before the relevant syllable: 'hat, 'letter, po'sition. Secondary stresses before the main stress are indicated by placing the mark ' before the relevant syllable: en'cyclo'pedia, 'unde'nomi'national. Other syllables with a certain degree of prominence (usually reflected by a pronunciation with a full vowel rather than a reduced vowel [ə]) are indicated by placing the mark , before them: ,fan'tastic, 'for,mat, 'e,xor,cise, 'in,can'tation. In the tables which follow, 'stressed' means 'when in a syllable preceded by ', ' or ,', 'unstressed' means 'when in a syllable not marked in this way'.

Occasionally we shall use a phonetic transcription conforming to the

Table 1.1

Symbol	Keyword	Symbol	Keyword
b	boy	aɪ	mine
d	day	aɪə	tyre
dʒ	jaw, gin	æ	hat
ð	that	ɑ:	car
f	for, phone	aʊ	cow
g	go	aʊə	tower
h	hay	ɒ	hot
j	you	ʌ	hut
k	key, cow	e	pet
l	lie	eɪ	late
m	may	ɛə	where
n	no	ə	about
ŋ	sing	əʊ	go
p	pie	ɜ:	bird
r	ray	i:	see
s	see, cite	ɪ	hit
ʃ	show	ɪə	hear
t	toe	ɔ:	saw
tʃ	chew	ɔɪ	boy
θ	thin	u:	too
v	view	ʊ	push
w	way	ʊə	tour
z	zoo, ease		
ʒ	leisure		

Table 1.2

	Combined with following r		Not followed by r	
	Stressed	*Unstressed*	*Stressed*	*Unstressed*
a	[ɑː(r)]	[ə(r)]	[æ]	[ə]
	ˈstar, ˈstarry	ˈpolar, ˈbinary	ˈbat	Aˈmerica
e†	[ɜː(r)]	[ə(r)]	[e]	[ə]
	conˈfer,	ˈafter,	ˈbet	ˈwoollen
	conˈferring	ˈalteˈration		
i	[ɜː(r)]	[ə(r)]	[ɪ]	[ɪ]
	ˈstir, ˈstirring	ˈextir,pate	ˈbit	ˈrabbit
o	[ɔː(r)]	[ə(r)]	[ɒ]*	[ə]
	ˈstore, ˈstorage	ˈfactory	ˈpot	ˈrandom
u	[ɜː(r)]	[ə(r)]	[ʌ]	[ə]
	ˈfur, ˈfurry	ˈconurˈbation	ˈbut	ˈminus
y	[ɜː(r)]	[ə(r)]	[ɪ]	[ɪ]
	ˈmyrrh	ˈmartyr	ˈpyx	ˈcity

* 'Short' **o** in most varieties of American English is pronounced [ɑː] or [ɔː], phonetically on a par with the long vowels rather than the short ones.

† Word-final **e** is unpronounced. It often has the effect of lengthening the vowel before it, if this is stressed: ˈhope [həʊp], ˈtape [teɪp].

system used by Gimson in his *Introduction to the Pronunciation of English* (London: Edward Arnold, 3rd edn, 1980) (and in the latest editions of Daniel Jones's *English Pronouncing Dictionary* (London: Dent, 14th edn, 1977)); such representations will appear within square brackets, as in [ˈɪn,kænˈteɪʃn]. A key to this transcription system is given in Table 1.1. Thus our transcriptions will almost always represent varieties of the RP type (Standard Southern British English); other varieties (notably American) may be transcribed sporadically, though no systematic attention will be given to vowels and consonants

Table 1.3

	Pronunciation	Examples
ă	[æ]	ˈcărry, aˈspăragus, ˈănalogue
ĕ	[e]	ˈshĕrry, teˈmĕrity, ˈcrĕdit
ĭ	[ɪ]	ˈstĭrrup, ˈlĭver
ŏ	[ɒ]	ˈsŏrry, ˈhŏnest
ŭ	[ʌ]	ˈhŭrry, ˈpŭnish
ў	[ɪ]	ˈlуric, ˈanaˈlуtic

The mark ˘ appears only in stressed syllables, and is accompanied by no difference in pronunciation before a following **r**.

Table 1.4

	Combined with following r	Not followed by r
ā	[ɛə(r)] 'stāre, 'stāring	[eɪ] 'pāper
ē	[ɪə(r)] 'hēre, re'vēring	[iː] 'scēne, 'ēvil
ī	[aɪə(r)] 'fīre, 'wīry	[aɪ] 'bīte, 'īvy
ō	(Not distinct from unmarked **o** in this context)	[əʊ] 'wrōte, 'tōken, 'vetō
ū stressed	[jʊə(r)] 'pūre, 'fūrious	[juː] 'tūne, 'mūsic
ū unstressed	[jə(r)] 'penūry	[jə] 'regūlar
ȳ	[aɪə(r)] 'bȳre, 'tȳre	[aɪ] 'Hȳde, 'cȳcle, 'al,lȳ

in these varieties. On the other hand, where American stressings differ from British, this will always be explicitly stated.

Often the spelling of a word gives sufficient indication of how it is pronounced, provided that some fairly general conventions are understood (for example, that the ending **-tion** is usually pronounced [ʃn]). Where further guidance is called for, we adopt one of two solutions:

(a) The addition of diacritic marks (see below for a full description);
(b) The use of hybrid 'semi-phonetic' representation, sometimes appearing within slant lines: thus **pharmacopoeia** is assigned the representation /farmăkŏpēa/.

The remainder of this section deals with the system of diacritics which we use both in 'semi-phonetic' representations and in normal spellings of words to indicate exact pronunciation. Unmarked single vowels indicate the 'short' pronunciation of the letter concerned, as in Table 1.2. Where there is a need to emphasise that a vowel is short rather than long, the short mark ˘ may be used: Table 1.3 gives details. The macron ¯ means that the vowel has its long pronunciation, as

Table 1.5

	Combined with following r	Not followed by r
ä	(Not distinct from unmarked **a** in this context)	[ɑː] 'dräma, ‚ä'men
ë	[ɪ] ë'rase	[ɪ] ca'tastrophë, ë'quip, 'nuclëus
ï	[ɪə(r)] na'dïr	[iː] ma'chïne
ö	[ɜː] 'wörd	[ʌ] 'cöver
ü	[ʊə(r)] 'lürid	[uː] 'jübi‚lee

shown in Table 1.4. The double-dot diacritic ¨ has no systematic meaning of its own: the implications of its combinations with the various vowel letters are seen from Table 1.5. Notice that ä and ï are long, ü is long phonetically but may count as short, and ë and ö are short; also that ë normally occurs in unstressed syllables, ä and ï in stressed syllables only, and ö and ü in both stressed and unstressed syllables.

For most RP-type varieties, a letter r occurring after a vowel merges with the vowel, usually affecting its quality; a consonant sound [r], however, occurs only when the sound following the r is a vowel (either in the same word, or the initial sound of the next word). Even when the sound [r] does not occur, the written r needs to be taken into account as a consonant letter in determining the phonological structure of the word containing it. Most American varieties, on the other hand, together with Scots and Irish varieties, and the speech of many speakers from south-western England, have r after a vowel pronounced as a retroflex approximant after all vowels.

A combination of vowel letters sometimes indicates a vowel sound which forms the centre of a single syllable. Table 1.6 shows how vowel sequences of this kind should be pronounced when no diacritics are present, while Table 1.7 gives those combinations with diacritics which commonly occur as centres of a single syllable. All vowel sequences not mentioned in either of these tables represent centres of two distinct

Table 1.6

2nd element	1st element a-	e-	o-
-a		=ē	=ō
	[ɑ:] 'Saar	[i:] 'beat	[əʊ] 'boat
		[ɪə] 'rear	[ɔ:] 'soar
-e	=ā	=ē	=ō
	[eɪ] 'brae	[i:] 'beet	[əʊ] 'toe
	[ɛə] 'aeroplane	[ɪə] 'beer	
-i, -y	=ā	=ā	
	[eɪ] 'aim, 'day	[eɪ] 'rein, 'grey	[ɔɪ] 'coin, 'boy
	[ɛə] 'air	[ɛə] 'heir	
-o	—	=ë	
		[e] 'leopard	[ʊ] 'good
-u, -w		=ü*	
	[ɔ:] 'sauce, 'lawn	[juː] 'few, 'neuter	[aʊ] 'cloud, 'down
		[jʊə] 'neural	[aʊə] 'flour

* Replaced by ü after r, l, ch, j, s, z (and after t, d, n in some American varieties): crew, pleurisy, chew, jewel, sewer, (dew, neuter).

Table 1.7

	Combined with following r	Not followed by r
äu		[ɑu] 'säuerkräut
eā	[ɛə(r)] 'beăr, 'beāring	[eɪ] steāk
ĕa	[ɜ:] sĕarch	[e] brĕad
ēi	[ɪə] wēird	[i:] sēize, re'cēive
ëy		[ɪ] 'donkëy
iē	[ɪə(r)] piēr	[i:] shriēk
īe	[aɪə(r)] flīer	[aɪ] līe
ōō	[ʊə(r)] 'bōōrish	[u:] fōōd
oü	[ʊə(r)] toür, 'toüring	[u:] woünd ('injury')
öu	[ə(r)] 'laböurer	[ʌ] 'döuble stressed [ə] 'grievöus unstressed
ōw		[əu] lōw
uā	[wɛə(r)] 'squāre, 'squāring	[weɪ] per'suāde
üe		[ju:] 'valüe
üe		[u:] trüe
uï		[wi:] suïte
üi	[jʊə(r)] Müir	[ju:] 'nüisance
üi		[u:] früit

syllables (e.g. hīātus [ˌhaɪ.'eɪ.təs], musēum [ˌmju:.'zi:.əm], where a single dot represents a boundary between two syllables), with the following exceptions:

   (a) ia, ie and io (without diacritics) become monosyllabic when *both* the following conditions hold:
      (i)   They are preceded by c, g, s, t, or x;
and (ii)   No stress is placed on the a, e or o.
When this happens, preceding c, s, t, and x become palato-alveolar in pronunciation and usually coalesce with the i. Thus in Christian both conditions are fulfilled, and the pronunciation is ['krɪs.tjən] or ['krɪs.tʃən] with two syllables; in Christianity main stress falls on the a, violating condition (ii), and the pronunciation is therefore ['kris.tɪ.'æ.nɪ.tɪ]. The word previous is normally pronounced with three syllables, as it does not meet condition (i).

   (b) ua may be monosyllabic when *both* the following conditions are satisfied:
      (i)   The a is part of the suffix -al;
and (ii)   No stress is placed on the a.
When this happens, preceding d, s, t, or x *may* become palato-alveolar. Thus individual may be pronounced ['ɪn.dɪ.'vɪ.djʊ.əl] or

['ɪn.dɪ.'vɪ.djʊl] or ['ɪn.dɪ.'vɪ.dʒʊl], whereas in **individuality** condition (ii) is violated, and the only possible pronunciations are ['ɪn.dɪ.ˌvɪ.djʊ.'æ.lɪ.tɪ] or ['ɪn.dɪ.ˌvɪ.dʒʊ.'æ.lɪ.tɪ].

1.3   Kingdon's Innovations

We next proceed to the study of the main essentials of some other approaches to the question of English stress. 'The field of English word stress is practically virgin soil,' claims Kingdon (*Groundwork of English Stress*, 1958, p. xii), 'it having been generally held that it follows no rules.' In fact his investigations showed that there were a number of principles that could be stated, and that the main problems arose from what he referred to as 'compounds'. He distinguishes three types of these:

    (i) 'Romanic' – consisting of root plus affixes;

    (ii) 'Greek' – consisting of root plus root, where the roots are not able to stand on their own as complete words;

    (iii) 'English' – consisting of root plus root, where the roots are independent words.

The great contribution of Kingdon's work is to show how suffixes affect stress-placement in Romanic-type compounds, and how the final root of a Greek-type compound exerts the greatest influence in that type of word. He demonstrates, furthermore, that in many cases the suffix or the final root can have only one possible effect on the overall stress pattern: the suffix -**ity** always causes stress to be placed one syllable back in the word, while the ending -**metric** invariably attracts stress on to its own first syllable. In fact just over one-third of the book is devoted to a listing of suffixes of Romanic-type compounds and elements of Greek-type compounds.

A number of ways suggest themselves in which Kingdon's conclusions might be refined and strengthened. First, he does not distinguish 'strong' and 'weak' syllables; a number of common affixes cannot be accounted for without this distinction. He claims, for instance, that -**al** 'is too weak to show a definite stress habit when it is added directly to a root' (p. 64), whereas the pattern is quite clear once the 'strong'/'weak' distinction is established (cf. p. 21 below). Second, he does not explicitly recognise that an affix which normally places stress two syllables back will inevitably place stress one syllable back if there are not two syllables there, and that therefore this does not constitute a separate pattern of stress assignment. Third, the part played by individual suffixes in combinations of suffixes is never sorted out; thus the stress effects of the ending -**metric** (see previous paragraph) can be accounted for in terms of the properties of the single affix -**ic**.

1.4 The approach of Chomsky and Halle

In *The Sound Pattern of English* (1968), Chomsky and Halle aim to show that it is possible to predict where stress will fall in an English word on the basis of two types of information:

(a) The segmental make-up of the word, i.e. whether particular vowels are long or short ('tense' or 'lax' in their terms), and whether consonants occur singly or in sequences of more than one. Each word is divided into 'clusters', i.e. sequences beginning with a vowel and ending immediately before the next vowel, or at the end of the word if there are no further vowels. The difference between 'weak clusters' (which consist of a short vowel followed by at most one consonant) and 'strong clusters' (short vowel followed by two or more consonants, or long vowel followed by any number of consonants) is crucial in determining certain differences in stress-placement.

(b) The internal structure of the word, i.e. whether the word can be divided into smaller parts, and what relations hold between the various parts. Chomsky and Halle reject Kingdon's 'suffix-based' approach as unnecessary; they assert that their rules account directly for stress-placement without the need for classifying suffixes as 'placing stress two syllables back' or the like. Instead they invoke the principle of the 'cycle': certain rules apply in order, first to the root, then over again to the next larger constituent, and so on until the boundaries of the word are reached. Thus in **theatricality**, the rules apply first to **theatre** (the root of the word) giving primary stress on the first syllable: **théatre**; then to **theatrical**, giving primary stress on the antepenultimate syllable, and weakening the primary stress on the **e** to secondary: **thèátrical**; and finally to **theatricality**, giving primary stress on the antepenultimate syllable and weakening the other stresses by one degree: **thèátricálity**.

I have incorporated the 'strong v. weak' distinction into the present work in the slightly different form 'strong syllable v. weak syllable' (see Section 2.2). There is no doubt that some such distinction is indispensable. Another feature of the Chomsky and Halle proposals which I have adopted (with modifications) is the set of rules for lengthening short vowels in certain contexts, shortening long vowels in others, and for applying vowel reduction. These rules account for alternations such as those affecting the vowel of the root in **explain** [eɪ], **explanatory** [æ] and **explanation** [ə] (see Section 7).

On the other hand I have not followed Chomsky and Halle's thoroughgoing use of the cyclic principle (restricting its applicability in effect to certain combinations of suffixes – see Section 4.5), nor have I rejected Kingdon's 'suffix-based' approach: from a practical point of view, it makes a great deal of sense to remember the stress patterns of words in terms of the properties of endings like **-ity**, **-ology**, etc.

1.5   The Work of Paul Garde

In addition to his work with Chomsky on stress in English, Halle has done extensive work on the corresponding features of the Slavic language-group. Interestingly, another very stimulating approach to stress has come from the pen of another Slavicist, the French scholar Paul Garde. In his fairly short but substantial book *L'Accent* (1968), and in a number of articles, he has outlined a method of assigning word-stress in languages with 'free stress' (i.e. languages in which there are no rules specifying that stress is *always* initial, etc.). The basis of this method is to consider the *accentual properties* of each morpheme, which in general are twofold:

(a) Every morpheme (i.e. prefix, root or suffix) in such a language has its *place of stress*, i.e. the propensity to place stress in a certain position in the word. Thus, some attract stress on to themselves, others place stress one syllable after them, others cause stress to fall on the first syllable of the word they occur in, and so on.

(b) There is a hierarchy of *accentual strength* of morphemes, i.e. certain morphemes have the power to impose their 'place of stress' on the other morphemes in the word they occur in.

My own approach to English stress owes a great deal to this. As far as English is concerned, aspect (b) of the matter is relatively simple: it is the last suffix in the word (ignoring inflections and a few other suffixes) that imposes its properties on the word (see Section 4 below). If there are no suffixes, then a different principle operates (see Section 3); stress falls on the last syllable but one of the word, or the last but two, depending on properties of the various syllables (and not those of morphemes). There are exceptions to this principle, most of them finally stressed.

Aspect (a) of Garde's approach, on the other hand, is much more complex for English than is aspect (b), so much so that I use the term *accentual properties* almost as being synonymous with Garde's 'place of stress'. The accentual properties of English morphemes (especially suffixes) need to be stated in considerable detail. For some suffixes, several different principles of stress-assignment need to be recognised (see Appendix 4.1). It is clearly such properties that Kingdon was aiming to state in his *Groundwork* (see Section 1.3), and, like him, I have devoted a great deal of space to a statement of them.

Notes: Section 1

1 There are two types of exception to this principle:

   (*a*) Cases where the word was not properly perceived by the hearer ('I said *ar*rived not *de*rived');

   (*b*) Certain types of phrase require a shift in word-stress in one of their components – this matter is discussed in detail in Section 5.3 below.

2 Such terms include 'phonological word' as used by Chomsky and Halle in *The Sound Pattern of English*.

3 Experiments have shown that in a sentence as actually spoken it quite often happens that no syllable shows the physical properties normally associated with prominence.

4 For example, D. B. Fry, 'Experiments in the perception of stress', *Language and Speech*, vol. 1, (1958), pp. 126–52.

5 See C. Adams, *English Speech Rhythm and the Foreign Learner* (The Hague: Mouton, 1979), p. 87.

6 The actual timings are affected by other factors (number of syllables occurring between stressed syllables, number of sounds in each syllable, etc.).

7 See L. E. Armstrong, *The Phonetics of French* (London: Bell, 1932), pp. 140–1, 'Emphasis for Intensity'. The word 'intensity' is used by Armstrong and many other writers on French phonetics to denote affective or emotional intensity, but it must be noted that such shifts of stress placement in French occur in many contexts where this kind of factor is not present. Thus in such phrases as **l'année dernière**, 'last year', stress most often falls on the *first* syllable of **année**, even when there is no emphasis on the phrase.

Exercises

1 Transcribe the following words phonetically, using Gimson's notation:

   (*a*) let, (*b*) thick, (*c*) ball, (*d*) grace, (*e*) home, (*f*) wash, (*g*) write, (*h*) right, (*j*) through, (*k*) though, (*l*) thought, (*m*) power, (*n*) cheese, (*o*) ginger, (*p*) finger.

2 What diacritics would need to be added to the spelling of the following words in order to specify the pronunciation given?

   (*a*) 'ar‚row ['æ‚rəu]   (*g*) ‚Lou'ise [‚lu:'i:z]

   (*b*) 'borough ['bʌrə]   (*h*) 'oven ['ʌvən]

   (*c*) 'breakfast ['brekfəst]   (*j*) re'frige‚rator [rɪ'frɪdʒə‚reɪtə]

   (*d*) ‚ca'shier [‚kæ'ʃɪə]   (*k*) 'staff ['stɑːf]

   (*e*) de'fy [dɪ'faɪ]   (*l*) 'suitable ['suːtəbl]

   (*f*) 'granular ['grænjələ]   (*m*) 'suitable ['sjuːtəbl]

3 Divide the following set of words into three categories:

   (*a*) Those for which the spelling predicts the pronunciation with no need for stress marks or diacritics;

    (*b*)   Those for which the spelling would predict the pronunciation with the introduction of appropriate stress marks and/or diacritics (state the diacritics needed in each such case);

    (*c*)   Those for which the pronunciation cannot be predicted from the spelling even if stress marks and diacritics are added (suggest if you can a hybrid representation which would predict the pronunciation in each case).

(i)	bleak	(x)	honest	(xix)	rush
(ii)	both	(xi)	lamb	(xx)	sour
(iii)	calculate	(xii)	make	(xxi)	suet
(iv)	camomile	(xiii)	nitric	(xxii)	through
(v)	door	(xiv)	plough	(xxiii)	trail
(vi)	enormous	(xv)	prove	(xxiv)	tread
(vii)	freezing	(xvi)	pseudonym	(xxv)	trough
(viii)	great	(xvii)	pseudonymous	(xxvi)	volcanic
(ix)	growl				

Further Reading

1.1   What Is Stress?

The classic work on the physical cues which English hearers use to determine the place of stress is D. B. Fry's article, 'Experiments in the perception of stress', *Language & Speech*, vol. 1, 1958, pp. 126–52; also reprinted in D. B. Fry (ed.), *Acoustic Phonetics: a Course of Basic Readings* (Cambridge: Cambridge University Press, 1976), pp. 401–24. A more accessible summary of Fry's findings is given by A. C. Gimson, *An Introduction to the Pronunciation of English*, 3rd edition (London: Edward Arnold, 1980), pp. 221–6.

Some more recent treatments of stress may be found in L. M. Hyman (ed.), *Studies in Stress and Accent* (Los Angeles: University of Southern California Linguistics Department, 1977). The papers by Hyman himself (pp. 37–82), J. J. Ohala (pp. 145–68) and L. Nessly (pp. 121–44) are of particular interest.

The rhythm of English speech is dealt with by K. L. Pike in *The Intonation of American English* (University of Michigan Press, 1945) and D. Abercrombie, 'Syllable quantity and enclitics in English', in D. Abercrombie *et al.*, *In Honour of Daniel Jones* (London: Longman, 1964), pp. 216–22, also reprinted in D. Abercrombie, *Studies in Phonetics and Linguistics* (London: Oxford University Press, 1965), pp. 26–34. A more specialised treatment (though one which is concerned particularly with the problems of the non-native speaker) is to be found in C. M. Adams, *English Speech Rhythm and the Foreign Learner* (The Hague: Mouton, 1979).

1.2   The Notation

The phonetic transcription used is that of Gimson (*An Introduction to the*

Pronunciation of English, pp. 93–4, 151–2), which is also that of the latest editions of D. Jones's *English Pronouncing Dictionary* (London: Dent, 14th edn, 1977). The standard work for American pronunciation is still J. S. Kenyon and T. A. Knott *A Pronouncing Dictionary of American English* (Springfield, Mass: Merriam, 1944); this uses a rather different transcription system.

The system of diacritics which we apply in this book to orthographic forms to indicate how they are pronounced is similar, but not identical, to that used in the *Concise Oxford Dictionary*.

1.3 Kingdon's Innovations

R. Kingdon *The Groundwork of English Stress* (London: Longman, 1958) is relatively easy reading, and needs no commentary; slightly more detailed from the historical point of view, though less complete as a work of reference, is O. Jespersen, *A Modern English Grammar on Historical Principles* (London: Allen & Unwin) Part I (1909), Chapters V and IX; and Part VI (1942).

1.4 The Approach of Chomsky and Halle

The basic work is N. Chomsky and M. Halle, *The Sound Pattern of English* (New York: Harper & Row, 1968); Chapters 2 and 3 relate to the topic of stress. This is not an easy book. Chapter I of M. Halle and S. J. Keyser, *English Stress: its Form, its Growth, and its Role in Verse* (New York: Harper & Row, 1971) gives a rather simpler and clearer exposition of the matter, though at the same time it must be noted that the approach has been modified at a number of points.

The Sound Pattern of English generated a great deal of specialist discussion, much of which is represented in the book *Essays on the Sound Pattern of English* (Ghent: Story-Scientia, 1975), edited by D. L. Goyvaerts and G. K. Pullum. As well as four detailed reviews of the whole book (each with something of interest to say about the question of word-stress assignment), this contains several articles specifically on English stress, including a further modified version of the original proposals (M. Halle, 'Stress rules in English: a new version', pp. 261–76), and the theoretical article on which much of the practical approach of our present book is based (E. C. Fudge, 'English word-stress, an examination of some basic assumptions', pp. 277–323). One important critical article not included in these *Essays* is J. R. Ross, 'A re-analysis of English word-stress: part I', in M. K. Brame (ed.), *Contributions to Generative Phonology* (Austin, Texas: University of Texas Press, 1972), pp. 229–323.

For those who read French, there is an invaluable work which combines a theoretical treatment of English stress with word lists of rather more practical value, and that is L. Guierre, *Essai sur l'accentuation en anglais contemporain* (Paris: Université de Paris VII, 1979).

Finally, a highly influential new development in stress-assignment is to be found in M. Liberman and A. Prince, 'On stress and linguistic rhythm', *Linguistic Inquiry*, vol. 8 (1977), pp. 249–336.

1.5   The Work of Paul Garde

P. Garde, *L'Accent* (Paris: Presses Universitaires de France, 1968) says rather less about English than a number of other languages, but is to date the author's most complete treatment of stress. Those who do not read French will prefer to read the briefer treatment in Garde's translated article, 'Principles of the synchronic description of stress', in E. C. Fudge (ed.), *Phonology* (Harmondsworth: Penguin Books, 1973), pp. 309–19.

Preliminaries

2.1 General Outline of the Approach

In principle, the method consists in counting back a number of syllables from the end of a certain part of the word. We will refer to that part of the word as the *stressable portion* (or SP). The SP is what is left of the word when certain suffixes and prefixes have been removed from it. These suffixes and prefixes include:

(a) All inflectional suffixes:
    (nouns) plural **-s**, **-es**, possessive **-'s**, **-s'**, **-es'**;
    (verbs) 3rd person singular **-s**, **-es**, past **-ed**, past participle **-ed**, **-en**, present participle **-ing**.
(b) A number of derivational suffixes (many of them highly productive);
    (nouns) **-ness**;
    (adjectives) **-y** (**-i-** when not word-final), **-ly** (**-li-**), **-less**;
    (adverbs) **-ly**, **-wise**. (For a full list of these suffixes see Sections 4.1 and 4.5.)
(c) A number of derivational prefixes, notably the negative prefixes **un-**, **in-** (**im-**, etc.). (For a full list see Section 6.1.)

Examples

The parenthesised portions of the words shown below are excluded from the SP. The boundaries of roots and affixes are shown by the sign + (see below, Section 2.3):

    ordin+anc (+es)
    clar+ify (+ing)
    (im+) practic+abil+ity
    specul+at+ive (+ly)
    (un+) man (+li) (+ness)

In cases like the following, the SP is identical with the whole word:

    hullabaloo
    republic+an
    equi+voc+at+ion

The next step depends on the structure of the SP.

1   If the SP is monosyllabic, there is no choice of stress-placement: the single syllable receives stress:

> 'ship
> 'eat (+ing)
> (un+) 'man (+li) (+ness)

2   If the SP contains one or more suffixes, then the last suffix determines how main stress is placed – see Sections 4.2, 4.3 and 4.4 for more details. It should be noted that some endings which are not strictly suffixes act like suffixes in the assignment of stress.

Examples

> re'al+ity (since -**ity** causes main stress to be placed one syllable back into the stem)
> 'com+pens+ate (since -**ate** causes main stress to be placed two syllables back into the stem)
> millio'n+aire (since -**aire** attracts stress on to the syllable containing it)
> hullaba'loo (since the ending -**oo** has accentual effects comparable with those of a suffix – it attracts stress on to the syllable containing it)

If the SP contains two or more suffixes, the suffix before the last often influences the placement of secondary stress (see Section 4.5).

Examples

> e'qui+vo'c+at+ion (secondary stress applied by the properties of -**ate**: two syllables back from main stress)
> fa'mili+'ar+ity (secondary stress applied by the properties of -**ar**: for details see pp. 46–8)

3   If the SP is polysyllabic but contains no prefixes or suffixes, main stress will normally be placed according to the principles given for simple roots in Section 3. There are exceptions, such as **hullabaloo** (see preceding paragraph), **Japan**; nearly all of these are finally stressed.

4   If the SP contains no suffixes, but does contain at least one prefix, the rules of Section 3 may be modified as shown in Section 6.

Examples

> per+'mit (verb – the prefix **per-** does not take stress in verbs, except by the 'suffix' rule as in 'per+col+ate)
> 'per+mit (noun – in nouns the prefix **per-** is stressable by the rules of Section 3)

2.2 Words and Syllables

From the foregoing it is obvious that the reader needs to be able to recognise the syllables into which an English word is to be split up. Furthermore, it is important to know not only how many syllables there are but also exactly where the syllable boundaries are to be placed; this is so because stress-placement is often dependent on the number of sounds occurring in a particular position within a syllable. In what follows we shall designate syllable boundaries by the sign ., thus: *win.dow*, *ath.lete*.

Syllables in general consist of:

(a) A vowel portion, which we shall say occupies the *peak* of the syllable. In many languages there are times when, phonetically speaking, the peak is occupied not by a vowel but by some consonant (most commonly this is a nasal (**m**, **n**, etc.) or a liquid (**l**, **r**, etc.), but in some languages fricatives may act in this way). Thus, in the English word **sudden**, the **e** is not normally pronounced, and the **n** becomes the peak of the second syllable (from a purely phonetic point of view): [sʌ.dn]. For phonological purposes, however, including stress-assignment, it is better to treat that syllable of the word as if it contained a vowel; we would thus syllabify *sudden* at this level as /su.den/, or perhaps /sud.den/. In many cases this vowel is shown in the spelling of an English word, and occurs in the place where the syllabification requires it. The main exception is the case of the ending -**le**, as in **ample**. It is best to think of this as having the basic shape /el/ rather than /le/ so that the phonological form of **ample** would be /am.pel/. The suffixes -**able**, -**ible**, -**uble** have the phonological forms /a.bil/, /i.bil/, /ū.bil/ respectively, cf. **probable – probability**, **visible – visibility**, **soluble – solubility**.

(b) A string of consonants occurring before the peak: we shall call this the *onset* of the syllable. In English this string may contain as many as three members (as for instance **str-** in the word **string** itself), and as few as zero members (as in words like **up**, **ice**).

(c) A string of consonants occurring after the peak: we shall call this the *coda* of the syllable. In English this string may contain one, two, three, or, occasionally, four members (as in **sixths**, which is phonologically /siksθs/), and again may be empty (as in **see**, **low**, and in both syllables of **coda**). A syllable with an empty coda is called an *open syllable*, while a syllable with at least one consonant in the coda is called a *closed syllable*.

The following principles operate in determining the extent of each syllable and in placing syllable-boundaries in English words.

1 In general, for words considered singly (as they have to be for stress-assignment), every word-boundary can be taken as also forming a syllable-boundary. This situation may not hold in connected speech,

however, where consonants at the end of a word may be carried over to the syllable beginning the next word. Thus, in English, **at all** is usually syllabified [ə.'tɔ:l]; in such cases we might say that a word-boundary has been suppressed (so that **at all** is treated in connected speech as being a single word).

2   If a consonant cluster within a word can be divided into two parts, such that the first is a possible word-final cluster and the second is a possible word-initial cluster, then a syllable-boundary may be placed between these two parts.

Examples

> **ath.lete** but not **a.thlete**, since **thl-** is not a permitted word-initial cluster, and not **athl.ete**, since **-thl** is not a permitted word-final cluster.
>
> **ob.struct** but not **o.bstruct**, since **bstr-** is not a permitted word-initial cluster, and not **obs.truct** or **obst.ruct** or **obstr.uct**, since these all exhibit non-permitted word-final clusters (the word-final spelling **-bs** as in **jobs**, in fact represents /-bz/, not /-bs/).

3   Sometimes alternatives are possible, especially where sequences of **s** plus consonant occur in the middle of a word. The pronunciation may indicate one permissible syllable division as being preferable to another. As a general rule, stressed syllables tend to attract consonants more than unstressed ones. Such criteria do not necessarily coincide with the conventions for the division of words in printed English.

Examples

> **roos.ter** is to be preferred to **roo.ster**, since the length of the **oo** vowel is comparable with that of **loose** rather than that of **moo**. The **s** belongs to the stressed syllable.
>
> **mi.stake** is to be preferred to **mis.take**, since the pronunciation of the **t** is more like the **t** of **stake** than the **t** of **take**. Again, the **s** belongs to the stressed syllable. For further instances, see comments on **-cratic** in Appendix 4.1 and on the Strong Initial Syllable Rule in Section 7.2.3.

4   A single consonant between two vowels is normally taken as being the onset of the syllable containing the following vowel.

Examples

ba.con	(even though the first syllable is stressed and [beɪk] is a possible syllable)
com.pe.ti.tive	(even though the second syllable is stressed and [pet] is a possible syllable)

5 A doubled consonant between two vowels is normally pronounced single, unless one of the identical consonants is within the SP and the other outside it, as in (**un**)**natural** [ˌʌnˈnætrəl], **mean**(**ness**) [ˈmiːnnəs]. For this purpose **ck** counts as doubled **k**, **tch** as doubled **ch**, and **dg** as doubled 'soft' **g** ([dʒ]). However, there are times when such doubled consonants act as two consonants for stress-assignment purposes. For example, the stressings **Kenˈtucky**, **toˈbacco**, **Caˈmilla** require the penultimate syllable to be closed: /ken.tʌk.ki/, /to.bak.ko/, /ka.mil.la/. The phonological forms /ken.tʌ.ki/, /to.ba.ko/, /ka.mi.la/, with short vowels in the penultimate syllable, would lead to antepenultimate stress: [ˈkentəkɪ] [ˈtɒbəkəʊ] [ˈkæmɪlə] (for details, see Section 3.1).

6 Exceptions to the principle stated in 2 above may occur. The most frequent case is a medial syllable with a short vowel and no coda. Such syllables cannot occur word-finally if they are stressed (a stressed word-final vowel has to be long).

Example
    com.ˈpe.ti.tive [kəmˈpetɪtɪv], even though [.pe.] is not a possible word-final stressed syllable.

Sometimes the spelling of a word obscures the syllabic division. The letter **x**, for example, usually represents the sound sequence [ks] or [gz], and the syllable boundary often comes in the middle of this sequence. Thus **example** is /eg.zäm.pel/, and **extraction** is /ek.strak.ʃon/. Obviously when stress marks are applied to the orthographic form of such words they cannot indicate such boundaries properly. The convention we adopt in this book is to write **eˈxample** (where **x** is followed by a vowel) with the stress before **x** (in some kind of conformity with principle 4 above), but **exˈtraction** (where **x** is followed by a consonant) with the stress after **x** (since that would be a possible syllabification under principle 2).

Syllabic division should, of course, strictly be carried out with reference to a phonemic representation (one which shows the systematic features of pronunciation); in many cases, though, it is not misleading to syllabify orthographic forms (as we have been doing in this section).

Another very important distinction, which operates in a large number of languages, is that of *syllable strength* (sometimes called *syllable weight*). The structural details may differ from one language to another, but the basic principle is that the peak and coda of a weak syllable contain less material than those of a strong syllable. In English, a *weak syllable* is defined as one with a short vowel peak and no coda with, for word-final syllables, the additional possibility of a one-consonant coda. The word **oblivious**, for instance, consists of four weak syllables: /ŏblĭ.vĭ.ŏs/. A *strong syllable* is a syllable of any other type; it may contain a long vowel, in which case the content of the coda is immaterial: thus, **trainee** consists of two strong syllables of this kind /trā.nē/. A syllable with a short vowel will also be strong if it has at least one consonant in its coda (at least *two* consonants if it is word-final): thus **stagnant** has two strong syllables of this type /stăg.nănt/.

In determining syllable strength, a phonemic representation is, strictly speaking, necessary; as with syllable division, though, orthographic representations often give the correct results. However, the following points should be borne in mind:

(a)   **r** after a vowel counts as a consonant for this purpose, even if it is not pronounced as a consonant (see p. 8);

(b)   Combinations of two letters representing single sounds, such as **sh**, **ch**, **th**, count as single consonants, except that **ng** counts as two consonants, whether pronounced as [ŋg] as in **finger**, or as simply [ŋ] as in **singer**, **along**;

(c)   Word-final doubled consonants, including **ck**, **tch**, **dge**, are always pronounced as single consonants; unlike medial doubled consonants (see principle 5 above), they do not act as two consonants for the purposes of determining syllable strength or stress placement – thus the single syllables of words like **odd**, **back**, **catch**, **judge** are weak, not strong. Word-final **-ng**, on the other hand, counts as two consonants, and a syllable ending with **-ng** is therefore strong.

Even when we work with a phonemic notation, or with a phonetic representation, there are still some anomalies. For example, although [ju:] (/ū/ in our phonemic notation) is clearly a long vowel on *phonetic* grounds, there are times when it acts as a short vowel from the *phonological* point of view:

(a)   The rule of trisyllabic shortening (Section 7.3) never changes this vowel. Thus even where the rule shortens other vowels, for instance before the suffix **-ity**, as shown below, it leaves /ū/ as /ū/.

di'vīne	di'vĭnity
se'rēne	se'rĕnity
ur'bāne	ur'bănity
ver'bōse	ver'bŏsity
But im'mūne	im'mūnity [ɪ'mju:nɪtɪ]

(b)   Many syllables containing /ū/ are weak rather than strong for purposes of stress-assignment and vowel reduction. For example **ridiculous** would be stressed **'ridi'culous** if ū counted as long, since the suffix **-ous** causes stress to be placed on the preceding syllable if it is strong, but two syllables back if the preceding syllable is weak;

ri`dicŭlous is the correct pattern, indicating that **cū** is a weak syllable. (For fuller details see Section 4.3). That this vowel is in fact /ū/ and not /ŭ/ is shown by the fact that it reduces to [ju] or [jə] rather than to [ə] (see Section 7.1). This example illustrates well the importance of the weak v. strong distinction; our examples of **Kentucky**, etc., discussed under principle 5 above are further relevant instances.

The other phonetically long vowel which may count as short from the point of view of stress assignment is [əu], the vowel of **go**; this is sometimes written **o** (as in **veto**, **calico**), and sometimes as **ow** (as in **window**, **fellow**). This vowel counts as short only in word-final position (as in the examples just cited); in all non-final positions it is always long phonologically as well as phonetically. Thus **memento** is not stressed by rule 3(a) of Section 3.1, but by rule 3(b)(i): **me`mento**. Final short **o** then becomes lengthened in the pronunciation, and is *protected* from reduction (see Section 7.2). (Note that in some colloquial varieties this final **o** may reduce in certain words: **fellow**, **window** are often pronounced ['felə], ['wɪndə]. However, other words in **o**, **ow** always maintain a full vowel: **elbow** is always ['el,bəu].)

2.3 Words and Morphemes

Syllabification is not the only way of dividing words into parts. Some words may be segmented according to their morphological formation, i.e. into affixes and roots. Each of the basic parts into which a word may be divided in this way is called a *morpheme*. Sometimes morpheme boundaries will coincide with syllable boundaries, as in **kindly**, which is morphologically **kind+ly** as well as syllabically **kind.ly**. But there is no guarantee that this will always be the case: **farmer** is morphologically **farm+er**, but syllabically **far.mer**; **goes** is morphologically **go+es**, but cannot be divided syllabically at all.

For stress-assignment purposes, it is better to syllabify the SP of a complex word rather than the whole word itself; in other words, the affixes that do not affect stress should be removed before syllabification takes place. To do things the other way round would result in some strange syllable-boundary locations: **interpreted** would have the structure **in.ter.pre.ted**, which would in turn yield the undesirable **in.ter.pre.t** (implying four syllables, the last being merely a fragment) when the past tense affix was removed.

Words may exhibit several layers of morphological complexity. Five layers is about the upper limit for English (as exemplified by **ungentlemanliness** in Figure 2.1), but some other languages permit their words to be a good deal more complex even than this. The precise meanings to be attached to the terms *stem*, *root*, and *compound* are as follows:

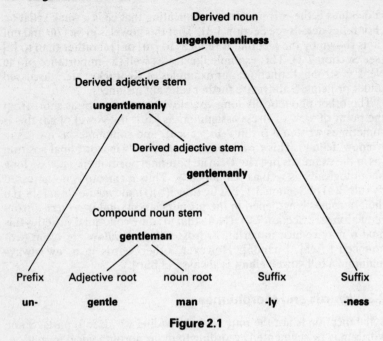

Derived noun

ungentlemanliness

Derived adjective stem

ungentlemanly

Derived adjective stem

gentlemanly

Compound noun stem

gentleman

Prefix	Adjective root	noun root	Suffix	Suffix
un-	**gentle**	**man**	**-ly**	**-ness**

Figure 2.1

A *stem* is what is left when an affix has been removed from a form: **gentlemanly** is the stem of **ungentlemanly**.

A *root* is a form which is not an affix and which cannot be further subdivided morphologically: **gentle, man**.

A *compound* is a form which may be subdivided into some combination of stems and roots: **gentleman** is **gentle+man**, where both parts are roots; **motheaten** is **moth+eaten**, where **moth** is a root and **eaten** is a stem further subdivisible into **eat+en**.

The notation of Figure 2.1 has the disadvantage of being very space-consuming, and we shall normally use a system of labelled brackets:

$$_N[\ _A[\ un\ _A[\ _N[\ _A[\ gentle\ ]_A\ _N[\ man\ ]_N\ ]_N\ li\ ]_A\ ]_A\ ness\ ]_N$$

In a case as complex as this, the bracket notation is less clear than the branching structure of Figure 2.1, but the vast majority of the words we shall be dealing with are considerably less complex, and the notation will be found to serve its purpose well. The other examples cited in this section, for instance, will have the following structures:

$$_{Adv}[\ _A[\ kind\ ]_A\ ly\ ]_{Adv}$$
$$_N[\ _V[\ farm\ ]_V\ er\ ]_N\ \text{or}\ _N[\ _V[\ _N[\ farm\ ]_N\ ]_V\ er\ ]_N$$

$_V[$ $_V[$ go $]_V$ es $]_V$
$_N[$ $_A[$ gentle $]_A$ $_N[$ man $]_N$ $]_N$
$_A[$ $_N[$ moth $]_N$ $_A[$ $_V[$ eat $]_V$ en $]_A$ $]_A$

Brackets occur in pairs enclosing words, stems, or roots, and are labelled with the word-class ('part of speech') to which the particular form belongs.

Within this framework, a *stem* can be characterised as a form which, although completely within brackets of its own, does not constitute a complete word.

A *root* is a form completely within brackets of its own, but with no brackets within it.

A *compound* is a form which divides at a point where two brackets appear next to each other back to back, thus: $]_A$ $_N[$. For instance **gentleman** is a compound, but **ungentlemanliness** (which also contains the configuration $]_A$ $_N[$) is not; the latter word divides between **ungentlemanli-** and **-ness**, i.e. not at the $]_A$ $_N[$ place.

An *affix* is a form which does not have a pair of brackets of its own; a *prefix* has an opening bracket immediately to its left, but no closing bracket immediately to its right; a *suffix* usually has a closing bracket immediately to its right, but no opening bracket immediately to its left. Occasionally, a sequence of two suffixes may act as a single suffix from the word-formation point of view:

$_N[$ $_V[$ relax $]_V$ at+ion $]_N$ (no intermediate form **relaxate** exists)

In these cases the first suffix (**-ate** in this instance) has no closing bracket immediately to its right.

Many roots and stems can occur as independent words; such roots and stems are referred to as *free forms*. For example, in **ungentlemanliness** (Figure 2.1) the roots **gentle** and **man** are free, and so are the stems **gentleman**, **gentlemanly** and **ungentlemanly**. Other roots and stems cannot occur as independent words, and are called *bound forms*. Examples of bound forms are the root **toler-** which appears in **tolerable**, **tolerant** and **tolerate**, and the stem **superflu-** (prefix **super-** + root **-flu-**) which appears in **superfluous** and **superfluity**. The proportion of free roots to bound roots varies very much from language to language – quite high in English, very high in Chinese, and comparatively low in Latin (where it is extremely rare for a noun-, adjective- or verb-root to occur uninflected).

The meaning of a stem usually bears a very close relation to the meaning of the same stem when standing alone or with some different affix. Thus **farm-** in **farmer** is clearly the same semantically as the noun or more probably the verb **farm**, and the same as **farm** in **farming**; **demonstr-** in **demonstrate** is clearly the same as **demonstr-** in **demonstrable**. However, occasionally this does not hold, even in pairs which follow the rule for stress-placement – thus **ignorance** behaves as if it were formed from the verb **ignore**, though the meaning link between them has become tenuous or non-existent in the contemporary language.

Another problem arises from the fact that, while every word splits into syllables, and it is not too difficult a matter to decide how many syllables each contains, the same cannot be said of a division into morphemes. There is a scale of 'divisibility into morphemes' in a sense in which there is not a scale or divisibility into syllables.

For example, no one would hesitate to divide **employee** into **employ** and **-ee**, where the suffix **-ee** denotes 'person undergoing the action of the verb' (cf. **divorcee, payee, addressee, licensee**, etc.). The word ˌgranˈdee, 'Spanish nobleman', does not consist etymologically of **grand** plus **-ee** (it is a straight borrowing of the Spanish adjective ˈgrande, 'great'), but in fact, to the present-day speaker of English without a training in the history of his language, an analysis of the root-plus-affix type is highly plausible. This, of course, would account for the shift from penultimate stress in the Spanish original to final stress in the borrowing. In this case, though, the suffix **-ee** does not have quite the same meaning as in the main list of examples above; its meaning is something like 'person exhibiting the property referred to by the adjective', though with further specification as to nationality and rank.

The word **guarantee** is a different type of case again: if the ending **-ee** is taken to be a suffix in this word, it presupposes a bound stem **guarant-**. While it is true that this stem recurs with a very similar meaning in the form **guarantor**, the ending **-ee** means something very different when attached to it – something like 'result of the process expressed by the verb'. Even here, whatever the actual meaning of **-ee**, it makes some sense to recognise a break between this suffix and the stem. However, with words like **settee** and **repartee**, even the presence of a break before **-ee** is very difficult to justify: **sett+ee** 'place on which someone is set'? **repart+ee** 'witty words shared between two people'?

Finally, for a number of words ending in **-ee** no analysis into stem plus **-ee** even suggests itself as a remote possibility. The stem in such words never recurs either alone or in other combinations: for example, **buckshee, fricassee, jamboree**. In the lists given in this book, words whose divisibility into morphemes is problematic may appear both as simple roots and as stem+affix; thus **grandee** and **guarantee** occur in Appendix 3.1 as simple roots and in Appendix 3.2 under words ending in the suffix **-ee**. Words which are duplicated in this way are shown by the sign § in the word lists. Similarly **repast** occurs on the list in Appendix 3.2 as a simple root and on the list in Appendix 6.1 as

re+past, with a prefix **re-**. Words of this type are marked ‡ in the word lists.

Another complication in the analysis of words into morphemes is the fact that parts of certain words may not belong clearly either to a stem or to the affix attached to it. For example, in **fiftieth** ['fɪftɪəθ] there is no *a priori* reason to prefer the analysis **fifty+eth** to the analysis **fiftie+th** ['fɪftɪə+θ]. Clearly **fifty** ['fɪftɪ] is a free form, and it occurs in combination with other morphemes [fɪftɪ+z], but nevertheless *th* also recurs in other contexts with the same meaning as in **fiftieth**, e.g. **seventh** which is quite clearly [sevən+θ]. In practice, linguists seem to prefer to assign two forms to suffixes rather than roots: thus they have preferred to say that **fifty** always has the shape ['fɪftɪ] while the ordinal-number suffix may vary in shape between [θ] and [əθ]. Since in this book we are concentrating on the properties of suffixes, it is quite as important to us (and certainly advantageous for the learner) to recognise *one and the same* suffix in **fiftieth** and **seventh**. We can do both of these as long as we assign the [ə] of ['fɪftɪəθ] neither to the root nor to the suffix, but regard it as a kind of 'cushioning' element between the root ['fɪftɪ] and the suffix [θ]. In this instance this element has a phonological function, and its use can be accounted for in phonological terms: 'Insert [ə] between the cardinal number and the suffix [θ] when the cardinal number ends in an unstressed vowel'. Sometimes, however, there is no such phonological rationale, as in the case of the three stems **accent-**, **torrent-** and **parent-** when the suffix **-al** is added: **accent-** takes a 'cushioning' element **-u-**, **torrent-** a 'cushioning' element **-i-**, and **parent-** adds the suffix directly to the stem without a 'cushioning' element – **accentual, torrential, parental**. The **e** of **fiftieth**, the **u** of **accentual** and the **i** of **torrential** will be referred to as *inserts*. Other examples of inserts are **i**, **e** in **personify**, **liquefy** (cf. the stems **person-** and **liqu-**) and **c** in **personification** (cf. the stem **personify-** and the ending **-ation: personify+c+ation**).

Exercises

1 State the SP (stressable portion) of the following words:
   (*a*) crowded, (*b*) impossible, (*c*) detrimental, (*d*) unfortunately, (*e*) carelessness, (*f*) splintery, (*g*) otherwise, (*h*) inverting.

2 Which of the four procedures 1–4 of Section 2.1 applies in each of the examples given in Exercise 1 above?

3 Divide the following into syllables, stating alternatives where more than one division is possible:

   (*a*) local, (*b*) hackney, (*c*) winter, (*d*) vintner, (*e*) explanation, (*f*) substantial, (*g*) framework, (*h*) motto, (*j*) purple.

4 Which of the syllables in the examples of Exercise 3 are open syllables? Which are weak syllables?

5 Divide the following words into morphemes, and state whether each morpheme is a root, a prefix or a suffix:

(*a*) backwater, (*b*) long-haired, (*c*) dirtier, (*d*) admittance, (*e*) nationalisation, (*f*) incomprehensible, (*g*) undemonstrative.

Give a bracketing, or a branching structure as in Figure 2.1, illustrating the construction of each word.

6 Which of the roots involved in the words in Exercise 5 are free? What other free forms occur in the process of putting these words together (corresponding to the words **ungentlemanly**, **gentlemanly** and **gentleman** in Figure 2.1)?

7 Which of the following words contain inserts?

(*a*) fourteenth, (*b*) professorial, (*c*) tumultuous, (*d*) continuous, (*e*) European, (*f*) classification.

Further Reading

2.2 Words and Syllables

On syllables and syllable divisions see L. M. Hyman, *Phonology: Theory and Analysis* (New York: Holt, Rinehart & Winston, 1975), pp. 187–93, A. Sommerstein, *Modern Phonology* (London: Edward Arnold, 1977), pp. 199–203, and the works cited in those pages.

2.3 Words and Morphemes

On the principles governing the way in which words may be divided into morphemes, see e.g. E. A. Nida, *Morphology* (Ann Arbor, Mich.: University of Michigan Press, 1949), pp. 192–209, D. J. Allerton, *Essentials of Grammatical Theory* (London: Routledge & Kegan Paul, 1979), pp. 49–52, 210–16.

Stress in Simple Roots

In this chapter, we deal with words whose SP contains no prefixes or suffixes.

3.1 The Basic Rules

1 If the SP is *monosyllabic*, there is no choice of place for stress (as explained above, Section 2.1).

2 If the SP is *disyllabic*, stress is normally penultimate, as in examples *1–3* of Table 3.1 (there are exceptions; cf. Section 3.4 and also Section 6).

3 If the SP is *trisyllabic or longer*, its stress is either penultimate or antepenultimate, depending on a number of factors:

(a) If the final syllable is *strong*, stress falls two syllables back from that syllable, i.e. three syllables from the end of the SP of the word, as in examples *4* and *5* of Table 3.1

(b) If the final syllable is *weak*, then:

    (i) If the penultimate syllable is *strong*, then it is stressed, as in examples *6–8* of Table 3.1

    (ii) If the penultimate syllable is *weak*, then the syllable before it is stressed, as in examples *9* and *10* of Table 3.1

In written representations, strong final syllables are fairly easy to distinguish from weak final syllables. Final syllables ending with a single vowel letter or **y**, e.g. **tomato, macaroni, veranda**, with **ew, ow, ey**, or with a single vowel letter plus one consonant, e.g. **window, donkey, asparagus**, are almost always weak; the remainder are strong, i.e. those ending with two consonants, e.g. **asterisk, cummerbund**, with two vowel letters, e.g. **jubilee**, with two vowel letters plus consonant, e.g. **parakeet**, or with vowel plus consonant plus unpronounced **e**, e.g. **antelope**. This means it is fairly easy to determine from the written form whether a particular word is stressed by rule 3 (a) above or by rule 3 (b), without hearing the word actually pronounced.

However, if the final syllable is weak, there are many cases where spelling alone is not sufficient to determine whether the word comes under case (i) of rule 3 (b) or case (ii). A penultimate *closed* syllable, of

Table 3.1

Word	Syllabic structure	Main Stress placement
1 ozone	ō.zōn s s	ˈō.zōn
2 Arab	ă.răb w w	ˈă.răb
3 uncivil	(un.)sĭ.vĭl w w **un-** is not part of the SP	un.ˈsĭ.vĭl
4 antelope	an.tĕ.lōp s w s	ˈan.te.lōp
5 cummerbund	cŭ.mer.bŭnd w s s	ˈcŭ.mer.bund
6 veranda	vĕ.ran.dă w s w	ve.ˈran.da
7 panorama	pă.nŏ.rä.mă w w s w	pa.no.ˈrä.ma
8 spaghetti	spă.gĕt.tĭ w s w	spa.ˈgĕ.ti
9 asparagus	ă.spă.ră.gŭs w w w w	a.ˈspă.ra.gus
10 America	ă.mĕ.rĭ.că w w w w	a.ˈmĕ.ri.ca

course, is always strong, so words of this type are always stressed by (i) if the final syllable is weak. A penultimate *open* syllable, though, may be strong or weak, depending on whether its vowel is long or short. Comparing **panorama** with **asparagus** in Table 3.1, we can see that the third syllable is spelt -ra- in both cases, but has a long vowel in **ˈpanoˈräma**, and is therefore stressed, while in **asˈparagus** it has a short vowel (reduced to [ə]), and stress is antepenultimate. If the vowel of a penultimate open syllable is represented by two letters, as in **stegoˈsaurus**, then it is normally long, but a single letter representation is usually quite ambiguous, as in the above example. The only way to handle such ambiguous cases is to learn which of the two categories each word fits into.

Most of the exceptions to our rules are words with final stress. These have to be learnt as exceptions, though certain endings (as stated in Section 2.1.2) tend to attract stress on to themselves, e.g. -oo as in **kangaˈroo**, **hullabaˈloo**, or -een as in **canˈteen**, **smitheˈreen(s)** (though not -ene as in **ˈgangrene**, **ˈpolythene**). A complete listing of these finally-stressed simple roots is given in Appendix 3.1.

There is a smaller set of exceptions, in which penultimate stress occurs where the rules would predict antepenultimate; for example,

alpaca is syllabically ăl.pă.că (sww) and might be expected to bear stress on the syllable **al-**, whereas the actual pronunciation is **al'păca**, with stressed short [æ] in the second syllable. One way of making such words regular would be to assume a *double* consonant between the penultimate and final vowels. For the example just cited this would mean a representation like ăl.păc.ca (sww) (cf. **tobacco**, etc., cited above, p. 21). Appendix 3.2 lists words of this type.

3.2 Secondary Stress

In longer words syllables before the one with main stress may be made more prominent than their neighbours. The principle underlying this appears to be a rhythmic one: some alternation of relatively stressed and relatively unstressed syllables is the most natural situation for English (and for many other languages).

The normal rules for English seem to be somewhat similar to the rules for placing main stress:

4   If there is only one syllable before the one with main stress, no secondary stress is assigned, e.g. **la'pel, ve'randa, A'mĕrica**.
5   If there are two syllables before the one with main stress, secondary stress is always assigned to the first of these (i.e. two syllables back from main stress), e.g. **'ălū'mĭnium, 'păno'räma**.
6   If there are three or more syllables before the one with main stress, then:

   (i)   If there is a *strong* syllable two syllables back from main stress, it takes secondary stress.
   (ii) If there is a *weak* syllable two syllables back from main stress, the third syllable back from main stress takes secondary stress.

For examples of the operation of rule 6 see Table 3.2.
Certain prefixes may disturb this pattern; see Section 6.2 below.

Table 3.2

encyclopedia	en.'cy̆c.lo.'pē.di.a
	s
pharmocopoeia	'far.mă.co.'pē.a
	w
Septuagesima	'sep.tū.a.'gĕ.si.ma
	w (underlying short vowel)

3.3   Stress Shifts in Noun-Verb Pairs

Certain words exhibit different stress patterns depending on whether they are nouns or verbs. In the majority of cases the structure of such words is prefix+root, and these cases are dealt with in Section 6.3. Sometimes, however, no such analysis can be justified, as in the words listed in Table 3.3. In all such cases, whether the word contains a prefix or not, the stress is earlier ('further to the left') in the noun than in the verb. In the case of words where the prefix+root analysis is not possible, stress-shift has to be treated as idiosyncratic.

The unstressed vowel of the final syllable of the nouns **escort** and **torment** is not reduced to [ə]; thus we have ['eskɔːt], ['tɔːment], in contrast with the final vowels of **effort** ['efət] and **torrent** ['tɒrənt]. An analogous problem arises with prefix+root word pairs exhibiting stress-shift (for a full discussion see Section 7.2).

Table 3.3

Verb	Noun	Notes
ë'scort	'es,cort	Could be e+scort (prefix+stem)
fer'ment	'fer,ment	} Initial syllable of verb is reduced
sur'vey	'sur,vey	
,aug'ment	'aug,ment	
,tor'ment	'tor,ment	
,seg'ment	'segment	} Final syllable of noun is reduced
,frag'ment	'fragment	
'complë,ment	'complëment	⎫
'compli,ment	'compliment	⎪
'dĕcrĕ,ment	'dĕcrĕment	⎪
'dŏcū,ment	'dŏcūment	Final syllable of noun is reduced.
'implë,ment	'implëment	Main stress is sometimes placed
'incrĕ,ment	'incrĕment	on the final syllable in the verbs.
'orna,ment	'ornament	⎪
'rĕgi,ment	'rĕgiment	⎪
'supplë,ment	'supplëment	⎭

Exercises

1   State which of the basic rules of Section 3.1 (i.e. rule 1, 2, 3(a), 3(b)(i) or 3(b)(ii)) applies in each of the following words:

(*a*) mĕtal, (*b*) leave, (*c*) unfair, (*d*) dŏggĕrĕl, (*e*) cārelessness, (*f*) Nōvember, (*g*) imprŏper, (*h*) innūendō, (*j*) intĕger, (*k*) dăvenport.

2   State which (if any) of the basic rules of Section 3.2 (i.e. rule 4, 5, 6(i) or 6(ii)) applies in each of the following words:

(*a*) audĭtōrium, (*b*) ēmĕrĭtus, (*c*) rĕgatta, (*d*) cārelessness, (*e*) innūendō, (*f*) sarsăpărilla, (*g*) ămontillädō.

Give the correct main and secondary stress for each word.

3   Once main stress has been applied, rules 4, 5, 6(i) and 6(ii) apply also to words with irregular main stress, and also to those with suffixes in their SP. Given the place of main stress as shown in the following words, state which of rules 4, 5, 6(i), or 6(ii) applies to place secondary stress in each case:

(*a*) cătămă'ran, (*b*) persŏnĭfĭ'cation, (*c*) contempŏ'raneous, (*d*) gĕron'tocracy, (*e*) ecclēsĭ'astical, (*f*) trĭgŏnŏ'metric, (*g*) electrŏ'static.

Further Reading

(Where full bibliographical details of a work are not given, they may be found in the 'Further Reading' for Section 1. See pp. 14–16 above.)

3.1   The Basic Rules

With the approach in this chapter compare the treatments in Chomsky and Halle, *Sound Pattern*, pp. 69–80, and Halle and Keyser, *English Stress*, pp. 3–11, 26–9.

3.2   Secondary Stress

For this type of secondary stress compare Chomsky and Halle, *Sound Pattern*, pp. 113–120, Halle and Keyser, *English Stress*, pp. 49–54. Garde (*L'Accent*, pp. 53–7) also deals with this under the title of 'écho d'accent' – to be distinguished from his 'accent secondaire', which corresponds to our 'secondary stress by suffix' (Section 4.5); it has to be pointed out, however, that his claim (p. 54) that 'écho d'accent' in English always falls two syllables before main stress is too sweeping – in cases where there are three or more syllables before main stress, and the second syllable back from main stress is weak, secondary stress falls on the *third* syllable before main stress (cf. our examples in Table 3.2).

3.3   Stress-Shifts in Noun-Verb Pairs

See 'Further Reading' for Section 6.3 below.

Appendix 3.1 Finally-Stressed Simple Roots

This appendix consists of three parts:

(a) Words other than proper nouns (exhaustive list)
(b) Geographical proper names (select list)
(c) Personal proper names (select list)

The following signs are used:

* There is an alternative pronunciation with main stress on a non-final syllable.
† Stress is final because of an autostressed ending (see Section 4.2).
§ Final stress is possibly accounted for by the presence of an autostressed suffix (see Section 4.2).
‡ Final stress is possibly accounted for by the presence of a stress-neutral or stress-repellent prefix (see Section 6).

(a) Words Other than Proper Nouns

a'byss, †'acco'lāde, a'cūte, a'dieu [ə'dju:], *a'dult, ‡a'gree, ‡a'lert, †'ambu'scāde, ,ä'men (or ,ā'men), a'non, †,an'tïque [-k], †,ar'cāde, ,ar'cāne, 'arti'san [-'zæn], ,ar'tïste, ‡as'sïze, 'astra'khan [-'kæn], 'atta'ché [-'ʃeɪ] (American, in contrast with British at'tă,ché), ‡at'tack, ,au'gust, ,au'stēre.

†ba'bōōn (or ,bă'bōōn), †'băga'telle, ,bal'let [,bæ'leɪ] (Amer., ctr. Brit. 'bal,let ['bæ,leɪ]), †bal'lōōn, †'bally'hōō, *†'bălu'strāde, †,bam'bōō, ba'näl (or ba'nal), *,ban'shee, *,bap'tïse, 'barca'rolle [-'rəʊl] or [-'rɒl], ba'roque [bə'rɒk] or [bə'rəʊk], *†'bărri'cāde, 'bassi'net, †bas'sōōn, ba'ton (Amer., ctr. Brit. 'bă,ton), ba'zaar, bë'nign [-'naɪn], †bë'zïque [-k], bi'zarre, ,blas'phēme, 'bom'bard, §,bōō'tee, ,bou'quet [,bʊ'keɪ] or [,bu:'keɪ] or [,bəʊ'keɪ], bras'sière [brə'zɪər] (Amer., ctr. Brit. ['bræzɪə]), †bri'gāde, †bro'cāde, †'bucca'neer, ,buck'shee, ,bū'reau [-'rəʊ] (Amer., ctr. Brit. ['bjʊə,rəʊ]), ,bur'noüs.

ca'bal, ca'bōōse, ca'det, ca'goüle, ca'hōōts, ca'jōle, ,cam'paign [-'peɪn], ca'nal, ca'noe [-'nu:], †,can'teen, ca'prïce, ,cap'sïze, ca'răfe, *'căra'van, †ca'reen, †ca'reer, ca'ress, ca'rouse, 'că,roü'sel, ,car'tel, †,car'tōōn, †,cas'cāde, 'căsta'net, *'cătama'ran, ca'tarrh [-'tɑ:], *†'căval'cāde, 'căva'liēr, cë'ment, cë'rïse, cha'conne [ʃə'kɒn] or [,ʃæ'kɒn], ,cham'pagne [,ʃæm'peɪn], †cha'räde (Brit.) or †cha'rāde (Amer.) [ʃə-], ,chas'tïse, *,chauf'feur [,ʃəʊ'fɜ:], chë'mïse [ʃɪ-], che'rōōt [ʃə-], chi'cāne [ʃɪ-],'chimpan'zee (or -,pan-) (Brit., ctr. Amer. ,chim'pan,zee), cho'räle [kə-], ci'gar, 'clări'net, 'clien'tèle ['kli:ɒn'tel], §,coa'tee, ,cō'caine, †,coc'kāde, †'cocka'tōō, †co'cōōn, ‡,cō'erce, ,coif'füre [,kwæ'fjʊə], †,col'leen, †'cŏlon'nāde, †'comman'deer, cor'ral, cor'rŏbo'ree, ,cor'tège [,kɔ:'teɪʒ], 'courte'san ['kɔ:tɪ'zæn], cra'vat, crë'vasse, †cri'tïque [-k], †,crŏ'quette [-'ket], †,crü'sāde, †cui'sine [kwɪ'zi:n], †,cü'lotte, ,cur'tail.

da'coit, 'dĕbo'nair, *†dë'cāde, ‡dë'cree, ‡dë'gree, †,den'telle [,dɒn'tel], dës'sert, dë'tail (Amer., ctr. Brit. 'dē,tail), ‡§,dī'lāte, ‡§,dī'lūte, ‡dis'creet,

‡dis῾dain, ‡di῾sease [dɪ῾ziːz], ‡di῾spatch, di῾van, di῾vīne, ‡di῾vorce, ‡ˌdī῾vulge, do῾main (or ˌdō῾main), †῾dŏmi῾neer, †ˌdöu῾blōōn, †dra῾gee [drə῾ʒeɪ] or [drə῾dʒiː], †dra῾gōōn, §ˌdū῾et, †῾dunga῾rees, ˌdū῾ress.

‡ë῾clipse, ë῾līte, †ël῾lipse, *ë῾mïr, ë῾nough [ɪ῾nʌf], ‡῾enter῾tain, ë῾quip, ‡ë῾rāse, *†῾ësca῾pāde, ‡ë῾scāpe, ës῾chew [ɪs῾tʃuː], ‡ë῾scort (verb), ë῾squīre, ë῾steem.

†fa῾çade [fə῾sɑːd] or [ˌfæ῾sɑːd], ˌfai῾ence [ˌfaɪ῾ɒns], fa῾roüche [-῾ruːʃ],fa῾tïgue [-῾tiːg], †ˌfes῾toōn, fi῾nance (or *ˌfī῾nance), ῾flăgeo῾let, †῾fonta῾nelle, frë῾quent (verb), ῾fricas῾see, *ˌfrön῾tiēr, ˌful῾fil [ˌfʊl῾fɪl], †῾fūsil῾lāde.

*†῾găber῾dïne, gal῾lant (=῾amorous'), †gal῾lōōn, ga῾loot, ga῾lore, ga῾losh(es), ga῾lumph, ˌgam῾bōge, ga῾räge (Amer. [gə῾rɑːʒ], ctr. Brit. [῾gærɪdʒ] or [῾gæˌrɑːʒ]), †ga῾rotte, †ga῾votte, †ga῾zelle, †ga῾zette, ga῾zump, ˌgen῾teel, ger῾māne, gi῾raffe [dʒə῾ræf] or [dʒə῾rɑːf], †ˌgoa῾tee, §ˌgran῾dee, †grë῾nāde, gri῾māce, §῾guaran῾tee [῾gæ-], guf῾faw or ˌguf῾faw, gui῾tar [gɪ῾tɑː].

ha῾rangue [-῾ræŋ], ha῾rass (Amer., ctr. Brit. ῾hărass), ˌhä῾rēm, †ˌhar῾pōōn, hel῾lō, ˌhō῾tel, †῾hullaba῾lōō, ˌhū῾māne, hur῾räh, hur῾ray, hus῾sar.

§ig῾nīte, ig῾nore, ‡i῾nāne, ῾inas῾much, in῾trïgue [ɪn῾triːg] (noun may be ῾in,trïgue).

῾jambo῾ree, jë῾jüne, *§῾jübi῾lee, ˌJü῾lȳ (or Ju῾lȳ).

†῾kanga῾rōō, ka῾put [kə῾pʊt], †ka῾zōō, Ko῾rän.

la῾crosse, †la῾gōōn, ˌlam῾bast, la῾ment (noun as well as verb), †ˌlam῾pōōn, la῾pel, †la῾teen, †la῾trïne, li῾aise, ˌlō῾cäle, ˌlȳ῾chee.

†῾măca῾rōōn, †ma῾chīne [mə῾ʃiːn], †῾mădemoi῾selle [῾mædəmə῾zel] or [ˌmæm῾zel], *†῾măga῾zïne, ma῾hout, ˌmain῾tain, ma῾laise, ma῾lign [-῾laɪn], ma῾mä, ῾măna῾tee, ˌman῾kīnd, ma῾nūre, ma῾raud, ῾margue῾rïte, †ma῾rïne, †ma῾rōōn, ˌmar῾quee [-῾kiː], ῾marti῾net, *῾marzi῾pan, †῾masque῾rāde [῾mɑːsk-] or [῾mæsk-], *ˌmas῾säge [-ʒ], ˌmas῾seur [-῾sɜː], ˌmas῾seuse [-῾sɜːz] or [-῾suːz], ma῾tūre, me῾ringue [mə῾ræŋ], ῾mīna῾ret, ῾mīnū῾et, ˌmī῾nūte (= ῾tiny'), mi῾sère [mɪ῾zɛə], ‡mi῾stāke, mo῾lest, †ˌmon῾sōōn, †ˌmō῾quette [-῾ket], mo῾raine, mo῾räle, mo῾rass, mo῾rōse [-῾rəus], ˌmō῾tel, ˌmō῾tet, ˌmō῾tif, mou῾stache [mə῾stɑːʃ] (Brit., ctr. Amer. [῾mʌs,tæʃ]), ῾mŭsca῾tel, †ˌmȳ῾stïque [-k].

†na῾celle, *na῾dïr, ˌnä῾ïve, në῾glect.

o῾bēse [ə῾biːs] (or ˌō-), ‡o῾bey (or ˌō-), ‡†o῾blïque [-k], o῾pāque [-k] (or ˌō-), o῾pīne, ˌor῾dain, *ˌor῾deal, *ˌō῾vert.

†῾păli῾sāde, pa῾năche [-ʃ], †῾panta῾lōōn, pa῾pä, pa῾pōōse (or ˌpă-), †pa῾rāde, *῾păra῾keet, pa῾rōle, §ˌPar῾see, ˌpar῾tāke, ˌpar῾terre [-῾tɛə], ῾parti῾san [-῾zæn], ˌpăs῾tïche [-ʃ], pa῾trōl, pa῾väne or pa῾väne, pë῾cän, per ῾cent, per῾haps, ῾person῾nel, pë῾tard, pe῾tïte, †῾pïo῾neer, pi῾läu, †pla῾tōōn, po῾lïce, §po῾līte, †ˌpol῾trōōn, †ˌpon῾tōōn, pos῾sess [pə῾zes], ‡ˌpōst῾pōne, †ˌpŏ῾teen, ˌpres῾tïge [-ʒ], *†῾prŏme῾nāde, ˌpur῾loin, pur῾vey.

qua῾drille, ˌqua῾drōōn [ˌkwɒ-], *†qui῾nïne.

†trac‛cōōn (or ‚rac-), ‚ram‛pāge, ra‛vīne, 'rĕcita‛tīve, ‚rĕ‛gīme ['re‛ʒi:m] (or [‚reɪ-]), 'rĕ‚par‛tee, ‡rĕ‛päst, ‡rĕ‛prīse, †'rīga‛dōōn, ri‛pŏste, ro‛bust or *‚rō‛bust, ro‛mance or *‚rō‛mance, ‚rō‛tund, †‚roü‛läde, †‚roü‛tīne, ‚rü‛pee.

sa‛läam, †sa‛lōōn, sa‛lüte, †‚sar‛dïne, sa‛rong, †sa‛teen, sa‛voy, ‚schot‛tische [‚ʃɒ‛ti:ʃ], ‡sĕ‛cond (verb), ‡sĕ‛cūre, sĕ‛dan, †'sĕre‛nāde, ‡se‛rēne, ‚set‛tee, ‡sĕ‛vēre, shal‛lot, †‚sham‛pōō, she‛bang, shel‛lac, ‚sin‛cēre, †'smïthe‛reens, *spi‛net, †spit‛tōōn, *‚squee‛gee [-‛dʒi:], †‚stoc‛kāde, ‚stam‛pēde, ‚sü‛perb, su‛prēme (or ‚sü-), ‡sur‛mīse, ‡sur‛päss, ‡sur‛prīse, ‡sur‛vey (verb).

†ta‛bōō, †'tambou‛rïne, †'tange‛rïne, †‚tat‛tōō, †‚tech‛nïque ['tek‛ni:k], ter‛rain, *§‚thug‛gee, †‚tï‛rāde, tra‛pēze, ‡tra‛verse, trë‛pan, ‚trom‛bōne, †‚tū‛reen, ††tÿ‛cōōn, †‚tÿ‛phōōn.

†‚ū‛nïque [-k], §‚ū‛nīte, ‚ur‛bāne, ‚ū‛surp [-‛zɜ:p].

va‛līse, ‚vä‛mōōse, *ve‛loür, †vë‛neer, *ver‛moüth, 'vīo‛lin, †'vŏlun‛teer.

‚zoü‛äve.

(b) Geographical Proper Names

'Äber‛deen, Ac‛crä, ‚Al‛gïers, *'Amster‛dam, ‚An‛nam, 'Ar‛dennes [‚ɑ:‛den], ‚Ar‛gÿll, ‚Ar‛magh [‚ɑ:‛mɑ:], ‚As‛sam, 'Astra‛khan [-‛kæn].

‚Bagh‛dad [‚bæg-], ‚Bäh‛rain, †'Bäker‛lōō, ‚Bang‛kok, 'Bangla‛desh, ‚Bas‛tïlle, ‚Bei‛rüt [‚beɪ-], *‚Bel‛fäst, Ben‛gal [-‛gɔ:l], ‚Ber‛lin, 'Birken‛hĕad, ‚Bom‛bay, ‚Bor‛deaux [-‛dəʊ], Bou‛logne [bə‛lɔɪn], 'Büca‛rest, *'Büda‛pest.

Ca‛diz, Ca‛prï, *‚Car‛lisle [-‛laɪl], ‚Car‛lÿle, *‚Căta‛lan, Cey‛lon [sɪ-], Co‛logne [kə‛ləʊn], ‚Cor‛fü.

†'Darda‛nelles, 'Dŏne‛gal [-‛gɔ:l], ‚Dun‛dee, ‚Dun‛kirk.

*‚Gātes‛hĕad, ‚Grāves‛end.

'Hong ‛Kong.

'Illi‛nois [-‛nɔɪ], I‛rän, I‛räq, 'Is‚tan‛bul [-‛bʊl].

Ja‛pan.

*Ka‛bul [kə‛bʊl] or ['kɑ:‚bʊl], *‚Kash‛mir [-‛mɪə], ‚Khar‛toum [‚kɑ:‛tu:m], Kil‛dāre.

Lë‛vant, Lor‛raine, ‚Lü‛cerne.

Ma‛dras, Ma‛drid, Ma‛lay, 'Manda‛lay, ‚Mar‛seilles [-‛seɪ] or [-‛seɪlz], Mi‛lan, ‚Mō‛bïle, 'Montrë‛al [-‛ɔ:l], †Mo‛selle.

Na‛tal, Në‛pal [-‛pɔ:l].

‚Os‛tend.

'Päki‛stän, *'Păna‛mä, ‚Pē‛king, ‚Pen‛zance, 'Prŏ‚ven‛çäl [prɒ‚vɒn‛sɑ:l], *'Pÿre‛nees.

Quë‛bec.

†‚Ran'gōōn, Ro'mansch.

Sa'voy, ‚Sca'fell [‚skɔ:-], Së'ville, ‚Shang'hai [-'haɪ], ‚Sī'am, 'Singa'pore, ‚South'end, ‚Stōne'henge, ‚Stran'raer [-'rɑ:], ‚Sü'dan or ‚Sü'dän.

‚Tai'wan [‚taɪ'wɑ:n], ‚Tan'gïer [-'dʒɪə], ‚Teh'ran [‚tɛə'rɑ:n], 'Tĕne'rïfe, Ti'bet, 'Tim‚buk'tü, To'bruk [tə'brʊk], ‚Tor'quay [-'ki:], ‚Toü'loüse, Tri'ëste, ‚Tü'rin, ‚Tÿ'rōne or Ty'rōne.

‚Ū'kraine.

Ver'mont, ‚Ver'sailles [‚vɛə'saɪ] or [‚vɜ:-], ‚Viet'nam or -'näm.

‚Wal'lōōn [‚wɒ-], ‚Walls'end [‚wɔ:lz-], 'Water'lōō ['wɔ:tə'lu:].

‚Zä'ïre.

(c) Personal Proper Names

§‚An'nette, §'Antoi'nette [-twə-].

§'Berna'dette, ‚Ber'nïce, ‚Bur'nett.

‚Că'mïlle, Ca'nūte, Ca'pōne, Ca'vell, *†‚Chris'tïne, §Cŏ'lette, ‚Cor'nell.

*†'Dăni'elle, De'nïse, *‚Dï'äne.

*†‚Eï'leen, Ë'laine.

‚Gal'braith [‚gɔ:l-].

*‚Ī'rēne (or ‚Ī'rēnë).

§Jean'nette, ‚Jō'anne.

‚Loü'ïse.

Ma'lōne, 'Margue'rïte, 'Mări'anne, *†‚Mau'reen, *†‚Ma'xïne, †Mi'chelle [mɪ'ʃel], Mo'ran, Mo'rell.

‚Par'nell, §‚Pau'lette, *†‚Pau'lïne.

‚Ră'vel or Ra'vel.

‚Sü'zanne.

§Y'vette, Y'vonne or *‚Ÿ'vonne.

Appendix 3.2 Simple Roots with Anomalous Non-Final Main Stress

This appendix consists of two parts:

(a) Words with penultimate stress where our rules predict antepenultimate stress

(b) Words with antepenultimate stress where our rules predict penultimate stress

The following signs are used:

* There is an alternative pronunciation with main stress where the rules predict.
‡ Penultimate stress is possibly accounted for by the presence of a stress-neutral or stress-repellent prefix (see Section 6).

(a) Words with Penultimate Stress where Our Rules Predict Antepenultimate Stress

ˌalˈpăca, Aˈpăchë, apˈpărel, atˈtă,ché [əˈtæˌʃeɪ] (Brit., ctr. Amer. ˈattaˈché).

ˌbanˈdăna (also has an alternative spelling *bandanna*, which predicts the place of stress correctly).

caˈdăver, Caˈrăcas.

‡dëˈcrĕpit, *‡dëˈfīcit, ‡dëˈlīver, ‡dëˈvĕlop, ˌDīˈăna, ‡disˈpărage [-rɪdʒ].

ëˈlĕven, ëˈnămel, ‡ënˈvĕlop.

Ferˈmănagh [fəˈmænə].

ˌhapˈhăzard (possibly a compound *hap+hazard*), Haˈvăna.

iˈmăgine, ˈIndiˈăna.

ˌLoüˈïsiˈăna.

Maˈnīla, ˌMonˈtăna.

pëˈsĕta (or [pɪˈseɪtə]), ˌpïˈănō (or pronounced with two syllables [ˈpjænəʊ] or [ˈpjɑːnəʊ]).

soˈlīcit.

ˌUrˈbăna.

(b) Words with Antepenultimate Stress where Our Rules Predict Penultimate Stress

ˈAlgerₐ₎non.

ˈbalderˌdash [ˈbɔːl-], ˈburgundy.

ˈcălendar, ˈCăvenˌdish, ˈCŏventry (or ˈCö-), ˈCrŏmarty, ˈcÿlinder (underlying form is possibly /silindr/, cf. **cylindrical**).

ˈDăventry, ˈdĕrringer [ˈderɪndʒə].

ˈHottenˌtot, ˈhowitzer.

ˈinterval.

ˈKissinger [ˈkɪsɪndʒə].

ˈmackinˌtosh, ˈMăcInˌtosh.

ˈpărafˌfin, ˈpăralˌlel, ˈpimperˌnel.

'Rafferty.

'tälisman (s is pronounced [z], which indicates that it does not belong to the final syllable, and therefore that the second syllable is strong; this would predict that it should be the stressed syllable).

Suffixes and Stress

4.1 Inflectional and Other Stress-Neutral Suffixes

When certain suffixes are attached to free forms (i.e. forms which can occur as words in their own right), they leave the stress-pattern unchanged. As briefly stated in Section 2.1, all inflectional suffixes behave in this way (subscript letters A, B, C refer to distinct suffixes with the same form – see Appendix 4.1):

-s/-es (plural)	-s/-es (3rd person singular)
-'s (possessive)	-ed (past tense, past part.)
-er$_C$ (comparative)	-en$_A$ (past participle)
-est (superlative)	-ing (present part., gerund)

Some derivational suffixes also behave in this way; some are always stress-neutral, while others (denoted by a parenthesised 'm' in the list below) are sometimes stress-neutral and sometimes not. These latter are referred to as 'mixed' suffixes – see Section 4.4, and, for fuller details, the Appendices 4.1 and 4.2. The following is intended as a full list of stress-neutral derivational suffixes:

-able (m)[1]	-er$_A$ (m)	-ist (m)	-some
-acy (m)	-er$_B$	-ite$_A$ (m)	-t (m)
-age (m)	-ery (m)	-less	-th$_A$
-al$_B$	-ess	-let	-th$_B$
-ance (m)	-ful$_A$	-ly	-ty$_A$
-ant$_B$ (m)	-ful$_B$	-ment (m)	-ty$_B$
-ary (m)	-hood	-ness$_A$	-ure (m)
-ce	-ier (m)	-or$_A$ (m)	-ward
-cy	-iour	-ory (m)	-ways
-dom	-ise$_A$/-ize (m)	-ous (m)	-wise
-en$_B$	-ish	-ry	-y$_A$
-en$_C$	-ism (m)	-s	-y$_B$ (m)

4.2 'Autostressed' Suffixes

The first type of suffix which affects stress does so by attracting the main stress on to itself, whence the name 'autostressed'. These suffixes may be added both to free forms (as in **millio`naire**) and to bound forms (as in **Portu`guese**).

A number of endings which are not strictly suffixes share the property of being autostressed, and many finally-stressed simple roots (cf. above Sections 2.1.2 and 3.1 and Appendix 3.1) can be accounted for in this way, e.g. **hullaba`lōō**, **can`teen**, **an`tīque**.

The following is intended as a complete listing of autostressed suffixes and endings (see also Appendices 4.1 and 4.2):

-ade	-eer	-esse	-ique	-oon
-aire	-elle	-et (m)	-ise$_B$	-ose (m)
-aise	-enne	-ette	-ite$_C$ (m)	-otte (m)
-ate$_A$ (m)	-esce	-eur	-ment (m)	-teen
-ee (m)	-ese	-ier (m)	-ness$_B$	
-een	-esque	-ine$_D$	-oo	

Secondary stress is placed according to the principles stated in Section 3.1. Sometimes this falls on the syllable which has main stress in the corresponding free form, e.g. `**million** – `**millio`naire**, but this is purely coincidental: the stress pattern of the free form may be completely changed, especially if main stress falls on the final syllable, e.g. **Ja`pan** – `**Jăpa`nese**, or **ci`gar** – `**cĭga`rette**. English shows a definite tendency not to have strong stresses on adjacent syllables within a word. Pronunciations like **Ja'pă`nese** and **ci'gä`rette** seem to be avoided.

This tendency to keep strong stresses separated from one another by one or two syllables with weaker stress also underlies the shifts of stress in phrases like `**fif,teen `pence** (with **fif** stronger than **teen**) as compared with the isolated word ,**fif`teen** (where **teen** is the stronger syllable of the two). Consider also `**Japa,nese `fan** (with the relative stresses on **Ja** and **nese** reversed by comparison with `**Japa`nese**). This phenomenon is dealt with in more detail in Section 5.3.

4.3 'Pre-Stressed' Suffixes

By far the largest group of suffixes is that in which stress is assigned to a syllable a certain number of syllables before the one containing the suffix. These 'pre-stressed' suffixes are best subclassified according to the number of syllables involved.

1 *Pre-stressed 1* suffixes (i.e. those in which stress falls on the syllable *immediately preceding* the one containing the suffix) are the following:

-erie, -ic, -id, -ion, -ish (m), -itory, -ity/-ety, -uble

2 *Pre-stressed 2* suffixes (i.e. those in which stress falls *two syllables before* the syllable containing the suffix) are the following:

-able (m)[2]	-ene	-ism (m)	-ment (m)
-acy (m)	-er$_A$ (m)	-ist (m)	-oir (e)
-ast	-fy	-ite (m)	-ose (m)
-ate$_A$ (m)	-gon	-ite$_B$	-tude
-ate$_B$	-ine$_C$	-ite$_C$ (m)	-y$_B$ (m)
-cide	-ise/-ize (m)		

3 A large group of suffixes place stress by a principle similar to that for simple roots ending in a weak syllable (see Section 2.1 rule 3(b)).

(i) If the syllable before the one containing the suffix is *strong*, then it is stressed, as in examples *1* and *2* of Table 4.1.
(ii) If the syllable before the one containing the suffix is *weak*, then the syllable before that is stressed, as in examples *3* and *4* of Table 4.1.

These will be referred to as *Pre-stressed 1/2* suffixes (P 1/2); the list of them is as follows:

-ad	-ate$_C$	-ide	-or$_A$ (m)
-age (m)	-ative	-ile	-or$_B$
-al$_A$	-ature	-ine$_A$	-or$_C$
-an	-ee (m)	-ine$_B$	-ory
-ance (m)	-ée	-ine$_E$	-our
-ant$_A$	-ence	-is	-ous (m)[4]
-ant$_B$ (m)	-ent	-ive	-um
-ar	-ery (m)	-oid	-ure (m)
-ary (m)	-ible[3]	-on	-us

Table 4.1

	Word	Syllabic and morphemic structure	Main Stress placement
1	tremendous	trĕ.mĕn.d+ŏs [P 1/2] w s w	tre.'men.dos
2	homicidal	hŏ.mĭ.+cī.d+ăl [P 1/2] w w s w	ho.mi.'cī.dal
3	benevolent	bĕ.nĕ.+vŏ.l+ĕnt [P 1/2] w w w s	be.'nĕ.vo.lent
4	original	ŏ.rĭ.gĭ.n+ăl [P 1/2] w w w w	o.'rĭ.gi.nal

Table 4.2

Word	Syllabic and morphemic structure	Predicted main stress and pronunciation	Actual main stress and pronunciation
1 thermostat	θĕr.mŏ.+stăt [P 2/3] s w w	['θɜ:məstət]	['θɜ:mə͵stæt]
2 telegram	tĕ.lĕ.+grăm [P 2/3] w w w	['telɪgrəm]	['telɪ͵græm]
3 microscope	mīk.rŏ.+skōp [P 2/3] s w s	['maɪkrə͵skəʊp]	(as predicted)
4 kaleidoscope	kă.lī.dŏ.+skōp [P 2/3] w s w s	[kə'laɪdə͵skəʊp]	(as predicted)
5 heliograph	hē.lĭ.ŏ.+grăf [P 2/3] s w w s	['hi:lɪə͵grɑ:f]	(as predicted)
	hē.lĭ.ŏ.+grăf [P 2/3] s w w w	['hi:lɪəgrəf]	['hi:lɪə͵græf]
6 telephonist	tĕ.lĕ.+fō.n+ĭst [P 2] w w s s	[tɪ'le͵fəʊnɪst]	[tɪ'lefənɪst]
7 telegraphy	tĕ.lĕ+g.ră.f+ĭ [P 2] w s s w	[tɪ'leg͵rɑ:fɪ]	[tɪ'legrəfɪ]
	tĕ.lĕ+g.ră.f+ĭ [P 2] w s w w	[tɪ'legrəfɪ]	(as predicted)
8 microscopic	mīk.rŏ.+skōp.+ĭk [P 1] s w s w	[maɪkrə'skɒpɪk] (ō shortened before -ic)	(as predicted)

Properties such as 'pre-stressed 1', 'autostressed', etc., will be referred to in what follows as the *accentual properties* of the suffix concerned.

4   There is a further large, probably open-ended, group of elements (mostly Greek in origin) which could from some points of view be treated as suffixes, and which could be said to place stress by a principle similar to the one stated in 3 above, but one syllable further back in each case:

(i)   If the syllable two syllables before the one containing the suffix is *strong* (or if it is the first syllable of the word), then it is stressed, as in examples *1–4* of Table 4.2.

(ii) If the syllable two syllables before the one containing the suffix is *weak* (and it is not the initial syllable), then the syllable before that is stressed, as in example *5* of Table 4.2.

Table 4.3

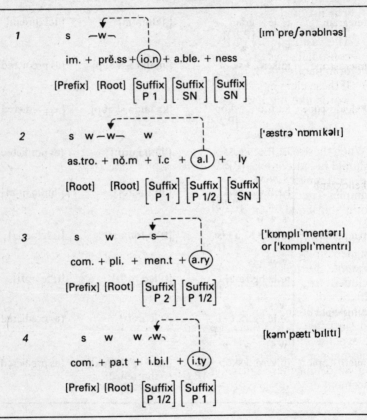

These could be referred to, analogously with the preceding set, as 'pre-stressed 2/3' suffixes. They combine some of the properties of suffixes with some of the properties of compound-forming elements; see Section 5 (especially 5.5) for a fuller treatment of the latter. The following facts support their classification as compound-forming elements:

(a) The rules (including the vowel reduction rules of Section 7) predict that when elements of this kind with short vowels are word-final they should end up with a reduced vowel (see column 3 of examples *1* and *2* and the second pronunciation of example *5* in Table 4.2); this is not the case (as shown in column 4 of the same examples). This rhythmic pattern is typical of initially-stressed compounds: cf. for instance **cricket-bat** ['krɪkɪt,bæt], **traffic jam** ['træfɪk,dʒæm] (for more details see Section 5.1).

(b) The list of elements involved is open-ended, as opposed to true suffixes, which form closed lists.

(c) The vast majority of these elements begin with a consonant or consonant cluster, whereas other pre-stressed suffixes are predominantly vowel-initial.

(d) If these elements were treated as suffixes, we would have to treat words like **digraph**, **misanthrope** as consisting of a prefix (**di-**, **mis-**) followed by a suffix (**-graph**, **-anthrope**), with no root in each case. These would be the only cases of rootless words.

When these elements are followed by genuine pre-stressed suffixes, it should be noted that their vowels are shortened (if basically long), and are reduced when stress is placed elsewhere by the suffix (see examples *6* and *7* (both pronunciations) in Table 4.2). The vowel of a root is shortened when it appears before **-ic** (see example *8* in Table 4.2).

When more than one suffix is attached to a root, main stress is assigned on the basis of the accentual properties of *the last suffix of the stressable portion* of the word. Thus, stress-neutral suffixes will be excluded from consideration, and the last of the stress-affecting suffixes will impose its stress pattern on the word; see Table 4.3 for examples. This may cause main stress to fall on the root (cf. examples *1* and *2* in Table 4.3), or it may result in the stressing of an earlier suffix at the expense of the root (cf. examples *3* and *4* in Table 4.3). It sometimes happens that earlier suffixes are irrelevant to the stress-pattern of a word, but there are a number of cases in which they affect the placement of secondary stress (see 4.5 below).

4.4 'Mixed' Suffixes

A number of suffixes (marked (m) in the lists given earlier in this section) have two or more distinct modes of operation. In certain words they belong to one of the categories described above, while in others they belong to a different category.

Thus, for instance, verb-forming **-ate** (**-ate**ₐ in the lists above) is *autostressed* in words of two syllables such as ,rō'tāte (in British English though not always in American English), but *pre-stressed 2* in words of three or more syllables, e.g. `dĕmon,strāte. Again, **-able** is in general *stress-neutral* if attached to a free stem (dë`fīnable, cf. dëfīne), but *pre-stressed 2* if attached to a stem that is not free (in`terminable, where there is no actual word **intermin(e)**).

'Mixed' suffixes will be treated in more detail in Appendix 4.1 below – the principles governing the categories to which they belong are explained fully there. Moreover, in Appendix 4.2 extended lists of words are given for each 'mixed' suffix.

4.5 Secondary Stress by Suffix

1 As explained above (Section 4.3), main stress is assigned on the basis of the accentual properties of the last suffix in the SP of the word. Other suffixes in the SP are sometimes involved in deciding where secondary stress is to be placed in the word. Often secondary stress is placed by this method on the same syllable as it would be placed by the rhythmic principle (see examples *1* and *2* of Table 4.4); sometimes, however, differing results are obtained by the two methods, as in examples *3–6* of Table 4.4. When this is the case, the correct stressings come sometimes from one method and sometimes from the other: examples *3* and *4* require secondary stress to be placed by the suffix, while examples *5* and *6* require the rhythmic principle in order to obtain the proper stressings.

2 In order to know which principle gives the correct secondary stress placement in any given case, it is necessary to take account of what combination of suffixes is involved. The following is a list of suffix combinations which utilise the accentual properties of the earlier suffix for the placement of secondary stress:

abil+ity
al+ity
ar+ity
ary+an
ate+ion (except in **-fication**, which is morphologically fy+c+ ate+ion)
cide+al
fact+ion (possibly morphologically analysable as fy+ct+ion)
fy+c+ate+ion (**-fication**, in which secondary stress is placed in almost all cases by **-fy** and not by **-ate**).
ibil+ity
ment+al
ment+ary
os+ity
ubil+ity

Table 4.4

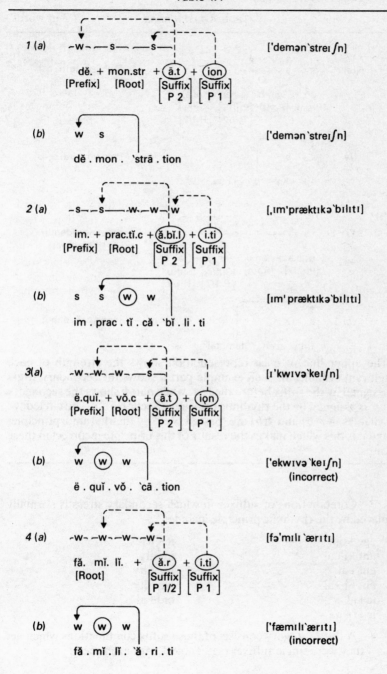

1 (a)   -w- — s— — s—| ['demən`streɪʃn]

dě. + mon.str + (ā.t) + (ion)
[Prefix]   [Root]   [Suffix P 2]   [Suffix P 1]

(b)   w   s   ['demən`streɪʃn]

dě . mon . 'strā . tion

2 (a)   -s—s——w-—w-—w   [,ɪm'præktɪkə`bɪlɪtɪ]

im. + prac.tǐ.c + (ǎ.bǐ.l) + (i.ti)
[Prefix]   [Root]   [Suffix P 2]   [Suffix P 1]

(b)   s   s   (w)   w   [ɪm'præktɪkə`bɪlɪtɪ]

im . prac . tǐ . cǎ . `bǐ . li . ti

3(a)   -w-—w-—w-—s—| [ɪ'kwɪvə`keɪʃn]

ë.quǐ. + vǒ.c + (ā.t) + (iọn)
[Prefix] [Root]   [Suffix P 2]   [Suffix P 1]

(b)   w   (w)   w   ['ekwɪvə`keɪʃn]
(incorrect)

ë . quǐ . vǒ . `cā . tion

4 (a)   -w-—w-—w-—w-| [fə'mɪlɪ`ærɪtɪ]

fǎ. mǐ. lǐ. + (ǎ.r) + (i.ti)
[Root]   [Suffix P 1/2]   [Suffix P 1]

(b)   w   (w)   w   ['fæmɪlɪ`ærɪtɪ]
(incorrect)

fǎ . mǐ . lǐ . `ǎ . ri . ti

Table 4.4 *continued*

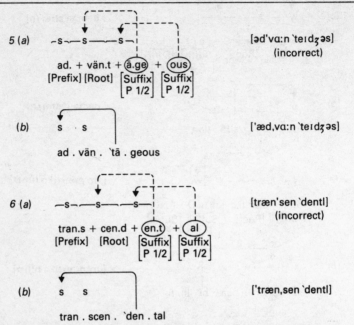

5 (*a*)   [əd'vɑːn ˈteɪdʒəs]
(incorrect)

(*b*)   ['æd͵vɑːn ˈteɪdʒəs]

6 (*a*)   [træn'sen ˈdentl]
(incorrect)

(*b*)   ['træn͵sen ˈdentl]

The upper line of each representation shows the strength of each relevant syllable. In each example part *a* shows the secondary stress assigned by the suffix before the last, while part *b* shows the secondary stress assigned by the rhythmic principle (Section 3.2). The circled 'w' syllables in *3*(*b*) and *4*(*b*) are 'passed over' by the rhythmic principle, and it is this which makes the results of this principle incorrect in these cases.

3   Combinations of suffixes in which secondary stress is normally placed by the rhythmic principle include:

age+ous	ic+ity
ant+i+al	id+ity
ent+al	ine+ity
ent+i+al	ive+ity
ic+al	oid+al
ic+i+an	

4   A third category consists of those suffix combinations which act as if they were single suffixes (see Table 4.5 for examples):

Table 4.5

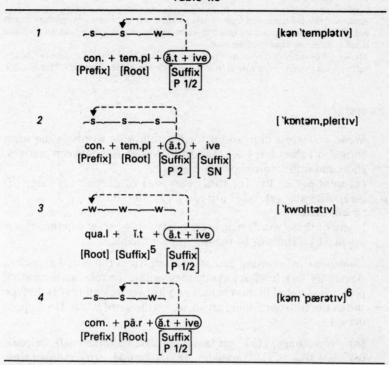

ate+ive
ate+ure

Occasionally in the combination **ate+ive**, the suffix **-ive** has to be taken as stress-neutral, and in that case, of course, main stress is placed by the suffix **-ate**, as in example *2* of Table 4.5. This particular example represents an alternative pronunciation to the regular one (cf. example *1*), but in some cases the treatment of **-ive** as stress-neutral is obligatory: ˌcreˈātive (from ˌcreˈāte) is a word of this kind.

Notes: Section 4

1 Phonologically /ăbĭl/, as shown when the suffix -ity follows: **probable** – **probability** [-'bɪlɪtɪ].
2 cf. note 1.
3 Phonologically /ĭbĭl/, as shown when the suffix -ity follows: **feasible** – **feasibility** [-'bɪlɪtɪ].

4　Phonologically /ŏs/, as shown when the suffix -**ity** follows: **generous – generosity** [-ˈɒsɪtɪ].

5　Assuming this is a truncated form of -**ity**; for the purpose of stress-assignment it does not in fact matter whether we make this assumption or not – we would get the same result if we treated **qualit** as the root.

6　The long ā of the root (the stem is pronounced [kəmˈpɛə] when it appears without a suffix) is shortened by the rule of 'trisyllabic shortening' (see Section 7.3 for details).

Exercises

1　Write out stress derivations for the following words in the form shown in Tables 4.1, 4.3, 4.4 and 4.5. Boundaries between prefixes, roots and suffixes are shown by the sign +.

(*a*) multĭpl+ĭc+ĭty, (*b*) ītĭnĕr+ary, (*c*) con+centr+āt+ing, (*d*) Nĕăpŏlĭt+an, (*e*) ĕlĭg+ĭbĭl+ĭty, (*f*) in+dĭvĭd+ū+ăl+īse, (*g*) răcont+eur.

If any of these words bears secondary stress, state whether this is applied by a suffix or by the rhythmic principle.

2　Consider the following exceptional stressings (all noted as such in Appendix 4.1); in what ways do they violate the rules and accentual properties stated in this chapter and its two appendices? Bold type shows the suffix or ending under which the word is listed in Appendix 4.1.

(*a*) ˈĕspio,näge, (*b*) galˈlant, (*c*) ˈnūme,rātor, (*d*) sëˈrēne, (*e*) ˈhōs,tess, (*f*) ˈămateur, (*g*) ˈpўramid, (*h*) ˈserpen,tīne, (*j*) imˈpŏverish, (*k*) ˈīsoˈmor,phism, (*l*) ˈobscūˈran,tist, (*m*) ĕxˈquĭsĭte, (*n*) ˈsўstema,tīze, (*o*) ˈflăgĕoˈlet, (*p*) ˈcom,ment, (*q*) ˈig,lōō, (*r*) ˈalli,gātor, (*s*) ˈdĕsultory, (*t*) ˈgrandiˈōse, (*u*) ˈŏvertūre, (*v*) atˈtrĭ,būte (verb).

3　In each of the following sets of words there is a common suffix. Look the suffix up in Appendix 4.1 of this chapter, and try to decide which of the principles given for that suffix operates for each word in the set. Give the correct stressing for each word; certain vowels have length or shortness marked to help you. Wait until you have done the exercise before you look at Appendix 4.2 which will provide you with a full solution to each part of this exercise.

(*a*)　-**able**: answerable, commūnĭcable, dĕmonstrable, disăgreeable, impĕnĕtrable, jŭstifīable, objectionable, sĕpărable, variable.

(*b*)　-**ance**: appurtĕnance, contĭnūance, disturbance, extrăvăgance, insignĭfĭcance, persĕvērance, surveillance, sustĕnance, tŏlĕrance.

(*c*) **-ant**: aberrant, applĭcant, clairvoyant, consultant, expectŏrant, incessant, lŭbrĭcant, observant, partĭcĭpant, signĭfĭcant.

(*d*) **-er**: abstainer, autobĭŏgrăpher, blackmailer, handĭcapper, icŏnŏlăter, messenger, philŏsŏpher, rejoinder, trespasser.

(*e*) **-ine**: adămantīne, cuĭsĭne, eglantīne, nitroglўcĕrĭne, nitroglўcĕrĭne, limousĭne, prēdĕstīne, strychnĭne, Valentīne.

(*f*) **-ite**: Areŏpăgīte, cosmŏpŏlīte, indĕfĭnĭte, mŏnŏphўsīte, rĕquīte, stălagmīte, theŏdŏlīte.
(Note: some words in this set may be capable of treatment by more than one of the principles given for -ite; not all possibilities are given in Appendix 4.2.)

(*g*) **-ize**: antăgŏnīze, căpĭtălīze, extempŏrīze, hўpŏstătīze, mătērĭălīze, părăsĭtīze, prŏpăgandīze, tantălīze, ūtĭlīze, vĭsūălīze.

(*h*) **-ment**: augment (verb), commăndment, dĭsarmăment, entertainment, incrĕment (verb), incrĕment (noun), prĕdĭcăment, rēĭnstātement, tournăment.

(*j*) **-or:** ⎱accĕlĕrător, aggressor, bĕhăvĭour, compĕtĭtor, en-
      -our: ⎰dĕavour, mīnor, proprĭētor, refrĭgĕrător, süpērĭor.

(*k*) **-ous**: ăvărĭcĭous, carbŏnĭferous, fĕlŏnĭous, inconspĭcūous, marvellous, rumbustious, trĕmendous, vertĭgĭnous, villainous, vŏcĭfĕrous.

(*l*) **-ure**: compōsūre, dĕbentūre, forfeitūre, invĕstĭtūre, mănūfactūre, pĕradventūre, prĕfectūre.

(*m*) **-y**: antĭpăthy, audĭŏmĕtry, băstardy, cătălepsy, Ēgyptŏlŏgy, fĕathery, haberdashery, indŭstry, lĭturgy, polyandry, Saxony, splintery, taxidermy, telegraphy.

Further Reading

(Where full bibliographical details of a work are not given, they may be found in the 'Further Reading' for Section 1. See pp. 14–16 above.)

4.1, 4.2, 4.3, 4.4 Suffixes and their Accentual Properties

On stress-neutral suffixes see also Chomsky and Halle, *Sound Pattern*, pp. 84-7. On autostressed and pre-stressed suffixes see Garde, *L'Accent*, pp. 127–8 and 'Principles', p. 315; and Guierre, *Essai*, pp. 579–701.

For historical information on English suffixes (though little on the effect of these on stress-placement) see Jespersen, *Modern English Grammar*, Part I, pp. 164–72, Part VI, pp. 208–464; and L. Urdang, *Suffixes and Other Word-final Elements of English* (Detroit: Gale Research Company, 1982). As its title implies, the latter goes beyond genuine suffixes to include a number of what we have called 'endings' (see pp. 18, 30 and 41 above).

Chomsky and Halle (*Sound Pattern*, pp. 100–4) treat the elements like **-scope, -graph** mentioned in our Section 4.3.4 as belonging to a category 'Stem' which stands alongside the generally accepted syntactic categories like Noun, Verb, Adjective; Halle and Keyser follow this approach (*English Stress*, pp. 74–5). For criticism of this treatment see reviews of *Sound Pattern* by Hill and Nessly (in Goyvaerts and Pullum, *Essays*, pp. 100–3) and by McCawley (ibid., pp. 152, 157–8); also, and especially, the remarks of Ross ('Reanalysis', pp. 294–305). In 1975 I actually adopted the analysis of these as 'pre-stressed 2/3' suffixes (see Goyvaerts and Pullum, *Essays*, p. 288); as stated on p. 45 I now prefer to analyse them as the second elements of a particular type of compound (see Section 5.5 below).

Appendix 4.1   List of Suffixes with their Properties

The following sign is used:

*There is an alternative spelling with main stress where the rules predict.

-ability
Consists of **-able** plus **-ity**: since **-ity** is pre-stressed 1, main stress falls on the second syllable of **-able** (which has the form **-a'bĭl-** in this context). Secondary stress is then assigned according to the properties of **-able** (see below), i.e. it occurs where main stress falls in the corresponding word ending in **-able**.

Examples: ac'ceptable – ac'cepta'bility
　　　　　　 'comparable – 'compara'bility

-able
Two distinct principles operate:

　1   *Stress-neutral*, if the stem is a free form.

Examples:

　dë'sīre – dë'sīrable – 'undë'sīrable
　in'terpret – in'terpretable
　'rĕcon,cīle – 'rĕcon,cīlable – ir'rĕcon,cīlable

Exceptions (pre-stressed 2 in each case):

'admirable ['ædmərəbl]	'lamentable ['læməntəbl]
'comparable ['kɒmpərəbl]	'prĕferable
dis'rĕpūtable	rë'mēdiable
in'comparable	'rĕpūtable
'irrë'mēdiable	'rĕvocable ['revəkəbl]
ir'rĕvocable	*'transferable (or träns-)

　2   *Pre-stressed 2*, where the stem is not a free form. Stress is placed two syllables before the suffix **-able**, unless this results in main stress falling on a

negative prefix, or unless there is only one syllable before -**able**. In both these cases stress is placed 1 syllable back.

Examples:

'exĕcrable
in'terminable
'prŏbable, ˌim'prŏbable

Exceptions (pre-stressed 1 in each case):

a'mēnable	*for'mĭdable
*ap'plĭcable	*ˌhos'pĭtable
dë'lectable	*'inë'quĭtable
dë'spĭcable	*'inëx'plĭcable
*ë'quĭtable	*'inëx'trĭcable
*ëx'plĭcable	'in'flammable
*ëx'trĭcable	*'inˌhos'pitable
	re'doubtable [rɪ'daʊtəbl]

-acy

Consists of -**ate**$_C$+-**cy**: three types of structure need to be distinguished.

1   [[Stem+**ate**]$_{free}$+**cy**]. The second suffix, -**cy**, is stress-neutral, so that stress is assigned according to the properties of -**ate**: -**acy** thus acts as *pre-stressed 2* in these cases.

Examples: 'accūrate – 'accūracy
lë'gĭtimate – lë'gĭtimacy
'test,āte – 'testacy
in'testate – in'testacy (Negative prefix is unstressable)

2   [[Stem]$_{free}$+**ate**+**cy**]. *Stress-neutral.*

Examples: su'prēme – su'prēmacy
con'spīre – con'spĭracy

3   [Stem$_{bound}$+**ate**+**cy**]. *Pre-stressed 2.*

Examples: 'efficacy
'lūnacy

Notes: (i)   If the ending -**acy** is part of the ending -**cracy**, the word must be treated as stem plus -**crat** plus -**cy** (pre-stressed 2 variety).

Examples: 'ări'stŏcracy
dë'mŏcracy

(ii)   The word **dĭ'plōmacy** is 'diplo,mat plus -**cy** (pre-stressed 2 variety).

-ad

Meaning 'group of a certain number', this suffix is *pre-stressed 1/2*. The vowel does not reduce.

Examples: 'dȳ,ad (='group of two')
'tĕ,trad (='group of four')

Exception: ˈmўriad (vowel of suffix reduces)

-ade

Where this is clearly a suffix, it is *auto-stressed*. In these cases it is usually pronounced [-eɪd].

Examples:　ˈcannoˈnāde
　　　　　　ˈharlëquiˈnāde
　　　　　　ˈlĕmoˈnāde

Exceptions:　*ˈdĕ,cāde
　　　　　　ˈrĕnë,gāde (if this is taken as derived from the verb **renegue** [rɪˈniːg] or [rɪˈneɪg] 'go back on one's word')

Even when it would be hard to argue that **-ade** is a suffix, it is in most cases an ending which attracts stress on to itself. It is sometimes pronounced [-eɪd] and sometimes [-ɑːd] in these cases.

Examples:　　　　　　　　ˈaccoˈlāde
　　　　　　　　　　　　ˌfăˈçäde (or faˈçäde)
　　　　　　　　　　　　ˈpäliˈsāde

Exceptions:　*ˈcăval,cāde　　　　　ˈmarma,lāde
　　　　　　ˈcom,rāde　　　　　ˈmōtor,cāde
　　　　　　*ˈesca,pāde　　　　　*ˈprŏme,näde
　　　　　　*ˈespla,nāde

Note: The ending **-ade** may be part of the compound-forming element **-grade**, in which case the rules for compounds should be consulted.

-age

Sometimes pronounced [-,ɑːʒ] but more often [-ɪdʒ]. Two distinct principles operate:

1　*Stress-neutral* if the stem is a free form. The suffix is always [ɪdʒ] in these cases.

Examples:　ˈbrĭgand – ˈbrĭgandage
　　　　　　perˈcent – perˈcentage

Exceptions (pre-stressed 1/2 in each case):
　　　　　　ˌconˈcūbinage (in spite of ˈconcū,bîne)
　　　　　　ˈëquipage (in spite of ëˈquip)

2　*Pre-stressed 1/2* if the stem is not a free form. Stress is placed on the syllable preceding the suffix, unless this is a weak syllable; in this case the syllable preceding this is stressed, if there is one.

Examples:　adˈväntage
　　　　　　ˈgărage (or ˈgă,räge)
　　　　　　ˈfōliage
　　　　　　ˈcămou,fläge [ˈkæmə,flɑːʒ]

Exceptions:　ˈen,toü,räge [ˈɒn,tuə,rɑːʒ]　　*gaˈräge (American pronunciation)
　　　　　　ënˈvĭsage　　　　　　　　　ˈout,räge
　　　　　　ˈespio,näge　　　　　　　　ˈram,päge

-ageous

Consists of **-age** plus **-ous**: **-age** is always pronounced [eɪdʒ] in this combination, forming a strong syllable and therefore being assigned main stress by the rule for **-ous** (pre-stressed 1/2). Secondary stress is then placed according to the rhythmic principle (cf. pp. 31, 46 above), and not by the properties of **-age**.

Examples: 'ad,vän'tāgeous ['æd,vɑːn'teɪdʒəs] (ctr. ad'väntage)
  cou'rāgeous [kə'reɪdʒəs] (ctr. 'cöurage)

-aire
Autostressed.

Examples: 'doctri'naire
  'millio'naire ['mɪljə'nɜə]

-aise
Autostressed.

Example: 'pŏlo'naise

-al
Two distinct suffixes must be recognized.

A Adjective-forming **-al**: 1 *Pre-stressed 1/2.*

Examples: me'dĭcinal (**cĭ** is a weak syllable)
  'ŭni'versal (**ver** is a strong syllable)
  'trībal (only one syllable available)

Exception: ba'nal (or ba'näl) (perhaps not stem+the suffix **-al** but a simple root)

Some free stems insert an additional vowel when this suffix is attached to them; this insert is usually **-i-**, though **-u-** is also found (counting as short in all cases). Stress in the resulting word is regularly assigned by the rule for **-al**.

Examples: 'tŏrrent – tor'rential [-ʃəl]
  'con,tract – con'trac,tūal

Exception: 'spĭritūal

B Noun-forming **-al**: 2 *Stress-neutral* (the stem is nearly always a free form).

Examples: bë'trŏthe – bë'trŏthal
  rë'fūse – rë'fūsal

Exceptions: rë'prīsal (no verb rë'prīse exists)

-ality
Consists of **-al**$_A$ plus **-ity**. Since **-ity** is pre-stressed 1, main stress falls on the syllable containing the **a** of **-al**. Secondary stress is then assigned according to the properties of **-al**$_A$ (see above).

Examples: 'arti'fĭcial [-'fɪʃl,] – 'arti'fĭci'ălity [-'fɪʃɪ-] or [-'fɪsɪ-]
  'indi'vĭdūal – 'indi'vĭdū'ălity

Exceptions: Secondary stress is not assigned in certain words of four syllables.

ë'quality [ɪ'kwɒlɪtɪ] (ctr. 'ēqual)

fa'tălity (ctr. 'fātal) mo'dălity (ctr. 'mōdal)
*for'mălity (ctr. 'formal) mo'rălity (ctr. 'mŏral)
*lë'gălity (ctr. 'lēgal) *to'nălity (ctr. 'tōnal)
*lo'călity (ctr. 'lōcal) *vë'nălity (ctr. 'vēnal)

Secondary stress is assigned according to the rhythmic principle in certain longer words:

'illë'gălity (ctr. il'lēgal)
'inë'quality [-'kwɒ-]

-an
Pre-stressed 1/2

Examples: 'Afrĭcan (rĭ is a weak syllable)
su'burban (ctr. 'sŭb,urb) (**bur** is a strong syllable)
,dī'ŏcësan (ctr. 'dīocëse) (**cë** is a weak syllable)

Some free stems insert an additional vowel when this suffix is attached to them; this vowel is usually -i-, though e is also found (long in most cases, but occasionally short). Stress in the resulting word is regularly assigned by the rule for -**an**.

Examples: 'Păris – Pa'rĭsian [-'rɪz-]
'rep,tĭle – ,rep'tĭlian
'Eūrope ['jʊərəp] – 'Eūro'pēan ['jʊərə'pi:ən]
'Euclid ['ju:klɪd] – ,Eu'clidean [,ju:'klɪdɪən]

Note: Some words ending in -**an** in fact contain the suffix -**man** [mən], and are dealt with under that heading.

-ance
Consists of -**ant**$_A$ + -**ce**; three types of structure need to be distinguished:

1 [[Stem]$_{free}$ + ant + ce]. The combined suffix is *stress-neutral*.

Examples: 'clear – 'clearance
dë'lĭver – dë'lĭverance
'rēas'sūre ['ri:ə'ʃɔ:] – 'rēas'sūrance ['ri:ə'ʃɔ:rəns]

Note: The five words con'cordance, dis'cordance, 'ignorance, im'portance, ,lŭ'xūriance derive their stress-patterns from the corresponding free forms in -**ant** (see principle 2 below) rather than the free stems 'con,cord, 'dis,cord, ig'nore, 'im,port and 'lŭxūry.

2 [[Stem + ant]$_{free}$ + ce]. The final suffix -ce is stress-neutral, so the stressing follows the pattern for -**ant**$_A$ (see below). Thus -**ance** in these cases is, in effect, *pre-stressed 1/2*.

Examples: 'dŏminant – 'dŏminance
im'portant – im'portance (cf. note to 1 above)

3 [Stem$_{bound}$ + ant + ce]. *Pre-stressed 1/2*.

Examples: ap'purtĕnance (**te** is a weak syllable)

           ,mal'feasance (**fea** is a strong syllable)

           ,im'bălance (only one syllable available, since the negative prefix **im-** is not part of the SP)

Exceptions: fi'nance (or ,fī'nance)

           re'connaissance [rɪ'kɒnɪsəns]

-ancy

Consists of **-ant** followed by **-cy** (stress-neutral), and therefore follows the same pattern as **-ant** (see below).

Examples: 'hĕsitant – 'hĕsitancy

           rĕ'dundant – rĕ'dundancy

-ant

Two distinct suffixes must be recognised.

  A Adjective-forming **-ant**:

  1 *Pre-stressed 1/2.*

Examples: a'bundant (**bun** is a strong syllable)

           'consonant (**sŏ** is a weak syllable)

           ,flam'boyant (**boy** is a strong syllable)

Exception: gal'lant (='amorous') (Note that 'gallant, 'brave', follows the rule.)

  B Noun-forming **-ant**:

  2 *Stress-neutral when the stem is free.*

Examples: ac'count – ac'countant

           dĕ'fend – dĕ'fendant

           in'hăbit – in'hăbitant

Exceptions (mainly pre-stressed 1/2):

           'aspirant (ctr. a'spīre)

           'combatant (ctr. 'com,bat with full vowel in the final syllable)

           'comman,dant (ctr com'mänd)

           'confi,dant (ctr. con'fīde)

         *'dispūtant (ctr. dis'pūte)

           ĕ'xĕcūtant (ctr. 'exĕ,cūte)

           'Prŏtĕstant (ctr. pro'test)

  3 *Pre-stressed 1/2 when the stem is not free.*

Examples: ap'pellant (**pel** is a strong syllable)

           'adjutant (**ju** is a weak syllable)

           'cĕlĕbrant (**le** is a weak syllable)

           'occūpant (**cū** is a weak syllable)

Exceptions: ,lieu'tĕnant [,lef] or [,lu:-] (even though **tĕ** is a weak syllable)

           Lĕ'vant

           'flagĕllant (in spite of the strong syllable **-gel-** arising from double **l**)

-anthropic
Consists of the compound-forming element (cf. Section 5) **-anthrope** plus **-ic**. Since **-ic** is pre-stressed 1, main stress falls on the second syllable of **-anthrope**, and in addition the vowel of that syllable is shortened (see 7.3 below).

Example: 'phĭlan'thrŏpic

-anthropism, -anthropist, -anthropise, -anthropy
Consist of the compound-forming element **-anthrope** plus a pre-stressed 2 suffix. Main stress thus falls on the first syllable of **-anthrope**.

Examples: ˌlȳ'canthropy
mĭ'santhropist

-ar
Etymologically a variant of **-al**$_A$ (see above), usually occurring after a stem containing **l**. *Pre-stressed 1/2.*

Examples: 'alvë'ōlar (ō is a strong syllable)
'curvi'līnëar (në is a weak syllable)
mo'lĕcūlar (ctr. 'mŏlë,cūle) (cū is a weak syllable)

-arch
Compound-forming element, pronounced [-a:k] (cf. Section 5). Suffix-like in being affected by the 'destressing' rule (see Section 7.2 below).

Examples: 'ŏli,garch
'pātri,arch
'mŏnarch ['mɒnək] ('destressed' after stressed weak syllable **mŏ**)

-archy
Consists of the compound-forming element **-arch** plus noun-forming **y** (stress-neutral variety). The place of stress is therefore the same as in the corresponding word ending in **-arch**.

Examples: 'ŏli,garchy ['ɒlɪ,ga:kɪ]
'mŏnarchy ['mɒnəkɪ]

-arian
Follows the rule for **-an**, i.e. places stress on the first **a**, which is then lengthened (see Section 7.4). This holds no matter what the derivational structure of the word is.

Examples: ˌlī'brārian   [[libr+ary]+an]
ˌBul'gārian   [[Bulgaria]+an]
gram'mārian   [[grammar]+i+an]

-arium
Follows the rule for **-um**, i.e. places stress on the **a**, which is then lengthened (see Section 7.4).

Examples: a'quārium
'plăne'tārium
so'lārium

-ary

Pronounced [-ˌeri] in American English (unless immediately preceded by main stress, in which case the first vowel is reduced); it has a reduced vowel in British English [-əri] and may even elide this if the preceding consonants can be satisfactorily arranged around the remaining vowels.

	American English	British English
voluntary	[ˈvɑlənˌteri]	[ˈvɒləntri]
dispensary	[dɪˈspensəri]	[dɪˈspensəri]
constabulary	[kənˈstæbjəˌleri]	[kənˈstæbjələri]

1 *Stress-neutral* if the stem is free.

Examples: ˌanˈtïque – ˌanˈtïquary [-əri]
'budget – 'budgetary (Amer. 'budgeˌtary)
iˈmăgine – iˈmăginary [-ənri] (Amer. iˈmăgiˌnary)
saˈlïva – saˈlïvary [-əri]

Exceptions: (a) Most words ending in **-mentary**, which follow principle 2 (pre-stressed 1/2) and therefore place main stress on the syllable **-men-**.
'Parliament [-mənt] – 'Parliaˈmentary
'elëment [-mənt] – 'elëˈmentary

Note: 'comˌment loses its secondary stress when **-ary** is affixed:
'comˌment [-ˌment] – 'commentary [-məntri]
(Amer. 'commenˌtary [-mənˌteri]

(b) Certain free forms insert **-i-** before **-ary**. These are *pre-stressed 1/2.*

Example: ˌstïˈpendiary (ctr. 'stïpend)

(c) ˌăˈxillary (ctr. 'ăxil)
'discipline – 'disciˈplïnary or 'disciˌplïnary
(Amer. 'discipliˌnary is regular)
rëˈsïdüary (Amer. rëˈsïdüˌary) (ctr. 'rësïdüe)

2 *Pre-stressed 1/2* if the stem is not free.

Examples: ˌanˈcillary (double **l** makes the second syllable strong)
'cülinary (or 'cülinary) (**li** is a weak syllable)
ˌcenˈtēnary (**tē** is a strong syllable)
conˈstăbülary (**bü** is a weak syllable)

Exceptions (stress one syllable further back than expected in each case):
'adversary (often 'adverˌsary in Brit. as well as Amer.)
'nĕcessary (often 'nĕcesˌsary in Brit. as well as Amer.)
'commissary
'ĕmissary
ˌinˈvŏluntary
'sĕdentary
'vŏluntary
'vĕterinary (often with elision of first **r** in Brit.: ['vetɪnri] or ['vetnri])

Note: **caˈnāry, conˈtrāry, vaˈgāry** are all treated as simple roots with long **ā**.

-ast

Suffix related to **-ist**. *Pre-stressed 2*, and pronounced [-ˌæst] with a full vowel.

Examples: ĕnˈthūsiˌast
ˈgymˌnast

-ate

Several affixes written **-ate** need to be distinguished.

A   Verb-forming **-ate**: always pronounced with a full vowel.

1   *Pre-stressed 2* in words of three or more syllables.

Examples: ˈdĕlëˌgāte (verb)
ˈdĕmonˌstrāte

Exceptions:

(a)	(pre-stressed 3)	aˈmēlioˌrāte	ˈoxygeˌnāte
		dĕˈtērioˌrāte	ˈperëgriˌnāte
		disˈorienˌtāte	ˈtergiverˌsāte
		ˈētioˌlāte	
		ˈorienˌtāte	
(b)	(pre-stressed 1)	ˈcircumˈvalˌlāte	*ˌimˈpregˌnāte
		*ˌdēˈhȳˌdrāte	sëˈquesˌtrāte

2   *Autostressed in disyllables.*

Examples: crëˈāte
ˌrōˈtāte
ˈrē-crëˈāte (stress-neutral **rē** is not part of the SP)

Exceptions: ˈaeˌrāte [ˈɛəˌreɪt]
In American English, some of these words have pre-stressed **-ate** (cf. pattern 1 above):
*ˈrōˌtāte

Note: Many words ending in **-ate** are in fact of the form prefix + stem e.g. ˌtransˈlāte.

B   Noun-forming **-ate** in chemical terms: almost always with full vowel: [eɪt].

3   *Pre-stressed 2.*

Examples: ˈhȳˌdrāte
perˈmangaˌnāte (or perˈmanganate)

C   Noun- or adjective-forming **-ate** (usually pronounced [ət]).

4   *Pre-stressed 1/2*

Examples: ˌalˈternate [ˌɔːl-] (Brit., cf. Amer. ˈalternate)
ˈclīmate
dĕˈgĕnerate
ˈdĕlëgate
ëˈpĭscopate

Exceptions: (a) (full vowel in the final syllable)
     *'candi,dāte
     'cardina,lāte
     'cog,nāte
     'man,dāte
     'pātri,ar,chāte
     'pōten,tāte
     'prō,bāte
     *a'pos,tāte
     'cau,dāte
     'den,tāte
     *in'vertë,brāte
     *'vertë,brāte
    (b) (finally stressed)
     in'nāte
     ,or'nāte
     së'dāte
    (c) 'pŏmë'grănate (although **gră** is a weak syllable)
     or 'pŏmë,grănate ('compound' pattern)
    *'consummate (although **sum** is a heavy syllable)

-ation

Consists of -ate$_A$ plus -ion; -ion is pre-stressed 1, so main stress falls on the syllable containing the **a** (the **a** is always made long by the rules of Section 7.4). Secondary stress is then assigned according to the properties of -ate$_A$, i.e. usually placed two syllables before the **a**. This works no matter what the derivational structure of the word is. The sequence -**ti**- is assigned the pronunciation [ʃ].

Examples: 'dĕmon'strātion [[de+monstr+ate]+ion]
    'rĕcon'cīli'ātion [[re+con+cile]+i+ate+ion]
    ë'quĭvo'cātion [[equi+voc+ate]+ion]
    'transfor'mātion [[trans+form]+ate+ion] (or 'träns-)

Notes: (i)   For a variety of reasons (discussed in Section 7.2), the syllable before -**ation** may, although unstressed, retain a full vowel.

    Examples: *'con,den'sātion
     'in,can'tātion
     'rē,lă'xātion

  (ii)   -**ation** is unusual among stress-affecting affixes in occurring with its normal value after a stress-neutral affix, such as -**īze** (stress-neutral variety): 'rēgiona,līse – 'rēgiona,lī'sātion

-ative

Consists of -ate$_A$ (with *reduced* vowel: [ət]) plus -ive ([ɪv]) but seems to form a single *Pre-stressed 1/2* suffix for stress purposes, irrespective of the derivational structure of the word.

Examples: dë'monstrative [[de+monstr+ate]+ive] (ctr. 'dĕmon,străte,
with prestressed 2 suffix -**ate**)
'ŏperative [[oper+ate]+ive]
prë'servative [[pre+serve]+ate+ive]
'qualitative ['kwɒ-] [[qual+ity]+ate+ive]

Note: 'Trisyllabic shortening' (Section 7.3) may operate after stress assignment:

dë'clărative (cf. dë'clāre)
ë'vŏcative (cf. ë'vōke)

Exceptions: (a) (Stress falls one syllable back in a manner parallel to the
'trisyllabic shortening' cases just mentioned, though there
is not a corresponding base form with a long vowel)
'inter'rŏgative
*pë'jŏrative
prë'rŏgative
(b) (pronounced [eitiv]: usually analysable as -ate$_A$ plus
stress-neutral -**ive**)
*'contem,plātive
crë'ātive
*'illu,strātive
,op'tātive

-ator
Four types of structure need to be distinguished, and these fall into two sets,
each containing two structures.

1(a) [[Stem+**ate**]$_{free}$+**or**]   (b) [[Stem]$_{free}$+**ate**+**or**]

Stress-neutral, consisting of -ate$_A$ plus -or$_1$.

Examples: (a) ([Stem+**ate**] a free form)
'ăgi,tātor (cf. 'ăgi,tāte)
,dic'tātor (cf. ,dic'tāte) (British English)
'dic,tātor (cf. 'dic,tāte) (American English)
'prŏmul,gātor (cf. 'prŏmul,gāte)
(b) (Stem is a free form)
'appli,cātor (ctr. ap'plȳ)
'rĕspi,rātor (ctr. re'spīre)

Exceptions: (a) (-**ate** plus -or$_2$ (pre-stressed 1/2): see principle 2 below)
con'spīrator (even though **conspīre** is free)
'ŏrator (even though **orate** is free)
(b) (-**ate** and -**or** both stress-neutral)
'tōta,lī,sātor [[total]+ise+ate+or]
'versifi,cātor [[[verse]+i+fy]+k+ate+or]

2(a) [[Stem+**ate**]$_{bound}$+**or**]   (b) [Stem$_{bound}$+**ate**+**or**]

Consist of **-ate** (sometimes short, sometimes long) plus **-or₂** (pre-stressed 1/2). Stress thus falls on the syllable containing **a** if **a** is long, or the syllable before that if **a** is short.

Examples: cū'rātor⎫
                   ē'quātor⎰(long **a**, therefore penultimate stress)
               'prĕdator (short **a**, therefore antepenultimate stress)

Exceptions: 'glădi,ātor (as if 'glădi,āte were an actually occurring English verb)
               'nūme,rātor

Note: 'alli,gātor is probably a simple root, but is stressed in a fashion resembling compounds.

-atory

Consists of **-ate** plus **-ory**. In American English the latter affix maintains its full vowel [ɔ:] while **-ate** has its vowel reduced; the whole suffix is thus pronounced [-ə,tɔ:ri] in all cases. The best way of accounting for this is to say that **-ory** is stress-neutral in American English. Main stress is then assigned according to the properties of **-ate** (pre-stressed 2).

Examples: 'ăma,tōry
             ,ar'tĭcūla,tōry
             'manda,tōry

In British English, on the other hand, the **o** or **-ory** is always reduced; the vowel of **-ate** is sometimes maintained (giving a pronunciation [-eɪtəri]), and sometimes reduced, in which case the reduced **o** is normally elided (giving a pronunciation [-ətrɪ]). Most pronunciations can be accounted for in terms of a stress-neutral **-ory**, but main stress can shift to the syllable containing the **a**, which would indicate a pre-stressed variety of **-ory**.

Examples: 'ămatory ['æmətrɪ]
            ,ar'tĭcū,lātory [,ɑ:'tɪkjə,leɪtərɪ]
      or ,ar'tĭculatory [,ɑ:'tɪkjələtrɪ]
      or ,ar'tĭcū'lātory [,ɑ:'tɪkjə'leɪtərɪ]

-ature

Consists of **-ate_A** (with reduced vowel: [ət]) plus **-ure**, but seems to form a single *pre-stressed* 1/2 suffix for stress purposes (cf. **-ative** above).

Examples: 'armatūre ['ɑ:mətʃə]
      or 'arma,tūre ['ɑ:mə,tjʊə]
           'temperatūre ['tempərətʃə] or ['temprətʃə]
Exceptions: *'nōmen,clātūre

Note: Several words that end in **-ature** are of the form stem+**-ure**, and do not belong in this category: 'featūre, ma'tūre, 'natūre, ,dē-'natūre. In spite of its clear relation to the verb **create**, the word 'creatūre should be classed with these because of its pronunciation ['kri:tʃə].

-ce

This suffix is most frequently found attached to stems in **-ant** or **-ent**, forming words ending in **-ance** or **-ence**. It also occasionally occurs after stems in [-t],

[-d], [-s] or [-z], forming words ending in [-s]: this is in a few cases spelt **-se** rather than **-ce**. It never affects the placing of stress.

Examples: 'tŏlerant – 'tŏlerance
'temperance (**-ce** attached to bound form)
dë'pendent – dë'pendence
'inference (**-ce** attached to bound form)
ad'vīse [əd'vaɪz] (verb) – ad'vīce [əd'vaɪs] (noun)
dë'fend (verb) – dë'fence (noun) (Amer. dë'fense)
rë'spond (verb) – rë'sponse (noun)

-chromatic
Consists of the compound-forming element **-chrome** plus **-ic**, together with an insert **-at-** which is assigned stress because of the pre-stressed 1 **-ic**. Secondary stress is then placed by the rhythmic principle, and the vowel of **-chrome** is reduced.

Example: 'pŏlychro'mătic ['pɒlɪkrə'mætɪk]

-chronic [-'krɒnɪk]
Consists of the compound-forming element **-chrone** plus **-ic**. Pre-stressed 1 **-ic** assigns main stress to **-chron-**, and the vowel of that syllable is shortened (see Section 7.3 below).

Examples: ,syn'chrŏnic
'hĕtero'chrŏnic

-chronism, -chrony
Consist of **-chrone** plus a pre-stressed 2 suffix. Main stress thus falls on the syllable before **-chrone**.

Examples: a'năchro,nism [ə'nækrə,nɪzm]
,dī'ăchrony [,daɪ'ækrənɪ]

-chronous
Consists of **-chrone** plus **-ous** (in theory pre-stressed 1/2, but in fact acting as if the vowel of **-chrone** had already been shortened).

Example: ,ī'sŏchronous (and not 'īso'chrŏnous, as would normally be the case with the suffix **-ous**)

-cidal
Consists of **-cide** (see below) plus **-al** (pre-stressed 1/2): main stress therefore falls on **-ci-**. Secondary stress is then placed according to **-cide**.

Examples: 'hŏmi'cīdal
'süi'cīdal

-cide
Pre-stressed 2.

Examples: 'in'fanti,cīde
'păra'sīti,cīde (long ī of **parasīte** is shortened by 'trisyllabic shortening'. See Section 6.3)

Note: Some words ending in **-cide** are of the form [prefix+stem]:

dë'cīde
'cō-in'cīde

-cracy
Consists of the compound-forming element **-crat** (see Section 5) plus noun-forming **-y** (pre-stressed 2 variety). Main stress thus falls on the syllable before **-cra-**.

Examples: dë'mŏcracy
'ări'stŏcracy

-cratic
Consists of **-crat** plus **-ic** (pre-stressed 1). Main stress therefore falls on **-crat-**. Secondary stress is assigned by the rhythmic principle.

Examples: 'dĕmo'crătic
'aristo'crătic (British) (syllabifying ri.sto)
a'rĭsto'crătic (American) (syllabifying ris.to)

-cultural [-'kʌltʃərəl]
Consists of the compound-forming element **-culture** plus **-al** (pre-stressed 1/2). Main stress is therefore placed on **-cul-**, and secondary stress is placed 2 or 3 syllables before that by the rhythmic principle.

Example: 'horti'cultūral

-cy
Stress-neutral; usually attached to stems in **-ate**, **-ant**, or **-ent** to form words in **-acy**, **-ancy** or **-ency**, but may occur in other contexts also.

Examples: 'obstinate – 'obstinacy
ëx'pectant – ëx'pectancy
'prĕsident – 'prĕsidency
'bank,rupt – 'bank,ruptcy
'ïdiot – 'ïdiocy
'minstrel – 'minstrelsy (different spelling)

Exception: di'plōmacy (ctr. 'dïplo,mat)

Note: Words ending in **-cracy** are probably best taken as formed by adding **-y** (pre-stressed 2 variety) to the corresponding words in **-crat**.

-dom
Stress-neutral.

Examples: 'martyr – 'martyrdom
'băchelor – 'băchelordom

-ean
Consists of **-an** preceded by an insert **-e-** (usually long but sometimes short). Main stress falls on **-e-** if it is long, and on the preceding syllable otherwise.

Examples: 'Hercū'lēan
'subter'rānëan

-ed
Stress-neutral. Pronunciation varies as follows:
[ɪd] when preceded by [t] or [d]

[t] when preceded by voiceless sounds other than [t]
[d] when preceded by voiced sounds other than [d]

Examples: 'wait – 'waited ['weɪtɪd]
'pick – 'picked ['pɪkt]
'rub – 'rubbed ['rʌbd]

Exceptions: In certain adjectival forms this suffix is pronounced [ɪd] even
when not preceded by [t] or [d]: some of these are variants of
verbal forms (past participles), while others have no connection
with any verb.

ac'cursëd
'āgëd ['eɪdʒɪd] (='old'; ctr. **aged** ['eɪdʒd], past of **to age**)
bë'lövëd
'blessëd
'crookëd
'cursëd
'cussëd
'doggëd (='persevering'; ctr. **dogged** [dɒgd], past of **to dog**)
'jaggëd
'learnëd ['lɜːnɪd] (='erudite'; ctr. ['lɜːnd], past of **to learn**)
(bow, etc)-'leggëd
'nākëd
'raggëd (='in rags'; ctr. **ragged** ['rægd], past of **to rag**)
'ruggëd
'sācrëd
'wickëd
'wretchëd

-edly, -edness
Consist of **-ed** plus a further stress-neutral suffix. In these contexts the **-ed** is
pronounced [ɪd]:

(a) (Obligatorily) when preceded by [t] or [d];
(b) (Obligatorily) when the stem is one of the exceptions listed under **-ed**
above;
(c) (Sporadically) in other cases.

Examples: (a) 'heatëdly
(b) 'wickëdly
(c) sup'pōsëdly

-ee
1 *Autostressed* when it is a genuine suffix. Secondary stress is two syllables
earlier; syllables stressed when the stem occurs alone may escape reduction in
the suffixed form.

Examples: 'absent – 'absen'tee
in'tern – 'in,ter'nee

Exception: 'dēdi,cāte – 'dēdica'tee

When this ending is not a genuine suffix, it varies between 2   *autostressed*
and 3   *pre-stressed 1/2*.

Examples:	2	(autostressed)	'rĕ,par'tee
			,set'tee
	3	(pre-stressed)	'coffee
			com'mittee
			'pĕdi,gree

-ée [-eɪ]
Pre-stressed 1/2.

Examples: fi'än,cée
'măti,née

-een
Not really a suffix in most cases, but attracts stress on to itself (cf. -ene, which is identical in pronunciation but is *pre-stressed 2*).

Examples: ,can'teen
'velve'teen

Exception: 'ever,green (compound)

-eer
Autostressed; secondary stress is placed two syllables earlier.

Examples: 'auctio'neer
'găzet'teer (ctr. ga'zette)

Notes: (i) This ending still takes stress on to itself even when it is not strictly a suffix:
ca'reer
ve'neer

(ii) 'ōver,seer is [[over+see]+er], and is therefore handled under **-er** (see below).

-elle
Not really a suffix, but attracts stress on to itself. Secondary stress is then placed by the rhythmic principle (Section 3.2).

Examples: 'băga'telle
'mădemoi'selle ['mædəmə'zel] or [,mæm'zel]

-en
Three suffixes are to be distinguished, though all of them are *stress-neutral*.

A Participle-forming

Example: for'säke – for'säken

B Adjective-forming

Example: 'wood – 'wooden

C Verb-forming

Example: 'fresh – 'freshen

-ence
Consists of **-ent+ce**. *Pre-stressed 1/2.*

Examples: 'inter'fērence (**fē** is a strong syllable)
                    bë'nĕvolence (**vŏ** is a weak syllable)

Exceptions: (a) (two syllables back instead of one syllable back as indi-
                    cated by the stem)
                    ,cō-'incidence (ctr. 'cō-in'cīde)
                    'confidence (ctr. con'fīde)
                    'excellence (in spite of strong syllable **çel**)
                    'prĕcedence (ctr. prë'cēde)
                    'prĕvalence (ctr. prë'vail with long vowel)
                    'prŏvidence   ⎫
                    ,im'prŏvidence⎬(ctr. pro'vīde)
                                       ⎭
                    'rĕsidence (ctr. rë'sīde)
                    'rĕverence   ⎫
                    ir'rĕverence⎬(ctr. rë'vēre)
                    'subsidence (ctr. sub'sīde)
        (b) (one syllable back, instead of the expected two)
                    'omni'prĕsence (ctr. the regular ,om'nĭpotence)

Notes: (i) Some words ending in **-ence** consist of a stem in **-end** followed by
              noun-forming **-ce** (stress-neutral):
              dë'fend – dë'fence
       (ii) The word **com'mence** is of the form [prefix+stem]

-ency

Consists of **-ent**+**-cy**. *Pre-stressed 1/2*, since **-cy** is always stress-neutral in this
combination.

Example: ë'mergency (**mer** is a strong syllable)

Exceptions: 'excellency (in spite of strong syllable **cel**)
                  'prĕsidency (ctr. prë'sīde, cf. 'prĕsident)
                  'rĕsidency (ctr. rë'sīde, cf. 'rĕsident)
                  ,trans'părency (in spite of weak syllable **pă**)

-ene

Pre-stressed 2.

Examples: a'cĕty,lēne
                'Naza,rēne

Exception: së'rēne

-enne

Autostressed.

Example: Pa'rīsi'enne [pə'rɪzɪ'en]

-ent

Pre-stressed 1/2.

Examples: ad'jācent (**jā** is a strong syllable)
                  in'cumbent (**cum** is a strong syllable)
                  in'telligent (**li** is a weak syllable)

Exceptions: (a) (Pre-stressed 1 in spite of weak syllable)
ap`părent (cf. ap`pear with long vowel)
`omni`prĕsent (in spite of the weak syllable **prĕ**)
,trans`părent (or ,trans`pārent, which is regular)

(b) (Two syllables back instead of one syllable back as indicated by the stem)
,cō-`incident (ctr. `cō-in`cīde)
`confident (ctr. con`fīde)
`excellent (in spite of strong syllable **cel**)
`prĕcedent (ctr. prĕ`cēde)
`prĕsident (ctr. prĕ`sīde)
`prĕvalent (ctr. prĕ`vail with long vowel)
`prŏvident
,im`prŏvident } (ctr. pro`vīde)
`rĕsident (ctr. rĕ`sīde)
`rĕverent
ir`rĕverent } (ctr. rĕ`vēre)

Notes: (i) Many words in **-ent** are of the form [prefix + stem]; most of them are verbs, and the prefix is usually stress-repellent (cf. Section 6.2):

in`vent
con`tent (adj.)

(ii) Some words in **-ent** are nouns of the form Verb stem in **-end** followed by noun-forming **-t** (stress-neutral):

in`tend – in`tent
a`scend – a`scent

(iii) Some words ending in **-ent** are of the form stem + **-ment**, and are dealt with under that heading.

-ential

Consists of **-ent** plus **-al**$_A$ with an insert **-ĭ-**; main stress is placed by **-al**$_A$ (pre-stressed 1/2) on the syllable containing **-en-**. The sequence **-ti-** is then assigned the pronunciation [ʃ].

Examples: `pĕni`tential [-`tenʃl]
`ĕxi`stential

-er

Three distinct suffixes of this shape need to be recognised.

A   Agent-noun-forming **-er**.

1   *Stress-neutral* where the stem is a free form.

Examples: com`mänd – com`mänder
in`terpret – in`terpreter
`căta,logue [-,lɒg] – `căta,lŏguer

Exceptions: `ōver`see – `ōver,seer (compound)
`under`tāke – `under,tāker (=`funeral agent') (compound)
`under`wrīte – `under,wrīter (compound)

2   *Pre-stressed 2* where the stem is not free.

Examples: a'strŏnomer
gë'ŏgrapher
'milliner

Exceptions: 'hăber,dăsher (compound?)
'inter,lōper
'nĕcro,mancer (compound)

B   Abstract-noun-forming -**er**.

3   *Stress-neutral.*
Examples: dis'claim – dis'claimer

C   Comparative-adjective-forming -**er**.

4   *Stress-neutral.*

Example: po'līte – po'līter

-erie
Pre-stressed 1.

Example: 'căma'răderie

-ery
Pronounced [-ərɪ]; [ə] may be elided if the preceding syllable is reduced. Two patterns must be recognised.

1   *Stress-neutral* where the stem is a free form.

Examples: 'brībe – 'brībery
buf'fōōn – buf'fōōnery
'jewel – 'jewellery ['dʒu:əlrɪ]

2   *Pre-stressed 1/2* where the stem is not free.

Examples: 'frippery
a'dultery (stem is not related to the phonetically identical free
form **adult**)
'mŏnastery ['mɒnəstrɪ] (assuming the syllabification -**na.ste**-)

Exception: 'dÿsentery ['dɪsəntrɪ] (although **sen** is a strong syllable)

Notes: (i)   Some words in -**ery** are of the form [stem in -**er** plus (stress-
neutral) -**y**]:

dë'līvery
dis'cŏvery
rë'cŏvery
,up'hōlstery

(ii)   Some words in -**ery** are of the form [stem+-**er**+(stress-neutral)
-**y**]:

'millinery
'presbytery

(iii) The word **peˈrɪ̆phery** is [**peripher**+-**y** (pre-stressed 2)]; cf. the same stem in **peripheral**.

(iv) The word **perˈfūmery** is based on the free verb stem **perˈfūme** rather than the noun stem **ˈperfume**.

(v) In some American varieties, some words in -**ery** are pronounced with a full vowel [e]:

ˈcĕme,tĕry

ˈmŏna,stĕry

-esce [-ˈes]
Autostressed.

Examples: ˈacquiˈĕsce
ˈconvaˈlĕsce

-escence, -escent
Consist of -**esce** plus a pre-stressed 1/2 suffix; main stress is therefore placed on the syllable containing **es**.

Examples: ˈincanˈdĕscent (or ˈin,can-)
ˈphosphoˈrĕscence

-ese [-ˈiːz]
Autostressed.

Examples: ˌChīˈnēse
ˈPortūˈguese [-ˈgiːz]

Note: ˈdīocĕse

-esque [-ˈesk]
Autostressed.

Example: ˈpictūˈresque [ˈpɪktʃəˈresk]

-ess
Stress-neutral (though this suffix may sometimes be autostressed in certain words: see my remarks on 'built-in contrastive stress' in Section 5.3). It is pronounced [-,es] with a full vowel, unless the preceding syllable has main stress, in which case the pronunciation is [əs] or [ɪs].

Examples: ˈprŏphĕt – ˈprŏphĕ,tess (or ˈprŏphĕˈtess)
ˈmănager – ˈmănage,ress [-dʒə,res] (or ˈmănageˈress)
ˈactor – ˈactress [ˈæktrəs]
ĕnˈchänter – ĕnˈchäntress [-trəs]

Exception: *ˈhōs,tess (or ,hōsˈtess)

-esse
Autostressed.

Examples: fiˈnesse
ˌlarˈgesse

-et (=ˈgroup of . . . performers')
Autostressed.

Example: ˌquinˈtet

-ette
Autostressed.

Examples: ˌbrüˈnette
             ˈnŏveˈlette

Exceptions: *ˈcĭgaˌrette (American; British pronunciation is normally regular)
             ˈĕtiˌquette [-ˌket]
             ˈpălette [ˈpælət]

-ety
Variant of **-ity** when preceded by **-ĭ-**, which is always lengthened (Section 7.4). *Pre-stressed 1.*

Example: vaˈrīety

-eur
Autostressed.

Examples: ˌconnoisˈseur [ˈkɒnəˈsɜ:]

Exceptions: ˈămateur [ˈæmətə] or [ˈæmətʃə]
             ˈgrandeur [ˈgrændʒə]
             *ˈchauffeur [ˈʃəufə] (or [ˌʃəuˈfɜ:])

-faction
Consists of **-fȳ** plus **-ion** (pre-stressed 1), with an insert **-ct-** between them, and almost always preceded by an insert **-ĕ-**. Main stress is assigned to **-fac-**, and secondary stress is placed two syllables further back by **-fȳ**. The sequence **-ti-** is pronounced [ʃ].

Examples: ˈliqueˈfaction
             ˈsatisˈfaction

-fication
Consists of **-fȳ** plus **-ation**, with an insert **-c-** between them, and preceded by an insert **-ĭ-**. Main stress is assigned to the syllable **-cā-** by the properties of **-ion** (pre-stressed 1), while secondary stress falls two syllables further back than **-fȳ**. The sequence **-ti-** is pronounced [ʃ].

Examples: ˈfortifiˈcātion
             perˈsŏnifiˈcātion

-ful
Two suffixes must be distinguished,
   A   Adjective-forming suffix **-ful**. This always has the reduced pronunciation [-fl] and is *stress-neutral*.

Examples: ˈpurpose – ˈpurposeful
             rëˈproach – rëˈproachful

   B   Measure-noun-forming suffix **-ful**. This varies freely between a reduced pronunciation [-fl] and a full vowel pronunciation [-ˌfʊl], and is *stress-neutral*.

Examples: 'pockët – 'pockët,ful (or 'pockëtful)
'tāble,spōōn – 'tāble,spōōn,ful (or -,spōōnful)

-fy
Prestressed 2. This is almost always preceded by an insert -ĭ- (occasionally -ĕ-).
A long vowel in the preceding syllable is shortened.

Examples: 'lĭquë,fȳ   'sătis,fȳ
per'sŏnifȳ   'rărë,fȳ (cf. 'rāre)

-gogy [-,gɒdʒɪ].
Consists of the compound-forming element **-gogue** plus noun-forming **-y**
(stress-neutral variety).

Example: 'pĕda,gŏgy

-gon
Pre-stressed 2. The normal pronunciation in British English has a reduced
vowel, but American English tends to prefer a full vowel.

Example: 'octagon (Amer. 'octa,gon)

-gram
Compound-forming element (see Section 5).

-graph
Compound-forming element (see Section 5).
   Pronounced [-,grɑ:f] (British English only) or [-,græf] (British and
American English).

-grapher, -graphist, -graphy
Consist of **-graph** plus a pre-stressed 2 suffix. Main stress is therefore placed on
the syllable before **-graph**, and the vowel of **-graph** is reduced.

Examples: pho'tŏgrapher [fə'tɒgrəfə]
të'lĕgraphist
'rādi'ŏgraphy

-graphic
Consists of **-graph** plus **-ic** (pre-stressed 1). Main stress therefore falls on
-gra-. The vowel of **-graph** is shortened because of **-ic** (Section 7.3), and is thus
pronounced [æ] even by speakers who have [ɑ:] in **-graph** when word-final.

Examples: 'ethno'grăphic
'stĕreo'grăphic (or 'stē-)

-hood
Stress-neutral.

Examples: 'chīld,hood
'neighböur,hood

-ial, -ian, -iant
Consist of **-al**_A, **-an**, **-ant**_A, preceded by an insert -ĭ-. Stress therefore falls on the
syllable before the insert; **-ci-** and **-ti-** may coalesce to [ʃ].

-ible
Pre-stressed 1/2.

Examples: in'telligible (**lĭ** is a weak syllable)
sus'ceptible (**cep** is a strong syllable)
in'dĕlible (**dĕ** is a weak syllable, but the negative prefix **in-** is not
part of the SP)

Exception: com'pătible (although **pă** is weak)

-ic

Usually forms adjectives, but may also form nouns. *Pre-stressed 1.* A long
vowel in the final syllable of the stem is usually shortened, unless (a) it is
written with two letters, or (b) it comes immediately before the vowel of **-ic**
(and is therefore automatically long – cf. Section 7.4).

Examples: ,ath'lĕtic (ctr. 'ath,lēte)
'mīcro'scŏpic (ctr. 'mīcro,scōpe)
'cūbic (shortening rules never apply to **ū** – see Section 2.2)
,hȳ'gienic [,haɪ'dʒi:nɪk] (written with two letters – but note
the alternative American pronunciation **'hȳgi'ĕnic** in which
the two letters are taken as belonging to separate syllables).
'algĕ'brāic (**a** immediately before **-ic**)

Exceptions: (a)   (vowel shortening expected but not operative)

a'cētic	pho'nēmic
a'phāsic	*'phōto'gēnic
'bāsic	'psȳchic ['saɪkɪk]
'brōmic	'Rōmic
'chrōmic	'rūbric⎫ (**ū** after **r** is always
'cȳclic	'rūnic ⎭ replaced by **ü**)
ën'cȳclo'pēdic	'scēnic
(variant spelling	së'mēmic
in -paedic)	stra'tēgic
'ĕpi'cȳclic	*sy'stēmic
'gnōmic	to'nēmic (or ,tō'nēmic)
,lĕ'xēmic	'Vēdic
,mor'phēmic	'vēlic
'nītric	
'ortho'pēdic	
(variant spelling	
in -paedic)	

(b)   (antepenultimate stress – many of these are nouns)

'ăgaric (noun)	'hĕretic (noun)
'Ărabic	'lūnatic
a'rithmetic (noun: adj.	'nūclĕic
'ărith'mĕtic is regular)	'pŏlitic
'arsenic (noun)	'rhĕtoric (noun)
'Cătholic	'turmeric (noun)
'chŏleric	

(c)   (short vowels although written with two letters)
*a'coustic [ə'kustɪk] (or [ə'ku:stɪk] with long vowel)

*'caustic ['kɒstɪk] (or ['kɔ:stɪk] with long vowel)
*,hỹ'draulic [,haɪ'drɒlɪk] (or [,haɪ'drɔ:lɪk] with long vowel)
*'Gaelic ['gælɪk] (or ['geɪlɪk] with long vowel)

Note: **bishopric** consists of **bishop** plus a (very unproductive) suffix **-ric** (stress-neutral).

-ical

Consists of **-ic-** plus **-al** (pre-stressed 1/2). Main stress therefore falls on the syllable before **-ic** (which normally has short i). Secondary stress is placed according to the rhythmic principle. The vowel of the syllable before **-ic** undergoes shortening on the same terms as when **-ic** is the final suffix.

Example: 'gēo'grăphical
        'mĕtrical (ctr. 'mētre)
        hë'rĕtical (regular, ctr. 'hĕretic)
        po'lĭtical (regular, ctr. 'pŏlitic)
        rhë'tŏrical (regular, ctr. 'rhĕtoric)
Exception: cer'vīcal

-ice

Pre-stressed 2, and pronounced [-ɪs].

Examples: 'cowardice
         'mălice
         'prĕcipice
Exceptions: po'lĭce
           'săcri,fīce

-ician

Consists of **-ic** plus **-an** (pre-stressed 1/2) with an insert **-i-**. Main stress thus falls on the syllable containing the first **i**. The sequence **-ci-** is pronounced [ʃ] in these cases.

Examples: a'căde'mĭcian
        'stăti'stĭcian

-icious

In this ending the **-ic** does not represent the suffix **-ic** but is usually part of the stem. Main stress is placed by **-ous** (pre-stressed 1/2) on the syllable containing the first **i** of this ending. The sequence **-ci-** is pronounced [ʃ] in these cases.

Examples: ma'lĭcious
        'ăva'rĭcious

-icity

Sometimes consists of **-ic** plus **-ity** (pre-stressed 1). In some words, however, the sequence **-ic-** is part of the stem. Main stress is placed on the syllable containing the first **-i-** in both cases. Secondary stress is always placed according to the rhythmic principle.

Examples: 'au,then'tĭcity
        'multi'plĭcity

-ics
Consists of **-ic** plus a stress-neutral suffix **-s**. Main stress is placed on the syllable preceding **-ic**. The vowel of the stressed syllable is usually shortened (as stated under **-ic** above).

Examples: 'callis'thĕnics
              'măthĕ'mătics

-id
When this is a genuine suffix (adjective-forming) it is *Pre-stressed 1*. This rule also governs the majority of the other cases, though there are exceptions.

Examples: 'splendid (genuine affix: cf. splend+our)
              ca'rŏtid (possibly the suffix **-id**)
              'căry'ătid (noun: probably not the suffix **-id**)

Exceptions: 'chrўsalid (noun)
               'invalid (='sick person': adjective in'vălid is regular)
               'pўramid

-idė
In chemical terms; *Pre-stressed 1/2*.

Examples: 'flüo,rīde (o is a weak syllable)
              ,mŏ'nŏ,xīde (/nok/ is a strong syllable)

-idity
Consists of **-id** plus **-ity** (pre-stressed 1). Main stress falls on the syllable containing the **i** or **-id**. Secondary stress is assigned according to the rhythmic principle.

Example: 'intre'pĭdity (ctr. in'trĕpid)

-ient
Consists of **-ent** preceded by an insert **-ĭ-**. Stress therefore falls on the syllable before the insert; **-ci-** and **-ti-** may coalesce to [ʃ].

-ier [-'ɪə].
Autostressed, except in disyllabic words, which usually have initial stress (implying that the suffix is pre-stressed).

Examples: 'bombar'diēr
                     'gondo'liēr
                     'clōthiēr
                     'prĕmiēr

Exceptions: (a) (pre-stressed 1 although trisyllabic)
                    ,cos'tūmiēr
                    ,fī'nanciēr
               (b) (autostressed although disyllabic)
                    ,că'shiēr

-ile [-,aɪl] (British), [-əl] (American)
Pre-stressed 1/2.

Examples: 'dŏmi‚cīle (Amer. 'dŏmicile) (**mǐ** is a weak syllable)
pro'jec‚tīle (Amer. pro'jectile) (**jec** is a strong syllable)
'hos‚tīle (Amer. 'hostile)

Exceptions: (a) (pre-stressed 2/3)
'flŭvia‚tīle
'infan‚tīle
'mercan‚tīle

(b) (pronounced [-‚i:l] in both British and American English)
'automo‚bīle
'imbe‚cīle

(c) (final **e** pronounced [ɪ])
'campa'nïlë
‚can'täbilë
‚fac'sïmilë
'sïmilë
'sal vo'lătilë

Note: 'rĕcon‚cīle is of the form [prefix+prefix+[stem **-cile**]] and is therefore
not subject to the rules for suffixes or endings.

-ine

Several different cases need to be distinguished.
A   Adjective-forming suffix pronounced [-‚aɪn]:
1 *Pre-stressed 1/2.*

Examples: 'alka‚līne (**kǎ** is a weak syllable)
'elë'phan‚tīne (**phan** is a strong syllable)
'inter'nē‚cīne (**nē** is a strong syllable)

Exceptions: crÿstal‚līne
di'vīne
'Flŏren‚tīne
'sătur‚nīne
'serpen‚tīne

B   Chemical-noun-forming suffix pronounced [-‚i:n]
2 *Pre-stressed 1/2.*

Examples: 'glÿce‚rïne
'mor‚phïne

C   Noun-forming ending (sometimes fairly suffix-like) pronounced [-‚aɪn].
3 *Pre-stressed 2.*

Examples: 'cŏlum‚bīne
'turpen‚tīne

D   Noun-forming ending pronounced [-i:n].
4 *Autostressed*

Examples: 'măga'zïne (Brit.: ctr. Amer. 'măga‚zïne)
'marga'rïne (Brit. ['mɑ:dʒə'ri:n], but ctr. Amer. ['mɑrdʒərɪn]
‚roü'tïne
'tambou'rïne ['tæmbə'ri:n]

Exceptions: 'auber,gïne [-,ʒi:n]   *'măga,zïne (Amer.)
           'běnë'dic,tïne   'měla,mïne
          *'brïgan,tïne   'mezza,nïne
          *'brillian,tïne   *'necta,rïne
          *'găber,dïne   *'plasti,cïne
          *'grěna,dïne   'pris,tïne (adj.)
          *'guillo,tïne ['gɪl-]   'quaran,tïne ['kwɒ-]
          *'lïber,tïne

E   Adjective-, noun-, or verb-forming ending pronounced [-ɪn]
5   *Pre-stressed 1/2.*

Examples: ,clan'děstine (**des** is a strong syllable)
         'dïscipline (**scĭ** is a weak syllable)

Exceptions: ë'xămine (although /ză/ is a weak syllable)
          i'măgine (although **mă** is a weak syllable)

Notes: (i)   A number of verbs of the form [prefix+stem ending in **-ine**] are
             finally-stressed, e.g. com'bïne, dë'fïne, ,in'clïne, ,ō'pïne (or
             o'pïne).
       (ii) A number of [root+root] compounds have penultimate stress,
             e.g. 'sun,shïne.

-ion
Pre-stressed 1, and pronounced [jən]. When this suffix is immediately preceded by **c, g, s, t,** or **x,** the initial [j] coalesces with the consonant as follows:

   -cion is pronounced   [ʃən]
   -gion is pronounced   [dʒən]
   -ssion is pronounced   [ʃən]
   -sion is pronounced   {[ʃən] after a consonant
                     {[ʒən] after a vowel (or **r** for some speakers)
   -tion is pronounced   {[tʃən] after an **s**
                     {[ʃən] elsewhere
   -xion is pronounced   [kʃən]

When the stem ends in vowel plus single consonant, this vowel is always long
(unless it is **i,** which is always short); see Section 7.4.2 for more details.

Examples: rë'lātion [-ʃən]
         per'mission [-ʃən]
         'indi'gestion [-dʒestʃən]
         dif'fūsion [-ʒən]
         ,dï'version [-ʃən] or [-ʒən]

Exceptions: 'rătion ['ræʃən]⎫
          com'pănion   ⎬with short **a**
                      ⎭

Notes: (i)   'ion, 'lïon, O'rïon, 'scïon, 'Zïon are simple roots
      (ii) 'dandë,lïon

-ional, -ionate
If **-io-** were taken as forming two syllabic nuclei in these cases, then the
accentual properties of both **-al** (clearly **-al**ₐ in this context, and therefore

pre-stressed 1/2) and -**ate** (clearly -**ate**$_C$, and therefore also pre-stressed 1/2) would cause main stress to fall on the **i**, which would be incorrect. The letter **i** must be taken as representing a semi-vowel [j] here, so that it belongs to the same syllable as the **o**. Alternatively, -**al**$_A$ and -**ate**$_C$ could be taken as stress-neutral in these combinations.

Examples: ˈrēgional
dēˈnŏmiˈnātional
ĕxˈtortionate

Note: ˈnătional [ˈnæʃnəl] has short **a** (ctr. ˈnātion).

-ious
Consists of -**ous** (pre-stressed 1/2) preceded by an insert -**i**-. Since the insert has a short vowel, the stress falls on the syllable before it. When this combination is immediately preceded by **c**, **g**, **t**, or **x**, the **i** coalesces with the consonant as follows:

-**cious** }
-**scious** } are pronounced [ʃəs]
-**gious** is pronounced [dʒəs]
-**tious** is pronounced { [tʃəs] after an **s**
{ [ʃəs] elsewhere
-**xious** is pronounced [kʃəs]

If the stem has long **i** as its vowel, this becomes short (see Section 7.4.2).

Examples: conˈtāgious [kənˈteɪdʒəs]
fēˈlōnious [fɪˈləʊnɪəs]
ˌjüˈdīcious [ˌdʒuːˈdɪʃəs]
ˈvĭcious [ˈvɪʃəs] (ctr. vīce with long **i**)

Note: ˌpresˈtīgious [ˌpresˈtɪdʒəs] from ˌpresˈtīge [ˌpresˈtiːʒ]

-ique
Autostressed. Pronounced [-ˈiːk]

Examples: ˌanˈtïque
oˈblïque

-is
Pre-stressed 1/2.

Examples: syˈnopsis (**nop** is a strong syllable)
ˈhaliˈtōsis (**tō** is a strong syllable)
ˈgĕnesis (**nĕ** is a weak syllable)
ˈchrўsalis (**să** is a weak syllable)

-ise
Two distinct suffixes must be recognised
   A   Verb-forming suffix, pronounced [-aɪz] and often written -**ize**; where this alternative spelling exists, the word can be stressed as if it ended in -**ize**.

Notes: (i)   The following words which do not have alternative spellings in -**ize** are best treated as simple roots:

,chas'tīse ⎫
'fran,chīse ⎰ pronounced [-aɪz]

'păra,dīse   pronounced [-aɪs]

'treatise   pronounced [-ɪz]

'mortise ⎫
'practise (verb) ⎪
'prĕmise ⎬ pronounced [-ɪs]
'prŏmise (verb and noun) ⎭

(ii) The following words which do not have alternative spellings in
-ize are probably of the form prefix+stem:

ad'vīse ⎫
ap'prīse ⎪
a'rīse ⎪
com'prīse ⎪
dë'mīse ⎪
dë'spīse ⎪
dë'vīse ⎬ pronounced [-aɪz]
dis'guīse ⎪
ëx'cīse (verb) (or ,ex-) ⎪
'ex,cīse (noun) ⎪
prë'mīse (verb) (or 'prĕmise) ⎪
rë'vīse ⎪
sur'mīse ⎪
sur'prīse ⎭

con'cīse ⎫
prë'cīse ⎰ pronounced [-aɪs]

B   Noun-forming suffix, pronounced [-iːz]. *Autostressed.*

Examples: chë'mïse [ʃɪ-]
'exper'tīse

-ish
Two distinct suffixes must be recognised.
  A   Adjective-forming, meaning 'rather X(-like)'. *Stress-neutral.*

Examples: 'kittenish cf. 'kitten
'yellowish cf. 'yellow

  B   Verb-forming suffix, with no fixed meaning. *Pre-stressed 1.*

Examples: a'bŏlish
dë'mŏlish

Exception: im'pŏverish

-ism
Two distinct principles operate.
  1   *Stress-neutral*, where the stem is a free form.

Examples: 'absen'tee – 'absen'tee,ism
'Phări,see – 'Phărisā,ism (with slight spelling change)

,im'pērial – ,im'pēria,lism
'Prŏtestant – 'Prŏtestantism
,in'cendiary – ,in'cendia,rism (drops -y of stem)
'anti-'sē,mīte – 'anti-'sĕmi,tism ⎫
'Phili,stīne – 'Philistĭ,nism ⎭ (change of quantity)

Exceptions: Că̆tholic – Ca'thŏli,cism
'infan,tīle – in'fanti,lism

2 *Pre-stressed 2*, where the stem is not a free form.

Examples: 'ănar,chism [-,kızm]
'ăpho'rism
'ĕ,xor,cism
më'tăbo,lism

Exceptions: 'anthropo'mor,phism
'īso'mor,phism
'mŏnothĕ,ism
'pŏlythĕ,ism

-ist

Two distinct principles operate.
1 *Stress-neutral*, where the stem is a free form.

Examples: ëx'treme – ëx'trē,mist
'sĕparate – 'sĕpara,tist
'mŏdern – 'mŏder,nist
'prŏpa'ganda – 'prŏpa'gandist (with slight spelling change)

Exceptions: All words ending in **-graphist**, **-phonist**, **-culturist**, e.g.
'tĕle,phōne – të'lĕpho,nist

2 *Pre-stressed 2*, where the stem is not free.

Examples: 'Bap,tist
rë'cĭdi,vist
,ven'trĭlo,quist

Exceptions: 'Ăna'bap,tist
'mŏnothĕ,ist
'obscū'ran,tist
'oppor'tū,nist
'pŏlythĕ,ist
'sўstema,tist
'tăxi,der,mist or 'tăxi'der,mist

-ite

Several suffixes written **-ite** need to be distinguished.
A Noun-forming **-ite** in words meaning 'native of X' or 'supporter of X';
always pronounced [aıt], with a full vowel.
1 *Stress-neutral*, where the stem is a free form.

Examples: 'Jācob – 'Jăco,bīte
'Bethlë,hem – 'Bethlë,hĕ'mīte

2   *Pre-stressed 2* in other cases.

Example: 'Musco,vīte

B   Noun-forming -**ite** in chemical terms; always pronounced [aɪt], with a full vowel.

3   *Pre-stressed 2.*

Examples: 'anthra,cīte
              'gĕlig,nīte
              'gră,phīte

C   Verb-forming -**ite**: always pronounced [aɪt], with a full vowel.

4   *Pre-stressed 2* in words of three or more syllables.

Example: 'expë,dīte

5   *Autostressed* in words of two syllables.

Examples: ,ig'nīte
              ,ū'nīte
              dis,ū'nīte (stress-neutral **dis**- is not part of the SP)

Note: Many verbs ending in -**ite** are of the form prefix+stem, e.g. in'cīte.

D   Noun- or adjective-forming -**ite**; usually pronounced [aɪt], but sometimes [ɪt] or [ət].

6   *Pre-stressed 2.*

Examples: 'her'măphro,dīte
              'păra,sīte
              'plĕbiscite

Exceptions: ,bī'par,tīte
                ,trī'par,tīte
                *rë'con,dīte
                *ĕx'quĭsite
                'archi'man,drīte
                'mētëo,rīte

-ition

Consists of -**ion** (pre-stressed 1) preceded by -**it**-, which is sometimes part of the stem and sometimes an insert. Main stress falls on the syllable containing the first **i**, which is always short. Secondary stress is placed by the rhythmic principle.

Examples: 'juxtapo'sītion (-**it**- is an insert, cf. **juxtapose**)
              ë'dītion (-**it**- is part of the stem, cf. **edit**)

-itious

Consists of -**ious** (see above) preceded by -**it**-, which is sometimes part of the stem and sometimes an insert. Main stress falls on the syllable containing the first **i**, by the accentual properties of -**ous**. Secondary stress is placed by the rhythmic principle.

Example: 'sŭrrep'tītious

-itis
Follows the rules for **-is** (pre-stressed 1/2); since the first **i** is long, it takes main stress. Secondary stress is placed by the rhythmic principle.

Example: 'pĕrito'nītis

-itive, -itor, -itory
Consist of a pre-stressed 1/2 suffix preceded by **-it-**, which is sometimes part of the stem and sometimes an insert. The vowel of **-it-** is short and so main stress falls on the syllable before it; the vowel of this syllable is subject to trisyllabic shortening.

Examples: com'pĕtitive (ctr. com'pēte)
so'lĭcitor
in'hĭbitory (Brit. – Amer. in'hĭbi,tōry)

-itous
Consists of **-ous** (pre-stressed 1/2) preceded by **-it-**, which is sometimes part of the stem, but usually represents the suffix **-ity** with loss of final **-y**. The **i** is always short, and so main stress falls on the syllable preceding it; the vowel of this syllable is always short.

Examples: prë'cĭpitous (**-it-** is part of the stem)
ca'lămitous (**-it-** represents **-ity**, cf. **calamity**)

-iture
Consists of **-ure** (pre-stressed 1/2) preceded by **-it-**, which is sometimes part of the stem and sometimes an insert. Main stress falls on the syllable before **-it-**. Pronounced [-ɪtʃə].

Examples: dis'cömfitūre
ëx'penditūre

Exceptions: 'forfeitūre ⎱(in which **-ure** operates as
'portraitūre ⎰stress-neutral)

-ity
Pre-stressed 1. The vowel of the preceding syllable is almost always shortened (see trisyllabic shortening, p. 204 below).

Examples: ,tran'quillity (ctr. 'tranquil)
ëx'trĕmity (cf. ëx'trēme)
'ūni'formity (ctr. 'ūni,form)
'clărity ⎱(vowel change, cf. **clear**,
pro'fundity ⎰**profound**)

Exceptions: o'bēsity
'prōbity
*a'mēnity ⎱(trisyllabic shortening
'falsity ['fɔ:l-] ⎰does not apply)
'scārcity
'paucity

Notes: (i) All words whose stressed vowel is **ū** keep the vowel long (cf. above pp. 22f.), e.g. ma'tūrity, 'incre'dūlity.

(ii)   All words whose stressed vowel immediately precedes the **i** keep a long vowel ('VV lengthening', Section 7.3.1(c)), e.g. 'lāity, 'dēity, 'sponta'nēity.

-ive

Pre-stressed 1/2. The vowel **ū** in a penultimate syllable counts as long, and is therefore stressed, except in the ending **-ūtive**, where it counts as short, causing stress to fall on the preceding syllable. The vowel of a stressed antepenultimate syllable undergoes trisyllabic shortening (Section 7.3).

Examples: ĕx'pensive (**pen** is a strong syllable)
'lōco'mōtive (**mō** is a strong syllable)
ĕf'fūsive (**fū** counts as a strong syllable)
con'sĕcūtive (**cū** counts as a weak syllable)
com'pĕtitive (ctr. com'pēte with a long vowel)

-ivity

Consists of **-ive** plus **-ity** (pre-stressed 1); main stress therefore falls on the **i** of **ive**. Secondary stress is placed by the rhythmic principle.

Examples: 'ob,jec'tivity   (For the treatment of **-jec-** and **-duc-**,
'prŏduc'tivity   see Section 7.2)

-izable

Consists of **-ize** (stress-neutral or pre-stressed 2) plus **-able** (stress-neutral); the stem ending in **-ize** is always a free form, and stress is placed according to the accentual properties of **-ize**.

Example: 'rĕcog,nīzable

-ization

Consists of **-ize** (stress-neutral or pre-stressed 2) followed by **-ate** plus **-ion** (pre-stressed 1). See **-ation** above, note (ii). Main stress is placed on the syllable containing the **ā** of **-ate**; secondary stress is placed by the properties of **-ize**. The vowel of **-ize** may be shortened and reduced in some varieties of English.

Examples: 'chăracte,rī'zātion (or 'chăracteri'zātion)
'cīvi,lī'zātion (or 'cīvili'zātion)

-ize

The spelling **-ise** is usually acceptable as an alternative. Some Scots speakers have this suffix autostressed, but in general its accentual properties are as follows:

1   *Stress-neutral* when the stem is a free form. If the final syllable of the stem has a long vowel, this is shortened and reduced.

Examples: 'chăracter – 'chăracte,rīze ['kæ-]
fa'mīliar – fa'mīlia,rīze
'mŏ,bīle – 'mōbi,līze
'prŏse,lȳte – 'prŏsely,tīze
'allĕgory – 'allĕgo,rīze (with loss of -y)

Exceptions: 'căna,līze (ctr. ca'năl)
de'mŏcra,tīze
'immū,nize (ctr. im'mūne)

2 *Pre-stressed 2* when the stem is not a free form.

Examples: 'frater,nīze
             'rĕcog,nīze
             ,an'tăgo,nīze

Exceptions: a'mor,tīze
              ,bap'tīze
              'systema,tīze

Note: as'sīze, ,cap'sīze are simple roots.

-later, -latry

Consist of the compound-forming element -**latr** (see Section 5) plus -**er** (pre-stressed 2) or -**y**$_B$ (pre-stressed 2), and words are therefore stressed on the syllable before -**la**-.

Examples: ,ī'dŏlater
             'Māri'ŏlatry

-less

Stress-neutral, and pronounced [-ləs]. The stem is almost always a free form, the only exceptions being monosyllabic.

Examples: 'bottom – 'bottomless
             dë'fence – dë'fenceless
             ëx'pression – ëx'pressionless
             'feckless
             'gormless
             'hăpless
             'listless }(stems are not free forms)
             'reckless
             'rŭthless
             'shiftless

Note: The adverb 'nĕverthe'less has final stress.

-let

Stress-neutral, and pronounced [-lət].

Examples: 'cöver – 'cöverlet
             'rīver – 'rīvūlet (with minor spelling change)

Exceptions: 'flăgëo'let ['flædʒɪə'let]
              'lan,dau'let

-like

Stress-neutral; stem is always a free form.

Examples: 'workman – 'workman,līke
             'lādy – 'lādy,līke

-lith

Compound-forming element (see Section 5).

-lithic

Consists of -**lith** plus -**ic** (pre-stressed 1); main stress therefore falls on -**lĭ**-.

Examples: 'mŏno'līthic
              'pälëo'līthic

-log(ue)
Compound-forming element (see Section 5).

-loger, -logism, -logist, -logy
Consist of **-log** plus a pre-stressed 2 suffix; main stress is therefore placed on the syllable before **-lo-**. The **g** is pronounced [dʒ] in all cases.

Examples: a'strŏloger
              në'ŏlogism
              'sōci'ŏlo‚gist
              'crīmi'nŏlogy

-logian
Consists of **-log** plus **-an** (pre-stressed 1/2), with an insert **-ĭ-** between them. Main stress is placed on **-lo-**, and the vowel is then lengthened by trisyllabic lengthening (Section 7.4.2).

Example: 'thēo'lōgian [-dʒən]

-logical
Consists of **-log** plus **-ic** plus **-al**$_A$ (pre-stressed 1/2); main stress is therefore placed on the syllable **-lo-**. Secondary stress is placed according to the rhythmic principle.

Examples: 'bīo'lŏgical
              ‚bac'tērio'lŏgical (or 'bac‚tēri-)

-ly
Stress-neutral, whether adjective-forming or adverb-forming.

Examples: 'coward – 'cowardly ⎱(adjective-forming)
              'fäther – 'fätherly ⎰
              'răpid – 'răpidly ⎱(adverb-forming)
              së'cūre – së'cūrely ⎰

-man
Combinations in which **man** is set off from the stem by a hyphen or a space are compounds, and **man** is pronounced [mæn] with a full vowel. When **man** is directly attached to the stem, it is normally pronounced [-mən] and may be regarded as a *stress-neutral* suffix.

Examples: 'anchor-‚man ⎱(compounds)
              'Spīder ‚Man ⎰
              'fīsherman ⎫
              'infantryman ⎬(stem plus suffix)
              po'līceman ⎭

-mancy
Consists of the compound-forming element **-mant** (see Section 5) plus **-y**$_B$ (stress-neutral). Main stress is then placed on the first element of the compound, and the vowel of **-man** is not reduced.

Example: 'nĕcro‚mancy

-ment

1 *Stress-neutral*, when the stem is a free form: the vowel of the suffix is reduced.

Examples: 'dĭsa`gree – 'dĭsa`greement
              ac`cömplish – ac`cömplishment

Exceptions: 'adver,tīse – ad'vertisement
                'aggran,dīze ⎫
                ag'gran,dīze ⎭ – ag'grandizement
                ,cha'stīse – 'chastïsement

When the stem is not a free form, one of the following patterns is normal:

2 *Autostressed* in disyllabic verbs.

Examples: fer'ment
              ,seg'ment
              ,tor'ment

Exception: 'com,ment

3 *Pre-stressed 2* in verbs of three or more syllables. The vowel of the suffix is not reduced.

Examples: 'dŏcū,ment
              ëx'pĕri,ment

4 *Pre-stressed 2* in nouns. The vowel of the suffix is reduced.

Examples: 'segment (ctr. verb ,seg'ment)
                   'dŏcüment (ctr. verb 'dŏcū,ment)
                   ëx'pĕriment (ctr. verb ëx'pĕri,ment)
                   ë'mŏlūment
                   prë'dĭcament

Exceptions: (a)   (Vowel of suffix not reduced)
                      'aug,ment (cf. verb ,aug'ment)
                      'com,ment (identical with corresponding verb)
                      'fer,ment (cf. verb fer'ment)
                      'tor,ment (cf. verb ,tor'ment)
                (b)   (autostressed)
                      cë'ment   (identical with the
                      la'ment   corresponding verbs)
                (c)   (pre-stressed 1)
                      dë'partment   (although **depart** and **deport** are free forms,
                      dë'portment   they are quite different in meaning from
                                    these two words)
                      com'partment
                      ën'jambment
                      ëm'bankment ⎫(stems are not free, though **bank** and **scarp**
                      ë'scarpment ⎭ *are* free forms, and their meaning recurs in
                                    these words)
                      in'stalment [-'stɔ:l-]
                      ,can'tonment [-'tu:n-]

,ac'couche,ment [,æ'ku:ʃ,mɒŋ]   ⎱ (French loans whose
*,dé'noue,ment [,deɪ'nu:,mɒŋ]   ⎰ pronunciation still
,rap'proche,ment [,ræ'prɒʃ,mɒŋ] ⎰ reflects their origin)

(d) (Pre-stressed 3)
    'lĭnëament
*'mĕdicament
    'temperament

-mental

Consists of **-ment** plus **-al** (pre-stressed 1/2). Main stress is placed on the strong syllable **-men-**. Secondary stress is placed sometimes by the rhythmic principle, and sometimes by the accentual properties of **-ment** (provided it does not fall on the syllable immediately preceding **-men-**).

Examples: 'dē,part'mental   (rhythmic principle only, since dë'part'mental
                                        has secondary stress adjacent to main stress)
             ëx'pĕri'mental   (by accentual properties of **-ment**)
         or 'ex,pĕri'mental   (by rhythmic principle: but non-reduction of
                                        -pĕ- is noteworthy)
        'tempera'mental (both principles give same result)

-mentary

Consists of **-ment** plus **-ary** (pre-stressed 1/2) (see p. 59 above). Secondary stress is placed by the properties of **-ment**.

Examples: 'compli'mentary
             ë'mōlū'mentary
Exceptions: *'fragmentary [-trɪ] (Brit.)
             'fragmen,tary [-,terɪ] (Amer.)

-meter

Two distinct suffixes must be recognised. In American English the situation is further complicated by the fact that the compound-forming element **-metre** (see below) is spelt **-meter**.

A Meaning 'measuring instrument'. Consists of the compound-forming element **-metr** (see Section 5) followed by **-er**$_A$ (pre-stressed 2). Main stress is placed on the syllable preceding **-me-**. Secondary stress is placed by the rhythmic principle.

Examples: ,al'tĭmeter
             'cǎlo'rĭmeter
             ,gǎs'ōmeter (storage tank for gas)
             ther'mōmeter

Note: Some words ending in **-meter** (meaning 'measuring instrument') are compounds involving the free form **mēter**: e.g.

             'gas ,mēter (for measuring flow of gas)
             'parking ,mēter
             'tǎxi,mēter
             'vōlt,mēter

B Meaning 'verse prosody'. Same structure as **-meter**$_A$.

Example: ,pen'tǎmeter

-metre
Compound-forming element (see Section 5): a measure of length. Spelt **-meter** in American English.

Examples: 'centi,mētre (Amer. -,mēter)
               'milli,mētre

Exception: *ki'lŏmetre (as if it were **-meter**$_A$)

-metric
Consists of **-metr** plus **-ic** (pre-stressed 1). Main stress falls on **-me-**. Secondary stress is placed by the rhythmic principle.

Example: 'trĭgono'mĕtric

-metrics
Consists of **-metric** (above) plus **-s** (stress-neutral). Main stress falls on **-me-**.

Example: ĕ'cŏno'mĕtrics

-metry
Consists of **-metr** plus **-y**$_B$ (pre-stressed 2). Main stress falls on the syllable before **-me-**.

Examples: gĕ'ŏmetry
              'anthro'pŏmetry

-monger
Compound-forming element (see Section 5); pronounced [-,mʌŋgə].

-mongery
Consists of **-monger** plus **-y**$_B$ (stress-neutral).

Example: 'īron,mŏngery

-monial, -monious
Consist of **-mony** plus a pre-stressed 1/2 suffix, with an insert **-i-** between them. Main stress thus falls on **-mo-**, and the vowel is lengthened (Section 7.4.2) in both British and American English.

Examples: 'cĕrĕ'mōnial
              'sancti'mōnious

-mony
Pre-stressed 2. Pronounced [-mənɪ] in British English, but the **o** may be long (and therefore unreduced) in American English.

Examples: 'testimony (Brit.) – 'testi,mōny (Amer.)
              'mătrimony (Brit.) – 'mătri,mōny (Amer.)

-morph
Compound-forming element (see Section 5).

-morphic
Consists of **-morph** plus **-ic** (pre-stressed 1). Main stress falls on **-mor-**. Secondary stress is placed by the rhythmic principle.

Examples: 'īso'morphic
              'anthropo'morphic

-morphism
Consists of **-morph** plus **-ism**, which is normally pre-stressed 2 but behaves as pre-stressed 1 in these cases.

Example: 'īso'mor,phism

-morphous
Consists of **-morph** plus **-ous** (pre-stressed 1/2). Main stress falls on the strong syllable **-mor-**. Secondary stress is placed by the rhythmic principle.

Example: 'pŏly'morphous

-morphy
Consists of **-morph** plus **-y**$_B$ (stress-neutral).

Examples: 'allo,morphy
              'pŏly,morphy

-ness
Two distinct suffixes must be recognised:
   A   A highly productive abstract-noun-forming suffix added to free forms: always pronounced [-nəs].
   1   *Stress-neutral.*

Examples: po'līte – po'līteness
              'thŏrough – 'thŏroughness [ˈθʌrənəs]

Exception: 'wilderness (attached to a bound form)

   B   In place names, meaning 'cape': always pronounced [-nes].
   2   *Auto-stressed.* Secondary stress is placed by the rhythmic principle.

Examples: 'Inver'ness
              'Shoebury'ness [ˈʃuːbərɪˈnes]
Exception: *'Hōlderness

-nome
Compound-forming element (see Section 5).

-nomer, -nomist, -nomy
Consists of **-nome** plus a pre-stressed 2 suffix. Main stress is therefore placed on the syllable before **-nom** and the vowel of **-nom** is reduced.

Examples: a'strŏnomer
              ĕ'cŏno,mist
              'Deute'rŏnomy

-nomic
Consists of **-nome** plus **-ic** (pre-stressed 1). Main stress falls on **-nom-** and the vowel of that syllable is shortened (see Section 7.3).

Example: 'găstro'nŏmic

-nomous
Consists of **-nome** plus **-ous** (in theory pre-stressed 1/2, but in fact acting as if the vowel of **-nome** had already been shortened).

Example: ˌauˈtŏnomous (and not ˈautoˈnōmous, as would normally be the case with the suffix **-ous**)

-nym
Compound-forming element (see Section 5).

-nymic, **-nymity**
Consist of **-nym** plus a pre-stressed 1 suffix. Main stress thus falls on **-nym**.

Examples: ˈpătroˈnȳmic
ˈănoˈnȳmity

-nymous
Consists of **-nym** plus **-ous** (pre-stressed 1/2). Main stress thus falls on the syllable before **-nym**.

Example: syˈnŏnymous (ctr. ˈsȳnoˌnym)

-nymy
Consists of **-nym** plus **-y**$_B$ (pre-stressed 2). Main stress thus falls on the syllable before **-nym**.

Example: mëˈtŏnymy

-oid
Pre-stressed 1/2.

Examples: ˈalkaˌloid (**kă** is a weak syllable)
ëlˈlipˌsoid (**lip** is a strong syllable)

-oir, **-oire**
Pre-stressed 2. Pronounced [-ˌwɑ:].

Examples: ˈăbatˌtoir
ˈëscriˌtoire

-ology
Consists of the compound-forming element **-log** plus **-y**$_B$ (pre-stressed 2), preceded by an insert **-o-**; the insert receives main stress. Secondary stress is usually determined by the rhythmic principle, but may also be affected by the place of main stress in words related to the first element of the compound.

Examples: ˈŏnomaˈtŏlogy (rhythmic principle)
phëˈnŏmëˈnŏlogy (cf. phëˈnŏmënon)

-on
Occurs in the names of some chemical elements and types of particles. *Pre-stressed 1/2*, and the vowel does not reduce.

Examples: ëˈlecˌtron
ˈnēˌon

Exception: ˈcarbon (vowel of suffix reduces)

Note: The ending **-on** may maintain a full vowel in a number of cases where it is not strictly on a suffix. See Appendix 7.1 for examples.

-oo

Strictly speaking, not a suffix; however, it is regularly *Autostressed*.

Example:　　'kanga'rōō

Exceptions:　'cuc͵kōō ['kᴜ͵ku:]
　　　　　　　'hōō͵dōō
　　　　　　　'ig͵lōō
　　　　　　　'vōō͵dōō

-oon

Strictly speaking, not a suffix; however, it is regularly *autostressed*.

Examples:　͵fes'tōōn
　　　　　　'măca'rōōn

Notes:　(i)　'fore͵nōōn, 'hŏney͵mōōn are compounds with initial stress.
　　　　(ii)　The ending **-zoon** is pronounced [-'zəᴜən] or [-'zəᴜ͵ɒn].

-or

For words ending in **-ator**, **-itor**, see under these suffixes above. For other cases, three distinct suffixes must be recognised.

　A　Agent-noun-forming suffix.
　1　*Stress-neutral* when the stem is a free form.

Examples:　con'fess – con'fessor
　　　　　　'gŏvern – 'gŏvernor
　　　　　　'prŏsĕ͵cūte – 'prŏsĕ͵cūtor

Exceptions:　ë'xĕcūtor (ctr. 'ĕxë͵cūte)
　　　　　　con'trĭbūtor (even when verb stem is pronounced 'contri͵būte)
　　　　　　'ŏrator

　2　*Pre-stressed 1/2* when the stem is not a free form.

Examples:　͵am'bassador (**să** is a weak syllable)
　　　　　　'inter'cessor (**ces** is a strong syllable)
　　　　　　'warrior ['wɒ-] (**rĭ** is a weak syllable)
　　　　　　'inter'lŏcūtor (**cū** is a weak syllable)

Exceptions:　'alli͵gātor
　　　　　　'an͵cestor (although **ces** is a strong syllable – note that it does not
　　　　　　　　　　reduce; moreover, **ancestral** suggests that its phono-
　　　　　　　　　　logical form is /ancestr/ with two syllables)
　　　　　　'appli͵cātor
　　　　　　'chăncellor (although **cel** is a strong syllable)
　　　　　　'bĕnë͵factor
　　　　　　'mălë͵factor
　　　　　　'prēdë͵cessor

Note:　A number of words in **-or**, not all of which are agent nouns, have a full
　　　　vowel in their final syllable:

　　　　　　　　　　͵con'quista͵dor
　　　　　　　　　　cor'rĕgi͵dor

'guăran,tor
'măta,dor
'pĭca,dor
'tŏrëa,dor
'can,tor
'con,dor
*'cŏrri,dor
*ëx'celsi,or
'Lăbra,dor
,mon'sï,gnor [-,njɔ:]
'rēal,tor

B Abstract-noun-forming suffix (see also **-our**).
3 *Pre-stressed 1/2.*

Examples: 'pallor
'stūpor
'trĕmor

Note: 'dé,cor ([ˈde,kɔ:] or [ˈdeɪ,kɔ:]) is a simple root (cf. **decorate**).

C Adjective-forming suffix.
4 *Pre-stressed 1/2.*

Examples: ,ëx'tērior
,in'fērior
'jūnior
'prīor
,ul'tērior

-orial, -orian, -orious
Consist of **-or** (or **-ory** or **-our**) plus a pre-stressed 1/2 suffix, with an insert -ĭ-between them. Main stress falls on the syllable containing **-or**; the vowel of this syllable is then affected by trisyllabic lengthening (see Section 7.4.2).

Examples: ,tū'tōrial (ctr. 'tūtor)
'prŏfes'sōrial (ctr. pro'fessor)
hi'stōrian (ctr. 'history)
la'bōrious (ctr. 'lābo(u)r)
,vic'tōrious (ctr. 'victory)

-orous
Consists of **-or**$_B$ or **-our** plus **-ous** (pre-stressed 1/2). Main stress falls on the syllable before **-or**.

Examples: 'glămorous
'vĭgorous

Exception: *so'nōrous

Note: 'dĕcorous has the corresponding abstract noun **dë'cōrum** rather than 'dĕcor, which could be confused with 'dé,cor.

-ory
Forms nouns and adjectives. Two patterns must be distinguished. Note that in

American English the **o** is long (and therefore unreduced) unless main stress immediately precedes.

   1 *Stress-neutral* when the stem is a free form.

Examples: ad'vīse – ad'vīsory
              'contra'dict – 'contra'dictory
              'prŏmise – 'prŏmissory (Brit.)
                   'prŏmis,sōry (Amer.)

Exception: con'trĭbūtory (Amer. con'trĭbū,tōry) (even when the corres-
              ponding verb is pronounced 'contri,būte)

Note: 'clēre,stōry is a compound with initial stress (**clere** for **clear**).

   2 *Pre-stressed 1/2* in other cases.

Examples: ëx'pŏsitory (**sĭ** is a weak syllable) (Amer. ëx'pŏsi,tōry)
              ,ol'factory (**fac** is a strong syllable)

Exceptions: 'dĕsultory
               'inventory
               'offertory
               'prŏmontory
               'rĕpertory

-ose

Two distinct suffixes must be recognised.
   A   Adjective-forming suffix.
   1 *Pre-stressed 2* in words of three or more syllables: pronounced [-,əuz] or [-,əus].

Examples: 'belli,cōse
              'cōma,tōse
              'lăchry,mōse ['læk-]

Exception: *'grandi'ōse

Note: 'ōti,ōse ['əutɪ,əuz] or ['əuʃɪ,əuz]

   2 *Autostressed* in disyllables; pronounced [-'əus]

Examples: jo'cōse
              mo'rōse
              ver'bōse

   B   Noun-forming suffix (chemical term); pronounced [-,əuz] or [-,əus].
   3 *Pre-stressed 2.*

Examples: 'glü,cōse
              'cellū,lōse

Note: There are two verbs ending in **-ose** [-,əuz] which appear to follow no
       particular pattern:

                      'dīag,nōse
                      'mĕta'mor,phōse

-osity
Consists of **-ous** (occasionally **-ose**) plus **-ity** (pre-stressed 1). Main stress falls on the syllable containing the **o**. Secondary stress is placed by the suffixes **-ous** or **-ose**. The ō of **-ose** undergoes trisyllabic shortening (Section 7.3).

Examples: ver'bŏsity
'cūri'ŏsity

Notes: (i) In **preciosity** ['presɪ'ɒsɪtɪ] and **religiosity** [rɪ'lɪdʒɪ'ɒsɪtɪ], the **ci** and **gi** do not coalesce as they do in **precious** ['preʃəs] and **religious** [rɪ'lɪdʒəs].

(ii) '**virtū'ŏsity** is connected with '**virtū'ōsō** rather than '**virtūous**.

-our
Abstract-noun-forming suffix with many resemblances to **-or**ᴮ, and spelt that way in American English. *Pre-stressed 1/2.*

Examples: 'fervour
dë'meanour (**mea** is a strong syllable)
bë'hāviour (the insert **-i-** gives a weak syllable **vi** and the **i** then becomes a semivowel [bɪ'heɪvjə]
ën'dĕavour (**en-** is a stress-neutral prefix and therefore not part of the SP)

Note: The agent-noun 'săviour (Brit. spelling) has a suffix resembling **-or**ᴬ rather than **-or**ᴮ.

-ous
Always pronounced [-əs] in spite of the two-letter vowel **ou**; its phonological form is probably /-ŏs/ (cf. **pompous – pompŏsity**).

1 *Stress-neutral* when the stem is a free form, and there is no insert.

Examples: 'căvern – 'căvernous
dë'sīre – dë'sīrous
'hăzard – 'hăzardous

Exceptions: ˌan'tŏnymous (ctr. 'antoˌnym)
'blasphëmous (ctr. ˌblas'phēme)
ˌcar'nĭvorous (ctr. 'carniˌvore) (cf. **-vorous** below)
cir'cūitous (ctr. 'circuit ['sɜ:kɪt])
'gangrënous (ctr. 'ganˌgrēne)
gë'lătinous (ctr. 'gĕlatin or -ˌtïne)
mo'mentous (ctr. 'mōment)
ˌpor'tentous (ctr. 'porˌtent)
ri'dĭcūlous (ctr. 'rĭdiˌcūle)
sy'nŏnymous (ctr. 'sўnoˌnym)

2 *Pre-stressed 1/2* in all other cases. Many words have an insert **-i-**, **-ū-** or **-ë-** between stem and suffix, forming a weak syllable; in this case main stress falls on the last syllable of the stem, and trisyllabic lengthening operates (Section 7.4.2) except where the insert is **-ū-**. See **-ious** above for details of coalescences of **ci**, **gi**, **ti**, and **xi**; coalescences with **e** occur as follows:

-ceous is pronounced [-ʃəs], e.g. ˌher'bāceous

-geous is pronounced [-dʒəs], e.g.   'gorgeous
-seous is pronounced [-sɪəs], e.g.   'gāseous, except 'nauseous ['nɔːʃəs]
-teous is pronounced [-tɪəs], e.g.   'pĭtëous, except 'righteous ['raɪtʃəs]

Examples: a'nŏmalous (**mă** is a weak syllable)
,stū'pendous (**pen** is a strong syllable)
'sĭmul'tānëous (**në** is a weak syllable, and **a** is lengthened)
la'bōrious (**rĭ** is a weak syllable, and **o** is lengthened)

Exception: 'chĭvalrous ['ʃɪ-] (although **val** is a strong syllable)

-path
Compound-forming element (see Section 5). Pronounced [-,pæθ].

-pathic
Consists of **-path** plus **-ic** (pre-stressed 1). Main stress falls on **-path**. Secondary stress is placed by the rhythmic principle.

Example: 'psȳcho'păthic ['saɪkə-]

-pathy
Consists of **-path** plus **-y**$_B$ (pre-stressed 2). Main stress falls on the syllable before **-path**. Secondary stress is placed by the rhythmic principle, and the vowel of **-path** is reduced.

Example: 'hōmë'ŏpathy

-phobe
Compound-forming element (see Section 5).

-phobia
Consists of **-phobe** plus the ending **-ia**. **-phobe** gets the main stress and the ō remains long (in the context for trisyllabic lengthening – cf. Section 7.4.2).

Example: 'ăgora'phōbia

-phobic
Consists of **-phobe** plus **-ic** (pre-stressed 1). Main stress falls on **-phobe**. Note that the ō of **-phobe** remains long in spite of the presence of **-ic**.

Example: 'claustro'phōbic

-phone
Compound-forming element (see Section 5).

-phonic
Consists of **-phone** plus **-ic** (pre-stressed 1). Main stress falls on **-phon-** and the ō is shortened because of the presence of **-ic**.

Example: 'stērëo'phonic (or 'stērëo-)

-phonist, -phony
Consist of **-phone** plus a pre-stressed 2 suffix. Main stress falls on the syllable before **-phon-** and the vowel of **-phone** is reduced.

Examples: të'lĕphonist (ctr. 'tĕle,phōne)
ca'cŏphony

-phor
Compound-forming element (see Section 5)

Examples: 'ăna,phor
'mĕta,phor (or 'mĕtaphor)

-phoric
Consists of **-phor** plus **-ic** (pre-stressed 1). Main stress falls on **-phor**, and the **o** is shortened by the presence of **-ic**.

Example: 'căta'phŏric

-ry
For words ending in **-ary**, **-ery**, **-ory**, see under those endings above. *Stress-neutral.*

Examples: 'mĭmic – 'mĭmicry
'wĭzard – 'wĭzardry
'căsŭist – 'căsŭistry

Exceptions: 'căvalry
'chĭvalry ['ʃɪ-] (stems are not free)
'bărratry

-s
Noun-forming suffix, possibly related to **-ce** (see above). *Stress-neutral*; the stem is not strictly free, **-ic** is present, and its accentual properties govern the placement of stress.

Examples: ,lin'guĭstic – ,lin'guĭstics [-'gwɪs-]
'măthë'mătics (although the adjective **mathematic** does not exist)

-scope
Compound-forming element (see Section 5).

-scopic
Consists of **-scope** plus **-ic** (pre-stressed 1). Main stress falls on **-scop-** and the **ō** is shortened by the presence of **-ic**.

Example: 'tĕle'scŏpic

-scopy
Consists of **-scope** plus **-y**$_B$ (pre-stressed 2). Main stress falls on the syllable before **-scop-**, and the vowel of **-scope** is reduced.

Example: ,mī'crŏscopy

-some
Two distinct elements must be recognised.
A   Adjective-forming suffix, pronounced [-səm]. *Stress-neutral.*

Examples: 'irk – 'irksome
'weary – 'wearisome
'cumbersome (cf. root of ën'cumber)
'handsome (even though this word cannot be related to **hand**).

B Compound-forming element (see Section 5); pronounced [-ˌsəʊm].

Example: 'chrōmo,sōme ['krəʊ-]

-sphere
Compound-forming element (see Section 5).

-spheric
Consists of **-sphere** plus **-ic** (pre-stressed 1). Main stress falls on **-spher-**, and **e** becomes shortened by the presence of **-ic**.

Example: 'atmos'phĕric

-t
Abstract-noun-forming suffix. *Stress-neutral.*

Examples: com'plain – com'plaint
               dë'scend – dë'scent
               pur'sūe – pur'sūit [pə'sju:t]
               rë'cēive – rë'cēipt [rɪ'si:t]

Exceptions: 'con,cept (ctr. con'cēive)
                'con,junct (ctr. con'join)
                'con,tent (ctr. con'tain)
                'per,cept (ctr. per'cēive)
                'por,tent (ctr. ,por'tend)
                'por,trait (or 'portrait) (ctr. ,por'tray)
                'prŏ,duct (ctr. pro'dūce)
                'tran,script (ctr. ,tran'scrībe)

-teen
Autostressed.
Example: ,four'teen

-th
Two distinct suffixes need to be recognised.
   A   Abstract-noun-forming suffix.
   1   *Stress-neutral.*

Examples: 'warm – 'warmth [wɔ:mθ]
              'deep – 'depth (note vowel shortening)

   B   Ordinal-number-forming suffix.
   2   *Stress-neutral.*

Examples: 'sĕven – 'sĕventh
              ,four'teen – ,four'teenth
              'thousand – 'thousandth

Note: After the suffix **-ty** (='multiple of ten') there is an insert **-e-** pronounced [ɪ] or [ə]:

              'fifty – 'fiftieth ['fɪftɪɪθ] or ['fɪftɪəθ]

-tude
Pre-stressed 2. There may be an insert **-ĭ-** (occasionally **-ĕ-**), and a long vowel in the syllable preceding this will be shortened.

Examples: 'atti,tūde
si'mīli,tūde

-ty

Two distinct suffixes must be recognised.

A Numeral-forming suffix (='multiple of ten').

1 *Stress-neutral.*

Examples: 'seven – sĕventy
'fīve – 'fifty }(with modifications to the stem)
'three – 'thirty

B Abstract-noun-forming suffix.

2 *Stress-neutral.*

Examples: 'admiral – 'Admiralty
'crüel – 'crüelty
ĕn'tīre – ĕn'tīrety
'nŏvel – 'nŏvelty

Notes: (i) 'făculty, 'pūberty, even though the stems are not free.
(ii) Words in **-ity** are dealt with under that suffix above.

-ual

Consists of **-al**$_A$ (pre-stressed 1/2) preceded by an insert **-ū-**, which counts as a short vowel. Main stress thus falls on the syllable before **ū**. Although the stressed vowel appears to be eligible for trisyllabic lengthening, this rule does not in fact apply (cf. Section 7.3.2). The **u** is pronounced [jʊ], and a stem-final **d**, **s**, **t**, or **x** often coalesces with the [j] as shown below (in which case the [ə] of the suffix often merges into the [ʊ]):

-dual is pronounced [-djʊəl] or [-dʒʊl]
-sual is pronounced {[-zjʊəl] or [-ʒʊl] after a vowel
{[-sjʊəl] or [-ʃʊl] elsewhere
-tual is pronounced [-tjʊəl] or [-tʃʊl]
-xual is pronounced [-ksjʊəl] or [-kʃʊl]

Examples: 'căsūal ['kæzjʊəl] or ['kæʒʊl]
'sensūal ['sensjʊəl] or ['senʃʊl]
'indi'vīdūal ['ɪndɪ'vɪdjʊəl] or ['ɪndɪ'vɪdʒʊl]
'intel'lectūal ['ɪntə'lektjʊəl] or ['ɪntə'lektʃʊl]

Exception: 'spĭritūal (stressed 3 syllables back from **-al**)

Note: In this combination, **u** is sometimes part of the stem, as in con'tĭnūal (cf. **continue**), re'sĭdūal (cf. **residue**), per'pĕtūal (cf. **'perpe'tūity**); after **g** or **q** it is pronounced [w], as in ,bi'lingual, 'ĕqual.

-uality

Consists of **-al**$_A$ followed by **-ity** (pre-stressed 1) and preceded by an insert **-ū-**. Main stress falls on the **-a-**, and secondary stress is placed by the accentual properties of **-al** on the syllable before **ū**.

Examples: ĕ'ventū'ălity [ɪ'ventjʊ'ælɪtɪ] or [-tʃʊ'ælɪtɪ]
'spĭritū'ălity ['spɪrɪtjʊ'ælɪtɪ] ot [-tʃʊ-]

-uant, -uate
Consist of **-ant, -ate** preceded by an insert **-ū-** which counts as a weak syllable, and therefore does not take main stress. A long vowel in the preceding syllable is shortened.

Examples: ˌacˈcentū͵āte
ëˈvăcūant
ˈgrădū͵āte (cf. ˈgrāde)
Exception: purˈsūant (**ū** is here part of the stem **purˈsūe**, and counts as long)

Notes: (i) There are other cases in which **ū** is part of the stem, but which follow the rule because **ū** counts as short: **conˈtĭnūant, ëˈvăcū͵āte,**
(ii) When **u** is preceded by **q**, it does not form a separate syllable: **ˈădëquate** [ˈæ.dɪ.kwət], **ˈpïˌquant** [ˈpiː.kɒŋ].

-uble
Pre-stressed 1, perhaps treated by analogy with **-uable** as in ˈvălūable [ˈvæljʊbl]

Examples: ˈvŏlūble
disˈsŏlūble

-uous
Consists of **-ous** (pre-stressed 1/2) preceded by an insert **-ū-** which counts as a weak syllable, and therefore does not take main stress. A long vowel in the preceding syllable is shortened.

Examples: conˈtĭnūous (**ū** actually part of stem here)
perˈspĭcūous

-ure
For words ending **-ature**, see above. This suffix is pronounced [jə] and the [j] coalesces with stem-final **d, s, t,** or **z** as follows:

-dure is pronounced [-dʒə]
-ssure is pronounced [-ʃə]
-sure is pronounced $\begin{cases} \text{[-ʒə] after a vowel} \\ \text{[-ʃə] after a consonant} \end{cases}$
-ture is pronounced [-tʃə]
-zure is pronounced [-ʒə]

1 *Stress-neutral* when the stem is a free form.
Examples: ˈclōse – ˈclōsūre [ˈkləʊʒə]
ˈmoist – ˈmoistūre [ˈmɔɪstʃə]
ˈportrait – ˈportraitūre [ˈpɔːtrətʃə]
proˈceed – proˈcēdūre [prəˈsiːdʒə]
ˈarchiˌtect – ˈarchiˌtectūre [ˈɑːkɪˌtektʃə]

Exception: ˈcreatūre [ˈkriːtʃə]

Note: ˈfixtūre, ˈmixtūre have an insert **-t-**.

2 *Pre-stressed 1/2* when the stem is not a free form.

Examples: ëmˈbrāsure [-ʒə] (**brā** is a strong syllable)
ˈfurnitūre [-tʃə] (**nï** is a weak syllable)

Exceptions: ˈăpertūre
,coifˈfūre [,kwæˈfjʊə]
ˈem,boü,chüre [ˈɒm,bu:,ʃʊə] (or ˈem,boüˈchüre)
ˈōvertūre
ˈtemperatūre (often pronounced [ˈtemprətʃə])

For notes see Appendix 4.2, p. 130.

-ute
Two distinct patterns must be recognised.

1 *Pre-stressed 2 in words of three or more syllables.*

Examples: ˈĕxёˌcūte
ˈrĕsoˌlüte

Exceptions: *conˈtrĭˌbūte
*disˈtrĭˌbūte
atˈtrĭˌbūte (verb – the noun ˈattriˌbūte is regular)

2 *Autostressed in disyllabic words.*

Examples: aˈcūte
polˈlüte

Exceptions: ˈhirˌsūte
ˈstăˌtūte
ˈtrĭˌbūte

-vore
Compound-forming element (see Section 5).

-vorous
Consists of **-vore** plus **-ous** (pre-stressed 1/2, but acting as if the vowel of **-vore** had already been shortened).

Example: ,carˈnĭvorous (and not ˈcarniˈvōrous, as would normally be the case with **-ous**)

-ward(s)
Stress-neutral, and pronounced [-wəd(z)].

Examples: ˈbackward(s)
ˈheavenward(s)

Exceptions: toˈward(s) (prep.) [təˈwɔːd(z)] or [ˈtɔːd(z)]
ˈuntoˈward (adjective)

Notes: (i) The following words are simple roots: ˈcoward [ˈkaʊəd], ˈsteward [ˈstjʊəd]
(ii) The following words are of the form prefix+stem: aˈward, rёˈward [-ˈwɔːd].

-ways
Stress-neutral.

Examples: ˈlength,ways
ˈsīde,ways

Exception: *ˈalways [ˈɔːlwɪz]

-wise
Stress-neutral.

Examples: ꞌclock,wīse
ꞌöther,wīse

-y
Two distinct suffixes must be recognised.
  A Adjective-forming suffix. The stem is usually a free form, but not invariably.
  1 *Stress-neutral.*

Examples: ꞌcream – ꞌcreamy
ꞌshĭver – ꞌshĭvery
ꞌanger – ꞌangry (slight spelling change)
bë'wāre – ꞌwāry (exact form of stem does not occur as a free form)
ꞌshabby ⎱(stem does not occur as a free form)
ꞌflimsy ⎰

  B Noun-forming suffix. Four patterns must be distinguished.
  2 *Stress-neutral* when the stem is a free form, and not a compound.

Examples: ꞌbutcher – ꞌbutchery [ꞌbʊ-]
ëx'pīre – ëx'pīry

Exception: ꞌblăsphëmy (ctr. ,blas'phëme)

  3 *Pre-stressed 2* when the stem is not a free form, and not a compound.

Examples: mis'cellany
ꞌlĕthargy
ꞌsubsidy

Exceptions: ꞌcon,tūmely
*ꞌcontro,versy
ꞌĕquerry
ꞌignominy
ꞌmĕlancholy [-kəlɪ] or -,chŏly

  4 *Pre-stressed 2* when the stem is a compound (whether a free form or not) whose final element gives rise to a weak penultimate syllable.

Examples: ꞌări'stŏcracy (**cră** is a weak syllable)
të'lĕgraphy (**gră** is a weak syllable)
gë'ŏmetry (**mĕ** is a weak syllable)
,bī'ŏlogy (**lŏ** is a weak syllable)

Exceptions: ꞌpĕda,gŏgy (even though **gŏ** is a weak syllable)
ꞌorthō,ĕpy (even though **ĕ** is a weak syllable)

  5 *Stress-neutral* when the stem is a free form, and a compound whose final element gives rise to a strong penultimate syllable. If the stem is a compound of this kind which is not a free form, the resulting stress pattern is the same.

Examples: ꞌhĕtero,dox – ꞌhĕtero,doxy (/dok/ is a strong syllable)
ꞌŏli,garch – ꞌŏli,garchy (**gar** is a strong syllable)

'pŏly,morph – 'pŏly,morphy (**mor** is a strong syllable)
'ĕpi,lepsy (**lep** is a strong syllable)
'ortho,prăxy (/prak/ is a strong syllable)
'nĕcro,mancy (**man** is a strong syllable)

Exceptions: *mĕ'tallurgy
            *con'trŏversy

Appendix 4.2   Lists of Words with Mixed Suffixes

Words cited as exceptions in Appendix 4.1 are indicated with a superscript
letter 'e', while superscript 2, 3, etc., denote that the word is stressed by the
principle bearing that number in the discussion of the suffix in Appendix 4.1.
Thus, a'bominable[2] means that the word **abominable** is stressed by principle 2
for **-able** (cf. p. 52 above). Absence of superscript means that the word is
stressed according to the first (or only) principle stated for the suffix.

-able
a'bŏminable[2], ac'ceptable, ac'countable, a'daptable, 'admirable[2e], a'dōrable,
ad'vīsable, 'affable[2], a'greeable, 'ālïenable, al'lowable, 'alterable ['ɔ:l-],
a'mēnable[e], 'āmiable[2], 'ămicable[2], 'ăna,lȳsable, 'ănswerable, ap'plĭcable[e] (or
'applicable[2]), ap'prēciable[2], ap'proachable, 'ărable[2], 'argūable, 'ascer'tainable, as'signable [-'saɪn-], as'sĭmilable[2], at'tachable, at'tainable, at'trĭbūtable,
a'vailable, a'voidable.

'beārable, bë'lievable, 'bendable, 'breăkable, 'burnable.

'calcūlable[2], 'cāpable[2], 'chāngeable, 'chargeable, 'chăritable[2], 'circum'năvig-
able[2], 'classi,fiable, 'cleanable, com'bīnable, 'cŏmfortable, com'mendable,
com'mensūrable[2], com'mūnicable[2], com'mūtable, com'pănionable,
'comparable[2e], com'pūtable, con'cēivable, con'formable, con'jectūrable,
con'sĭderable, con'signable [-'saɪn-], con'sūmable, 'contra'dictable, con'trŏl-
lable, 'countable, 'crēditable, 'culpable, 'cultivable[2], 'cūrable.

'dămageable, 'damnable, dë'bātable, dë'cīpherable, dë'clārable, 'dēcom'pōsable, dë'fīnable, dë'lectable[e], 'dĕmonstrable[2], dë'nīable, dë'pendable,
dë'plōrable, dë'sīrable, dë'spĭcable[e], dë'terminable, dë'testable, dë'vĕlop-
able, 'dīsa'greeable, dis'cŏverable, dis'honourable [dɪ'sɒnərəbl], dis'pōsable,
dis'pūtable, dis'rĕpūtable[2e], dis'tinguishable, dis'trĭbūtable, 'drinkable,
'dūrable.

'eatable, 'ēdūcable[2], ĕm'ployable, ĕn'dūrable, ĕn'forceable, ĕn'joyable,
'enviable, 'ēquable[2], ë'quĭtable[e] (or 'ĕquitable[2]), ë'rāsable, 'estimable[2],
ë'xăminable, ĕx'chāngeable, ĕx'cītable, ĕx'cūsable, 'ĕxĕcrable[2], ĕx'plĭcable[e] (or 'explicable[2]), ĕx'trĭcable[e] (or 'extricable[2]).

'falsi,fiable ['fɔ:l-], 'făshionable, 'făvourable, 'flammable[2], ,fore'seeable, for-
'gĭvable, for'mĭdable[e] (or 'formidable[2]), 'forti,fiable, 'frīable[2].

,get-'at-able.

'hăbitable², 'honourable ['ɒnərəbl], ,hos'pĭtableᶜ (or 'hŏspitable²).

il'līmitable, i'măginable; a large number of words beginning with negative **im-**, which is stress-neutral, and may therefore cause main stress to fall on the syllable immediately preceding **-able** (even pre-stressed 2 **-able**) – this set of words includes: im'movable [-'mu:-], im'mūtable², im'peccable², im'pĕnetrable², 'imper'turbable, im'plăcable², im'ponderable, im'pregnable², im'prŏbable²; im'pressionable; a large number of words beginning with negative **in-** (which has the same properties as **im-**, see above), including: in'ālïenable, in'căpable², 'incon'sōlable, 'incon'testable, in'cūrable, 'indë'fătigable², 'indë'scrībable, 'indis'pensable, in'dŏmitable², in'dūbitable², in'effable², 'inë'rădicable², 'inë'scăpable, in'ëvitable², in'ïmitable², in'nūmerable², in'sātiable², in'scrütable², in'sufferable, in'süperable², 'insup'portable, in'terminable², in'tractable², in'vīolable²; in'flammableᶜ, in'hăbitable, in'surable [-'ʃɔ:-], 'inter'chăngeable, in'terpretable; a number of words beginning with negative **ir-** (which has the same properties as **im-**, see above), including: 'irrë'fūtable, ir'rĕparable², 'irrë'proachable, 'irrë'triēvable, ir'rĕvocable²; 'irritable², 'īsolable².

,jus'tīciable², 'justi,fīable.

'knōwable, 'knowledgeable ['nɒlɪdʒəbl].

'lămentable²ᶜ, 'laudable, 'laughable ['la:fəbl], 'līable², 'līkeable, 'līveable, 'lövable.

'mallëable², 'mănageable, 'marketable, 'marriageable ['mærɪdʒəbl], 'measurable ['meʒərəbl], 'mĕmorable², 'mendable, 'mīserable², mi'stăkable, 'mŏdi,fīable, 'mōuldable, 'movable ['mu:-].

'năvigable², në'gōtiable², 'nōtable, 'nōticeable, 'nōti,fīable.

ob'jectionable, ob'servable, ob'tainable, 'ŏperable².

'pălatable, 'palpable², 'pardonable, 'pässable, 'pāyable, 'peaceable ['pi:səbl], per'cēivable, 'pĕrishable, 'permëable², 'personable, per'suădable, 'pītiable, 'pleasurable ['pleʒərəbl], 'plīable², 'portable², 'practicable², 'prĕdicable², prë'dictable, 'prĕferable²ᶜ, prë'sentable, prë'sūmable, 'prŏbable², pro'cūrable, 'prŏfitable, pro'nounceable, 'provable ['pru:-], 'pŭnishable.

'questionable.

'rateable ['reɪtəbl], 'readable, 'rēa,līsable, 'reasonable, 'rĕcog,nīsable, 'rĕcon,cīlable, rë'cöverable, 'recti,fīable, rë'deemable, rë'doubtableᶜ [rɪ'daʊtəbl], rë'fūtable, rë'grettable, rë'līable, rë'markable, rë'mēdiable²ᶜ, re'movable [rɪ'mu:vəbl], rë'newable, rë'pairable, rë'pāyable, rë'plăceable, 'rĕpūtable²ᶜ, rë'solvable, rë'spectable, rë'tainable, rë'tractable, rë'triēvable, rë'turnable, 'rĕvocable², rë'vōkable, ,rō'tātable.

'sāleable, 'seasonable, 'sĕparable², 'serviceable, 'shrinkable, 'sinkable, 'sīzable, 'sōciable² ['səuʃəbl], 'spĕci,fīable, 'stātable, 'suitable ['su:təbl], sus'tainable.

'tăxable, 'teachable, 'tĕnable², 'thinkable, 'tŏlerable², 'trāceable, 'tractable², 'trainable, 'transferable²ᶜ (or ,trans'ferable [-'fɜ:rəbl]), ,trans'lātable, 'treasonable.

A large number of words beginning with negative **un-** (which has similar properties to **im-**, see above), including: ,un'conquerable [-kərəbl], un'conscionable², 'unĕx'ceptionable, ,un'fathomable, ,un'gŏvernable, 'un-im'peachable, 'unrĕ'peatable, ,un'searchable [-sɜ:-], ,un'speakable, ,un'touchable [-'tʌtʃ-], ,un'utterable; 'under'standable, 'ūsable.

'vălūable, 'vāriable, 'vĕnerable², 'vĕri,fīable, 'vĕritable², 'vulnerable².

'warrantable ['wɒrəntəbl], 'washable ['wɒ-], 'weārable, 'winnable, 'wörk-able.

Notes:
1 dis'āble, ĕn'āble, ,un'āble are clearly of the form prefix+root 'able, and not root+suffix -**able**.
2 'un'stāble, 'mĕta'stāble are formed from the root **stable**.
3 A number of words ending in the sequence -**able** (where this is not the suffix -**able**) follow a similar rule to the suffix -**able** (pre-stressed 2): 'constable, 'Dunstable, 'pārable, 'syllable, 'vĕgetable, 'vōcable. However, 'dī-,syllable, 'mŏno,syllable, 'pŏly,syllable, etc., stress the prefix.

-acy (excluding words in -**cracy**)
'abbacy³, 'accūracy, 'ădĕquacy, 'advocacy.

'cĕlibacy, con'fĕderacy, con'spīracy², 'contūmacy³, 'cūracy.

dĕ'gĕneracy, 'dĕlĕgacy, 'dĕlicacy.

ĕf'fĕminacy, 'efficacy³, ĕ'pīscopacy³, ĕ'quĭvocacy³.

'fallacy³.

'illĕ'gītimacy, il'lĭteracy, im'mēdiacy, im'portūnacy, in'accūracy, in'ădĕquacy, in'dĕlicacy, in'efficacy³, in'testacy, 'intimacy, 'intricacy.

'lĕgacy³, lĕ'gītimacy, 'lĭteracy, 'lūnacy³.

'măgistracy.

'obdūracy, 'obstinacy.

'pāpacy³, 'pharmacy³, 'pīracy, 'prĕlacy, 'prīmacy, 'prīvacy (or 'prĭvacy), 'prŏfligacy.

,sü'prĕmacy².

'testacy.

-age
'ācreage ['eɪkərɪdʒ], 'ădage², ad'văntage², ap'pendage.

'bădi,näge², 'baggage, 'bandage, 'băr,räge², 'bondage, 'breākage, 'brĭgandage, 'brōkerage.

ˈcabbage², ˈcămouˌflāge² [ˈkæməflɑːʒ], ˈcarnage², ˈcarriage [ˈkærɪdʒ], ˈcleavage, ˈcoinage, ˌconˈcūbinage²ᶜ, ˈcordage, ˈcorˌsäge², ˈcottage², ˈcourage² [ˈkʌrɪdʒ], ˈcribbage².

ˈdămage², ˈdīsadˈväntage², ˈdōsage, ˈdōtage, ˈdrainage.

ˈenˌtouˌrageᶜ [ˈɒnˌtuəˌrɑːʒ], ënˈvīsageᶜ, ˈĕquipage²ᶜ, ˈĕspioˌnägeᶜ.

ˈfōliage², ˈfootage, ˈfŏrage², ˈfröntage, ˈfūseˌläge².

ˈgărage² (or ˈgăˌräge²; Amer. gaˈrägeᶜ), ˈgarbage².

ˈhaulage, ˈhermitage, ˈhŏmage², ˈhŏstage².

ˈīmage².

ˈlanguage², ˈleakage, ˈlīnëage² [ˈlɪnɪɪdʒ], ˈlinkage, ˈluggage².

ˈmănage², ˈmarriage [ˈmærɪdʒ], ˈmasˌsäge², ˈmĕˌnäge², ˈmessage², ˈmīleage [ˈmaɪlɪdʒ], ˈmīˌräge², ˈmortgage [ˈmɔːgɪdʒ].

ˈnōnage².

ˈoutˌrägeᶜ.

ˈpackage, ˈpārentage, ˈpăssage, ˈpeerage, perˈcentage, ˈpersiˌfläge², ˈpillage², ˈportage², ˈpōstage, ˈpŏtage², ˈpoundage, ˈprĕsage².

ˈramˌpāgeᶜ (or ˌramˈpāgeᶜ), ˈrăvage², ˈroughage [ˈrʌfɪdʒ], ˈrummage².

ˈsăboˌtäge², ˈsalvage², ˈsausage² [ˈsɒsɪdʒ], ˈsăvage², ˈscrimmage², ˈseepage, ˈsewage² [ˈsuːɪdʒ], ˈsewerage [ˈsuː-], ˈshortage, ˈshrinkage, ˈsīlage², ˈslippage, ˈspoilage, ˈsteerage, ˈstoppage, ˈstōrage, ˈsuffrage².

ˈtönnage.

ˈumbrage², ˈūsage.

ˈvăgaˌbondage, ˈväntage², ˈverbiage², ˈvīcarage, ˈvillage², ˈvintage², ˈvīsage², ˈvōltage.

ˈwāstage, ˈwreckage.

ˈyardage.

Notes:

(i) The sequence **-age** is part of the stem in asˈsuāge, ˈdisënˈgāge, ënˈgāge, ënˈrāge.

(ii) ˈgreenˌgāge is a compound.

-ance

aˈberrance², aˈbeyance³, aˈbundance², acˈceptance, acˈcordance, acˈquaintance, adˈmittance, alˈlēgiance³, alˈlīance, alˈlowance, ˈambūlance³, anˈnoyance, apˈpearance, apˈplīance, apˈpurtenance³, ˈărrogance², ˈassonance², asˈsurance [əˈʃɔːrəns], atˈtendance, aˈvoidance.

ˈbălance³, ˈbrilliance².

caˈpăcitance³, ˌclairˈvoyance², ˈclearance, ˈcognisance², comˈplīance, conˈcŏmitance², conˈcordance²ᶜ, conˈductance, conˈnīvance, conˈtīnūance, conˈtrīvance, conˈveyance, ˈcountenance³.

'dalliance, dë'fiance, dë'līverance, 'dĭsap'pearance, 'discon'tīnūance, dis'cordance²ᶜ, dis'countenance³, 'dissonance², 'distance², dis'turbance, 'dŏminance², 'dūrance³.

'ĕlĕgance², ĕn'cumbrance³, ĕn'dūrance, 'entrance (noun), ĕx'trävagance², ĕ'xŭberance².

'fī,nanceᶜ (or fī'nanceᶜ), 'flāgrance², ,for'beārance, 'frāgrance², 'furtherance.

'griēvance, 'guidance ['gaɪdns].

'hindrance.

'ignorance², im'pēdance, im'portance²ᶜ, in'ductance, in'hĕritance, 'in,sig'nīfi-cance², in'soŭciance², 'instance², in'surance [-'ʃɔ:-], in'temperance, in'tŏlerance², in'vāriance, ir'rĕlĕvance².

,lu'xuriance ²ᶜ [,lʌk'ʃʊərɪəns] or [,lʌg'ʒʊə-].

'maintenance³, 'mīsal'līance.

'non-at'tendance, 'nonchalance², 'nuisance³ ['nju:-].

o'beisance³, ob'servance, 'ordinance³, 'ordnance³.

'parlance³, 'pĕnance³, per'formance, 'persĕ'vērance, 'pĕtūlance², 'pittance³, 'plĕasance², prĕ'ponderance², pro'tūberance², 'prŏvenance³, pur'sūance.

'quittance³.

'rādiance², 'rĕap'pearance, 'rĕas'surance [-'ʃɔ:-], rĕ'calcitrance², rĕ'cognisance², rĕ'connaissanceᶜ, 'rĕlĕvance², rĕ'līance, rĕ'luctance², rĕ'membrance, rĕ'mittance, rĕ'monstrance², Rĕ'naissance³ (or 'Rĕnais,sanceᶜ [-,sɒŋs]), rĕ'pentance, rĕ'pugnance², rĕ'semblance, rĕ'sistance, 'rĕsonance², 'riddance.

'semblance³, 'sĕverance, ,sig'nīficance², 'substance³, 'sufferance, 'sŭpera'bundance², sur'veillance³, 'sustenance³.

'temperance, 'tŏlerance².

'utterance.

'vāriance, 'vengeance³ ['vendʒəns], 'vĭgilance.

Notes:
(i) In the following words, **-ance** is part of the stem and not a suffix: ad'vance, a'skance (or a'skänce), 'circum,stance (or -,stänce), en'hänce (or en'hance), en'tränce (verb), fī'nance (or 'fī,nance), ,mis'chänce, per'chänce, ro'mance (or 'rō,mance).
(ii) The following words are compounds: 'counter'bălance (verb), 'counter,bălance (noun), ,out'distance, 'ōver'bălance.
(iii) The word im'bălance is 'bălance preceded by the stress-neutral negative prefix **im-**.

-ant
,ăb'ĕrrant (or a'bĕrrant), a'bundant, ac'countant², 'ădamant, 'adjutant³,

a'dulterant[1,3], 'alternant[3] ['ɔ:l-], ap'pellant[3], 'applicant[3], 'ărrant, 'ărrogant, a'scendant[2], 'ăspirant[c], as'sailant[2], as'sistant[2], 'assonant, at'tendant[1,2].

bë'nignant, 'blātant, 'brilliant.

'cĕlebrant[3], ,clair'voyant[3], 'clămant, 'cognisant, 'combatant[c], 'comman,dant[c], com'mūnicant[3], com'plainant[2], com'plaisant, com'plīant, con'cŏmitant[1,3], 'confi,dant[c], 'consonant[1,3], 'constant[1,3], con'sultant[2], con'testant[2], con-'tĭnūant[1,3], con'versant, 'cormorant[3], ,cō'sēcant[3], 'cövenant[3], 'currant[3].

dë'fendant[2], dë'fīant, ,dē'ōdorant[2], dë'pendant[2], dë'pressant[2], dë'scendant[2], dë'terminant[2], dis'cordant, 'dĭsin'fectant[2], 'dĭspūtant[3c] (or dis'pūtant[2]), 'dis-sonant, 'distant, 'dŏminant, 'dormant.

'ĕlĕgant, 'ĕlĕphant[3], 'ĕmigrant[3], 'ēqui'distant (or 'ĕqui-), 'ĕrrant, ë'xĕcūtant[3], ë'xorbitant, ëx'pectant, ëx'pectorant[3], 'extant, ëx'trăvagant, ë'xūberant, ë'xultant.

'flăgellant[c], 'flāgrant, ,flam'boyant, 'flippant, 'fondant[3], 'frāgrant, 'fulminant.

'gallant (='brave'), gal'lant[c] (='amorous').

'hĕsitant.

'ignorant, il'lüminant[1,3], 'immigrant[3], im'portant, in'cessant, in'constant, in'dignant, in'ĕrrant, 'infant[3], in'formant[2], in'hăbitant[2], in'hālant[2], 'in,sig'nĭficant, in'soüciant, 'instant[1,3], in'tŏlerant, in'tŏxicant, in'vāriant[1,2], ĭr'rĕlevant, 'ĭrritant[3], ,ī'tĭnerant.

'jūbilant.

Lë'vant[c], ,lieu'tĕnant[c] [,lef-] or [,lu:-], 'lĭtigant[3], 'lübricant[3], ,lŭ'xūriant.

ma'lĭgnant, 'mēdiant[3], 'mendicant[3], 'merchant[3], 'mīgrant[3], 'mĭlitant, 'mĭnistrant, 'mĭscrĕant[3], 'mordant, 'mūtant[3].

'nonchalant.

ob'servant, 'occūpant[3].

'pageant[2] ['pædʒənt], ,par'tĭcipant[3], 'pĕasant[3], 'pĕdant[3], 'pendant[3], 'pennant[3], 'pĕtūlant, 'phĕasant[3], 'pĭquant ['pi:kənt] or ['pi:,kɒŋ], 'plĕasant, 'poignant ['pɔɪnjənt], 'pŏstūlant[3], 'prĕdicant[3], prĕ'dŏminant, 'pregnant, prĕ'ponderant, pro'pellant[2], 'Prŏtĕstant[c], pro'tūberant, pur'sūant.

'rādiant, 'rampant, rë'calcitrant, 'rĕcreant[3], rë'dundant, 'rĕlevant, rë'līant, rë'luctant, 'remnant[3], rë'pentant, rë'pugnant, rë'sistant, 'rĕsonant[1,3], rë'sultant, rë'verberant, 'rüminant.

'sēcant[3], 'sergeant[3] ['sɑ:dʒənt], 'servant[2], 'sextant[3], 'sĭbilant, ,sig'nĭficant, 'stagnant, 'stĭmūlant[3], 'süpera'bundant, 'suppliant, 'supplicant[3].

'tĕnant[3], 'termagant[3], 'tŏlerant, 'trans'mīgrant[3] (or ,träns-), 'trenchant, ,trī'umphant, 'tȳrant[3].

A number of adjectives beginning with the stress-neutral negative prefix **un-**, including: 'unim'portant, ,un'plĕasant.

'vācant, 'vāgrant³, 'văliant, 'vāriant², 'verdant, 'vĭgilant, 'vīsitant².

Notes:

(i) The following words are best treated as simple roots: 'crois,sant ['krwæ'sɒŋ], 'galli,vant, 'pen,chant ['pɒŋ'ʃɒŋ], 'restau,rant ['restə,rɒŋ], 'sȳco,phant, 'warrant ['wɒrənt].

(ii) The following words are of the form prefix+stem ending in **-ant**: dë'cant, 'des,cant, ën'chänt, im'plänt, rë'cant, sup'plänt, ,trans'plänt (verb), 'trans,plänt (noun).

(iii) The following words are compounds: 'maid,servant, 'man,servant, ,sub'tĕnant.

-ary

ac'cessary²ᶜ, 'actūary², 'adversaryᶜ, 'āli'mentary²ᶜ, ,an'cillary², 'anni'ver-sary², ,an'tĭquary, 'āpiary², a'pŏthecary², 'arbitrary², ,au'xīliary², 'āviary², ,ä'xillary²ᶜ.

'beggary, 'bĕnë'fīciary², 'bestiary², 'bī,cen'tēnary², 'bīliary², 'bīnary², 'boundary, 'brĕviary², 'budgetary, 'burglary, 'bursary².

'calvary², ca'pillary², ca'tēnary², 'cautionary, ,cen'tēnary², 'cīliary², 'cīnerary², 'circumlo'cūtionary, 'commentaryᶜ, 'commissaryᶜ, 'complë'mentary²ᶜ, 'compli'mentary²ᶜ, con'stăbūlary², con'temporary², 'contrary (='opposite'), con'trāry (='perverse'), co'rollary², 'cŏronary², 'cŭlinary² (or 'cūlinary²), 'customary.

'dēnary², dë'pŏsitary, 'dīary², 'dictionary, 'dietary, 'dignitary², 'disci'plĭnaryᶜ (or 'disciplinary), dis'crĕtionary, dis'pensary, 'dŏcū'mentary²ᶜ, 'dŏmi'cīliary², 'drŏmedary², 'dūo'dēnary.

ë'lectūary², 'ĕlee'mŏsynary², 'ĕle'mentary²ᶜ, 'ĕlo'cūtionary, 'ĕmissaryᶜ, ë'mŏlū'mentary²ᶜ, ë'pistolary², 'estūary², 'ēvo'lütionary, ë'xemplary², 'expĕ'dītionary, ĕx'temporary², 'extra'ordinary² (or [ɪk'strɔ:-]).

'February² (or ['febrʊ,erɪ], fi'dūciary², 'formūlary, 'fragmentary, 'frīary², fri'tillary², 'functionary, 'fūnerary².

'glossary², 'grănary².

hë'rĕditary², 'hŏnorary.

i'măginary, in'cendiary², in'firmary, in'sănitary², 'insur'rectionary, in'tĕgū-'mentary²ᶜ, in'tercalary², 'inter'mēdiary², in'vŏluntaryᶜ, ,ī'tĭnerary².

'jănissaryᶜ (or 'jănizary²), 'Janūary² (or ['dʒænjʊ,erɪ]), ,jü'dĭciary², ,jus'tĭciary².

'lăpidary², 'lectionary², 'lĕgendary, 'lēgionary, 'lībrary², 'lĭterary², 'lüminary².

'mammary², ,mă'xillary², më'dullary², 'mercenary², mil'lēnary², 'mīlitary², 'missionary, 'mōmentary, 'mŏnetary², 'mortūary², 'multi'tūdinary.

'nĕcessaryᶜ (or [-,serɪ]), 'nŏtary².

o'bītūary², 'octo'gēnary², 'ordinary², 'ossūary², 'ōvary².

pa'pillary², 'parlia'mentary²ᶜ, 'peccary², pë'cūniary², 'pĕni'tentiary², 'pessary², 'pigmentary, 'plāgiary², 'plănetary, 'plēnary², 'plĕnipo'tentiary², 'prĕbendary, prë'cautionary, prë'lĭminary², 'prīmary, pro'bātionary, pro'prīetary², 'prōto'nōtary², 'pulmonary².

'quandary², qua'ternary².

rë'actionary, 'rĕliquary², 'rĕsi'dentiary², rë'sīdūary²ᶜ, 'rĕtiary², rë'vĭsionary, 'rĕvo'lütionary, 'rōsary, 'rōtary², 'rüdi'mentary²ᶜ.

'sălary², sa'līvary, 'sălūtary², 'sanctūary², 'sanguinary, 'sănitary², 'sĕcondary, 'sĕcretary² (or [-,terı]), 'sectary, 'sĕdentaryᶜ, 'sĕdi'mentary²ᶜ, 'segmentary, 'sĕminary², 'sŏlidary, 'sŏlitary², 'stātionary, 'stătūary, ,stī'pendiary², ,sub'lünary², sub'sīdiary², 'summary², 'sumptūary², 'süper'nūmerary², 'supple'mentary²ᶜ, 'syllabary².

'temporary², 'ter,cen'tēnary², 'ternary², 'tertiary², 'testa'mentary²ᶜ, 'tītūlary², 'tōpiary², 'trībūtary¹·², ,tū'multūary², 'tūtelary².

'ūnitary, ,un'nĕcessaryᶜ (or [-,serı]), 'ūrinary, 'ūsu'fructūary².

va'gāryᶜ (or 'vāgary²), 'văle'tūdinary², 'vestiary², 'vĕterinaryᶜ, 'vĭsionary, vo'căbūlary² (or ,vō-), 'vŏluntaryᶜ, vo'luptūary², 'vōtary².

Notes:

(i)   ca'nāry, con'trāry (='perverse'), and va'gāry have long **ā** and might be best treated as simple roots.

(ii)   'casso,wary [-,werı] and 'vāry are clearly simple roots.

(iii)   The following words are of the form root ending in -**ar** followed by suffix -**y** (stress-neutral): 'bleary, 'chāry, 'dreary, 'hoary, 'scāry, 'smeary, 'sugary ['ʃugərı], 'wāry.

-ate

a'bāte², 'abdi,cāte, 'abnĕ,gāte, a'bŏmi,nāte, ac'cĕle,rāte, ac'centū,āte, ac'commo,dāte, 'accūrate⁴, 'ăcĕ,tāte³, 'acti,vāte, 'ădĕquate⁴, ad'jüdi,cāte, 'ădum,brāte, 'advo,cāte (verb), 'advocate⁴ (noun), 'aerāteᶜ ['ɛə,reıt], af'fectionate⁴, af'fīli,āte (verb), af'fīliate⁴ (noun), 'affri,cāte (verb), 'affricate⁴ (noun), 'ăgate⁴, 'ăgi,tāte, 'aggra,vāte, 'aggrĕ,gāte (verb), 'aggrĕgate⁴ (noun), 'allo,cāte,'alter,cāte ['ɔ:l-], 'alter,nāte (verb) ['ɔ:l-], ,al'ternate⁴ (Brit.) or 'alternateᶜ (Amer.) [ɔ:l-], a'mēlio,rāteᶜ, 'ampū,tāte, 'ăni,māte (verb), 'ănimate⁴ (adj.), 'anno,tāte, 'antĕ,pĕ'nultimate⁴, a'pos,tāteᶜ or a'postate⁴, a'pŏstolate⁴, ap'pellate⁴, ap'prēci,āte, ap'prōpri,āte (verb), ap'prōpriate⁴ (adj.), ap'prŏxi,māte (verb), ap'prŏximate⁴ (adj.), 'arbi,trāte, ,ar'tīcū,lāte (verb), ,ar'tīcūlate⁴ (adj.), as'sassi,nāte, as'sīmi,lāte, as'sōci,āte (verb), as'sōciate⁴ (noun), as'phy˘xi,āte, ,au'thenti,cāte, 'auto,māte.

'bacca'laurĕate⁴, 'bīfur,cāte.

'calcū,lāte, 'căli,brāte, ca'lumni,āte, 'campho,rāte³, 'candidate⁴ or 'candi,dāteᶜ, ca'pītū,lāte, 'capti,vāte, 'carbo,nāte³, 'cardinalate⁴ or 'cardina,lāteᶜ, 'căsti,gāte, ,căs'trāte² or 'căs,trāteᶜ, 'caudate⁴ or 'cau,dāteᶜ, 'cĕlĕ,brāte, 'cĕlibate⁴, 'cĕrĕ,brāte, 'chlŏr,āte³, 'chlōri,nāte, 'chŏcolate⁴, 'chrŏ,māte³, 'circū,lāte, 'circum'năvi,gāte, 'circum'val,lāteᶜ, 'clīmate⁴,

‚cō'ăgū‚lāte, 'cō‚ar'tĭcū‚lāte, 'cŏgi‚tāte, 'cog‚nāte[c], col'lăbo‚rāte, col'lāte[2], col'lēgiate[4], 'colli‚gāte, 'collo‚cāte, com'mĕmo‚rāte, com'mensūrate[4], 'commen‚tāte, com'mĭse‚rāte, com'mūni‚cāte, 'commū‚tāte, com'passionate[4], com'pănionate[4], 'compen‚sāte or 'com‚pen‚sāte, 'concen‚trāte, con'cĭli‚āte, con'fĕde‚rāte (verb), con'fĕderate[4] (adj., noun), 'confi‚scāte, con'glŏme‚rāte (verb), con'glŏmerate[4] (noun), con'grătū‚lāte, 'conju‚gāte (verb), 'conjugate[4] (adj.), con'sĭderate[4], con'sŏli‚dāte, 'consūlate[4] or 'consulate[4], 'consum‚māte (verb), 'consummate[c] (adj.), con'tămi‚nāte, 'contem‚plāte, 'con‚trāte[c], ‚cō'ordi‚nāte (verb), ‚cō'ordinate[4] (adj., noun), 'cŏpū‚lāte, 'cor‚dāte[c], 'cŏrre‚lāte (verb), 'cŏrrelate[4] (noun), 'cŏrus‚cāte, crē'māte[2], 'crenel‚lāte[c], 'culmi‚nāte, 'culti‚vāte, 'cūrate[4].

dë'bĭli‚tāte, dë'căpi‚tāte, ‚dē'carbo‚nāte, ‚dē'cĕle‚rāte, 'dĕci‚māte, 'dēfe‚cāte, ‚dē'fŏli‚āte, dë'gene‚rāte (verb), dë'gĕnerate[4] (adj.), 'dē‚hȳ‚drāte, 'dĕlë‚gāte (verb), 'delegate[4] (noun), dë'lĭbe‚rāte (verb), dë'lĭberate[4] (adj.), 'dĕlicate[4], dë'lĭnë‚āte, 'dē‚mar‚cāte, 'dĕmon‚strāte, 'dĕni‚grāte, 'den‚tāte[c], 'dĕprë‚cāte, dë'prēci‚āte, 'dĕsë‚crāte, 'dĕsiccāte, 'dĕso‚lāte (verb), 'dĕsolate[4] (adj.), 'dĕsperate[4], dë'tērior‚āte[c], dë'terminate[4], 'dĕto‚nāte, 'dĕva‚stāte, ‚dī'ācon‚ate[4], ‚dic'tāte[2] or 'dic‚tāte[c] (Amer.) (verb), 'dic‚tāte[c] (noun), 'diffe'renti‚āte, di'lăpi‚dāte, ‚dī'lāte[2], dis'consolate[4], dis'crĭmi‚nāte (verb), dis'crĭminate[4] (adj.), dis'intë‚grāte, 'dislo‚cāte, dis'ōrien‚tāte[c], 'disparate[4], dis'passionate[4], 'dispro'portionate[4], dis'sĕmi‚nāte, dis'sĭmi‚lāte, dis'sĭmū‚lāte, dis'sōci‚āte, 'doctorate[4], do'mesti‚cāte, 'dŏmi‚nāte, do'nāte[2], 'dūpli‚cāte (verb), 'dūplicate[4] (noun).

‚ē'den‚tāte[c], 'ēdū‚cāte, ëf'fĕminate[4], ë'jăcū‚lāte, ë'lăbo‚rāte (verb), ë'lăborate[4] (adj.), ë'lāte[2], ë'lectorate[4], ë'lĭmi‚nāte, 'ē‚lon‚gāte, ë'lūci‚dāte, 'ēma‚nāte, ë'manci‚pāte, ë'mascū‚lāte, 'ĕmi‚grāte, 'ĕmū‚lāte, ën'capsū‚lāte, 'ĕner‚vāte, ë'nunci‚āte, ë'piscopate[4], ë'quāte[2], ë'quĭvo‚cāte, ë'rădi‚cāte, 'esti‚māte (verb), 'estimate[4] (noun), 'ētio‚lāte[c], ë'văcū‚āte, ë'vălū‚āte, ë'văpo‚rāte, ë'visce‚rāte, ë'xăcer‚bāte, ë'xagge‚rāte, 'exca‚vāte, 'excom'mūni‚cāte, 'ex‚cul‚pāte, 'ĕxë‚crāte, ëx'hĭla‚rāte [ıg'zıl-], ëx'pātriate[4], ëx'pecto‚rāte, 'expi‚āte, ëx'pŏstū‚lāte, 'expur‚gāte, ëx'termi‚nāte, 'extir‚pāte, 'extri‚cāte.

'făbri‚cāte, fa'cĭli‚tāte, 'fasci‚nāte, 'fĕde‚rāte, 'fil‚trāte[c], 'flăgel‚lāte, 'fluctū‚āte, 'formū‚lāte, 'forni‚cāte, 'fortūnate[4], 'frĭgate[4], 'fulmi‚nāte, 'fūmi‚gāte.

'gĕmi‚nāte (verb), 'gĕminate[4] (adj.), 'germi‚nāte, ‚ges'tĭcū‚lāte, 'glăci‚āte, gra'dāte[2], 'grădū‚āte (verb), 'grăduate[4] (noun), 'grănū‚lāte, 'grăvi‚tāte, ‚gȳ'rāte[2].

hal'lūci‚nāte, 'hĕsi‚tāte, 'hĭber‚nāte, ‚hū'mĭli‚āte, 'hȳ‚drāte[3], ‚hȳ'pŏthë‚cāte.

'illë'gĭtimate[4], il'lĭterate[4], 'illu‚strāte, 'imbri‚cāte, 'imi‚tāte, im'măcūlate[4], im'mēdiate[4], im'mŏderate[4], im'perforate[4], 'impli‚cāte, im'portūnate[4], 'impre‚cāte, 'im‚preg‚nāte, in'accūrate[4], in'ădēquate[4], in'ănimate[4], 'inap'prŏpriate[4], 'in‚ar'tĭcūlate[4], in'augū‚rāte, 'inca'păci‚tāte, 'in‚car‚nāte (verb), in'carnate[4] (adj.), 'inchōate[4], 'incom'mensūrate[4], 'incon'sĭderate[4], in'crĭmi‚nāte, 'incū‚bāte, 'in‚cul‚cāte, 'in‚cul‚pāte, in'dĕlicate[4], 'indë'ter‚minate[4], 'indi‚cāte, 'indis'crĭminate[4], in'doctri‚nāte, in'fătū‚āte, 'infil‚trāte, in‛fūri‚āte, ‛in‚grāteᶜ, in‛grāti‚āte, ‛inner‚vāte, ‛inno‚vāte, in‛ŏcū‚lāte, in‛ordinate⁴, in‛sensate⁴, in‛sīnū‚āte, in‛spectorate⁴, ‛insti‚gāte, ‛insub-‛ordinate⁴, ‛insū‚lāte, ‛intë‚grāte, in‛temperate⁴, ‛intercom‛mūni‚cāte, in‛terpel‚lāte, in‛terpo‚lāte, in‛tĕrro‚gāte, in‛testate⁴, ‛inti‚māte (verb), ‛intimate (adj.), in‛tĭmi‚dāte, ‛intricate⁴, ‛ĭnun‚dāte (or -‚un-), in‛văli‚dāte, in‛vertebrate⁴, or in‛verte‚brāteᶜ, in‛vesti‚gāte, in‛vĕterate⁴, in‛vīgi‚lāte, in‛vīgo‚rāte, in‛vĭolate⁴, ‚ī‛rāteᶜ, ‛ĭrri‚gāte, ‛ĭrri‚tāte, ‛īso‚lāte, I‛tălian‚āteᶜ.

‚lac‛tāte², ‛lămi‚nāte (verb), ‛lăminate⁴ (noun), ‛laurëate⁴ [‛lɒrɪət], ‛lĕgate⁴, ‛lĕgis‚lāte, lë‛gītimate⁴, ‛lĕvirate⁴, ‛lĕvi‚tāte, ‛lĭbe‚rāte, ‛lĭqui‚dāte, ‛lĭterate⁴, ‛lĭti‚gāte, ‚lō‛cāte², ‛lübri‚cāte, ‚lū‛xūri‚āte.

‛măce‚rāte, ‛măgistrate⁴ or ‛măgi‚strāteᶜ, ‛magnate⁴ or ‛mag‚nāteᶜ, ‛man‚dāteᶜ, ma‛nĭpū‚lāte, ‛mări‚nāte, ‛masti‚cāte, ‛mastur‚bāte, ‛mēdi‚āte, ‛mĕdi‚cāte, ‛mĕdi‚tāte, ‛menstrü‚āte, ‚mī‛grāte², ‛mĭli‚tāte, ‛mīsap‛prōpri‚āte, mis‛calcū‚lāte, ‛mĭti‚gāte, ‛mŏde‚rāte (verb), ‛mŏderate⁴ (adj.), ‛mŏdū‚lāte, ‚mū‛tāte², ‛mūti‚lāte.

nar‛rāte², ‛nausë‚āte, ‛năvi‚gāte, në‛cessi‚tāte, në‛gāte², në‛gōti‚āte [nɪ‛gəʊsɪ‚eɪt] or [-ʃɪ-], ‛nī‚trāte³, no‛vĭtiate⁴, ‛nūmerate⁴.

‛obdūrate⁴, ‛obfus‚cāte, ‛objur‚gāte, o‛blāteᶜ or ‛ō‚blāteᶜ, ‛ŏbli‚gāte, ‛obstinate⁴, ‛obvi‚āte, of‛fĭci‚āte [-sɪ-] or [-ʃɪ-], ‛ŏper‚āte, ‛ōpi‚āte³, o‛pĭnio‚nāte, o‛rāte² or ‚ō-, ‛orches‚trāte, ‛orien‚tāteᶜ, o‛rĭgi‚nāte, ‚or‛nāteᶜ, ‛oscil‚lāte, ‛oscū‚lāte, ‛ō‚vāteᶜ, ‛ŏvū‚lāte, ‛ŏxi‚dāte, ‛ŏxyge‚nāteᶜ.

‛păgi‚nāte, ‛pălate⁴, Pa‛lătinate⁴, ‛pal‚māteᶜ, ‚pal‛pāte², ‛palpi‚tāte, ‚par‛tĭci‚pāte, ‛passionate⁴, ‛pästorate⁴, ‛pātri‚ar‚chāteᶜ, ‛pĕnë‚trāte, ‚pĕn‛ultimate⁴, per‛ambū‚lāte, ‛perco‚lāte, ‛pĕregri‚nāteᶜ, ‛perfo‚rāte (verb), ‛perforate⁴ (adj.), per‛manga‚nāte³, ‛permë‚āte, ‛per‚noc‚tāte, ‛perpë‚trāte, per‛pĕtū‚āte, ‚phō‛nāte², ‛phos‚phāte³, ‛Pīlate⁴, ‛pīrate⁴, pla‛cāte², ‛polli‚nāte, ‛p̌omë‛grănateᶜ or ‛pŏmë‚grănateᶜ, ‚pon‛tĭfi‚cāte (verb), ‚pon‛tĭficate⁴ (noun), ‛pŏstū‚lāte (verb), ‛pŏstūlate (noun), ‛pōten‚tāteᶜ, po‛tenti‚āte [-sɪ] or [-ʃɪ-], prë‛cĭpi‚tāte (verb), prë‛cĭpitate⁴ (noun), ‛prĕdi‚cāte (verb), ‛prĕdicate⁴ (noun), prë‛dŏmi‚nāte, ‛prĕlate⁴, ‚prē‛mĕdi‚tāte, prë‛ponde‚rāte, prë‛vări‚cāte, ‛prīmate⁴ or ‛prī‚māteᶜ, ‛prīvate⁴, ‛prō‚bāteᶜ, pro‛crasti‚nāte, ‛prōcre‛āteᶜ, ‛prŏfligate⁴, ‚prog‛nosti‚cāte, ‛prō‚lāteᶜ, pro‛lĭfe‚rāte, ‛prŏmul‚gāte, ‛prŏpa‚gāte, pro‛pĭti‚āte [-sɪ-] or [-ʃɪ-], pro‛portionate⁴, ‛pros‚tāteᶜ, ‚pros‛trāte² (verb), ‛pros‚trāteᶜ (adj.), pro‛tectorate⁴, ‛prŏximate⁴, ‛pullūlāte, ‚pul‛sāte², ‛punctū‚āte.

‚quad‛rüplicate⁴ [‚kwɒd-].

‛rādi‚āte, ‛răti‛ŏci‚nāte, ‛rēca‛pĭtū‚lāte, rë‛cĭpro‚cāte, ‛rē-cre‛āte², rë-‛crīmi‚nāte, rë‛cüpe‚rāte, rë‛düpli‚cāte, rë‛frīge‚rāte, rë‛gĕne‚rāte (verb), rë‛gĕnerate⁴ (adj.), ‛rēgū‚lāte, rë‛gurgi‚tāte, ‛rēha‛bĭli‚tāte, ‛rē‛in‚car‚nāte (verb), ‛rēin‛carnate⁴ (adj.), ‛rēin‛stāte², rë‛jüve‚nāte, ‛rĕlë‚gāte, ‛rĕmon-‚strāte, rë‛müne‚rāte, ‚rē‛pătri‚āte, ‛rĕpli‚cāte, ‛rĕpro‚bāteᶜ, rë‛pūdi‚āte, ‛rĕso‚nāte, rë‛susci‚tāte, rë‛tăli‚āte, rë‛verbe‚rāte, ‛rōsëate⁴, ‚rō‛tāte² (Brit.) or ‛rō‚tāteᶜ (Amer.), ‛rümi‚nāte, ‛rŭsti‚cāte.

‛săli‚vāte, ‛sătū‚rāte, ‛scintil‚lāte, së‛dāte² (verb), së‛dāteᶜ (adj.), ‛sĕgrë‚gāte, ‛sĕnate⁴, ‛sensate⁴ or ‛sen‚sāteᶜ, ‛sĕpa‚rāte (verb), ‛sĕparate⁴ (adj.), së'ques,trāte᷄, ser'rāte², 'sĭli,cāte³, 'sīmū,lāte, 'spătūlate⁴, 'spĕcū,lāte, 'spĭfli,cāte, ,stag'nāte² or 'stag,nāte᷄ (Amer.), 'stel,lāte᷄, 'stīmū,lāte, 'stĭpū,lāte, 'strangū,lāte, 'strĭdū,lāte, 'subju,gāte, sub'ordi,nāte (verb), sub'ordinate⁴ (adj., noun), sub'stanti,āte [-sɪ] or [-ʃɪ-], 'sub,strāte᷄, 'sul,phāte³, 'süper'annū,āte, 'süper'ordinate⁴, 'suppli,cāte, 'suppū,rāte, 'sŭrrogate⁴, 'synco,pāte, 'syndi,cāte (verb), 'syndicate⁴ (noun).

'tăbū,lāte, 'temperate⁴, 'tem,plāte᷄, 'tergiver,sāte᷄, 'tes,tāte᷄, 'tītil,lāte, 'tĭti,vāte, 'tŏle,rāte, ,trans'līte,rāte, ,trī'angū,lāte, 'trĭplicate⁴, ,trī'umvirate⁴, ,trun'cāte² or 'trun,cāte᷄ (Amer.).

'ulce,rāte, 'ultimate⁴, 'under'grādūate⁴, 'undū,lāte, ,un'fortūnate⁴, 'ungūlate⁴, 'unrë'gĕnerate⁴, 'ūri,nāte.

,vā'cāte² or va'cāte² or 'vā,cāte᷄ (Amer.), 'vacci,nāte, 'văcil,lāte, 'văli,dāte, 'vārie,gāte, 'vĕgĕ,tāte, 'vĕne,rāte, 'venti,lāte, 'vertebrate⁴ or 'verte,brāte᷄, 'vindi,cāte, 'vīo,lāte, 'vĭti,āte ['vɪʃɪ,eɪt], ,vī'tūpe,rāte, ,vō'cĭfe,rāte, 'vulgate⁴ or 'vul,gāte᷄.

Notes:
(i)   The following words are best treated as simple roots: ,can'tätë, e'stāte.
(ii) The following words are of the form prefix+stem ending in -āte:
      bë'lāt,ë(d), bë'rāte, dë'bāte, dë'flāte, in'flāte, in'nāte, 'rē,bāte, rë'lāte,
      ,trans'lāte.
(iii) The following words are compounds: 'antë'dāte, 'ōver'rāte, 'ōver'stāte,
      ,prë'dāte, 'under'rāte, 'under'stāte.

-ee (excluding -ée)
'absen'tee, 'ad,dres'see, 'ăpo,gee³, 'ap,pel'lee², 'ap,poin'tee.

,ban'shee², ,bar'gee, ,bōō'tee², ,buck'shee², ,bur'gee².

,Chal'dee² (or 'Chal,dee³), 'chicka,dee³, 'chimpan'zee² (or -,pan-) (Brit.) or ,chim'pan,zee³ (Amer.), ,coa'tee², 'coffee³, com'mittee³, 'con,sig'nee ['kɒn,saɪ'ni:], cor'rŏbo'ree².

'dē,bau'chee (or dë'bau'chee᷄), 'dĕdica'tee¹᷄, 'dĕvo'tee or 'dĕ,vō'tee), 'dĭ,vor'cee (or di'vor'cee᷄), 'dunga'ree².

'em,ploy'ee (or ĕm'ploy,ee³), 'ĕpo'pee² or 'ĕpo,pee³, ë'văcū'ee (see note (iii) below), ë'xămi'nee.

'fĭli,gree³, 'frĭcas'see², ,fū'see².

'Găli,lee³, ,goa'tee², ,gran'dee², ,grän'tee, 'guăran'tee².

'in,ter'nee, 'in,vī'tee.

'jambo'ree², 'jübi,lee³ (or 'jübi'lee²).

'kedge'ree² or 'kedge,ree³.

'lĕga'tee, ,les'see, 'lĕvee³, 'līcen'see.

'măna'tee², 'Măni,chee³ [-,ki:], ,mar'quee² [-'ki:], 'mortga'gee ['mɔ:gɪ'dʒi:].

'nŏmi'nee (see note (iii) below).

'ō,gee³.

'Par'see², 'pāten'tee, ,pay'ee, 'pĕdi,gree³, 'pĕri,gee³, 'Phări,see³, 'put,tee³.

'rä,nee³, 'rĕfe'ree, 'rĕ,fū'gee (or 'rĕfū'gee (Amer.)), 'rĕ,par'tee², ,rü'pee².

'Saddū,cee³, ,set'tee², 'snicker'snee², 'spon,dee³, 'squee'gee² or 'squee,gee³, 'stinga'ree² or 'stinga,ree³, ,sut'tee² or 'sut,tee³.

'tē,pee³, ,thug'gee² or 'thug,gee³, 'toffee³, 'trō,chee³ [-,ki:], ,trus'tee.

'warran'tee ['wɒrən'ti:].

'Yankee³.

Notes:
  (i) The following words are of the form prefix+stem: a'gree, dë'cree, dë'gree, 'dĭsa'gree, ,fore'see, 'ōver'see.
  (ii) 'căre,free is a compound.
  (iii) ë'văcū'ee and 'nŏmi'nee have been treated as stem+true suffix -ee, although the stems **evacu-** and **nomin-** are not free.

-er
(The following list would be unmanageably large if two-syllable words were included in it. Since all such words have initial stress, nothing is lost by restricting it to words of three or more syllables.)

ab'stainer, a'būser, ac'cūser, a'dapter, ad'juster, ad'mīrer, a'dulterer², ad'ventūrer, 'almoner², 'ampli,fier, 'ăna,lÿser, 'armourer, ,ar'tĭficer², as'sembler, a'strŏloger², a'strŏnomer², at'tacker, 'auto,bī'ŏgrapher², a'venger.

'bălancer, 'bărrister², bë'ginner, bë'hōlder, bë'liēver, ,bī'ŏgrapher², 'black-,mailer, 'blunderer.

,cam'paigner [-'peɪnə], ,car'tŏgrapher², 'căta,lŏguer, 'cāterer, 'chŏrister² ['kɒ-], 'cŏmforter, com'mänder, com'missioner, 'commoner, com'mūter, com'pōser, com'pūter, con'denser, con'fectioner, 'cŏnjurer, con'sūmer, con'tainer, con'tender, con'trŏller, con'vēner, con'verter, con'veyancer, con'veyer, 'cŏroner², 'cottager, 'counter,fēiter, 'cövenanter, 'cŭstomer.

dë'canter, dë'faulter, dë'fender, dë'lĭverer, dë'scender, dë'serter, dë'signer [dɪ'zaɪnə], dë'terminer, dë'vĕloper, dis'claimer³, dis'pōser, dis'senter, di'stiller, di'sturber, di'vīder.

ëm'bezzler, ëm'brācer, ën'chänter, ën'grāver, ë'rāser, ë'xăminer, 'ëxë'cūtioner, ëx'horter [ɪg'zɔ:tə], ëx'plōrer, ëx'porter, ëx'tinguisher.

'falconer ['fɔ:l-], 'fästener ['fɑ:s(ə)nə], 'ferti,līser, 'fĭnisher, 'follōwer, 'fŏrager, 'fŏreigner ['fɒrɪnə], 'fŏrester, 'forti,fier, 'free,hōlder, ,free'trāder, 'früiterer².

'gardener, 'gătherer, gë'ŏgrapher², 'gŏspeller.

'häber,däsher^c, 'hägi'ŏgrapher², 'handi,capper, 'harvester, 'hī,jacker, 'hĭstori'ŏgrapher² (or -,stŏ-).

'īco'nōlater², ,ī'dōlater², im'bīber, im'porter, in'former, in'hāler, in'sīder, in'surer [ın'ʃɔːrə], in'tensi,fīer, 'inter,lōperᶜ, in'terpreter, 'inter'rupter, 'inter,viewer, in'trüder, 'īslander ['aıləndə].

'jeweller.

'lābourer, 'lectūrer, 'lĕveller, 'lĕxi'cŏgrapher².

'magni,fīer, ma'lingerer, 'mănager, 'mănū'factūrer, 'marketer, 'messenger², 'milliner², 'missioner, 'multi,plīer, 'murderer.

'nĕcro,mancer.

ob'server, 'occū,pīer, 'officer, 'ōpener, op'pōser, out'sīder, 'over'tāker.

pa'rīshioner², ,par'tāker, 'păssenger², 'pensioner, 'pĕrisher, 'perjurer, per'suāder, pë'tītioner, 'petti,fogger, phi'lŏsopher², pho'tŏgrapher², 'pŏlisher, ,por'nŏgrapher², 'pŏulterer², ,prac'tītioner², prë'senter, prë'tender, 'prīsoner, pro'bātioner, pro'dūcer, pro'mōter, pro'peller, pro'tester, pro'vīder, 'pŭblisher, 'purchaser, 'pūri,fīer.

'questioner.

rë'cēiver, rë'corder, 'recti,fīer, rë'deemer, rë'fīner, rë'former, rë'fresher, rë'joinder³, rë'mīnder³, rë'mitter, rë'mover [rı'muːvə], rë'peater, rë'porter, rë'searcher [rı'sɜːtʃə], ,rë'setter, rë'specter, rë'tainer¹'³, rë'trĭēver, 'rĕveller, rë'viewer, rë'vīser, rë'volver, ro'mancer.

'scăvenger, 'sĕconder, së'dūcer, 'sīlencer, 'sŏjourner, 'sorcerer², 'stābi,līser, 'stammerer, 'stātioner², stë'nŏgrapher², 'stutterer, sub'scrīber, 'sufferer, sup'porter, sus'pender, 'swash,buckler² ['swɒʃ-], 'sweetener.

'thunderer, ,trans'former, ,trans'mitter, ,trans'porter, 'trăveller, tra'verser, 'trĕasūrer ['treʒərə], 'trĕspasser, 'trumpĕter, ,tȳ'pŏgrapher².

'unbë'liēver, 'under'tāker (='one who undertakes something'), 'under,tākerᶜ (='one who arranges funerals), 'under,wrīterᶜ, ,up'hōlder, ,up'hōlsterer, 'ūsūrer² ['juːʒərə], ,ū'surper.

'versi,fīer, 'victualler ['vıtələ].

'waggoner, 'wanderer ['wɒn-], 'whĭsperer.

'yōdeller.

Notes:
(i) A large number of polysyllabic words in -er are compounds with various stress-patterns (for full details see Section 5); the following is merely an illustrative selection from the total list: 'beef,eater, 'book,seller, 'bȳ,stander, 'eaves,dropper, 'gāme,keeper, 'grăss,hopper, 'hair,dresser, 'in-,swinger, 'land,ōwner, 'left-'hander, 'loud'speaker, 'mŏney,lender, 'out,fiēlder, 'over,seer, 'păper,hanger, 'part-'tīmer, 'ring,leader, 'sharp,shooter, 'stŏry,teller, 'tȳpe,wrīter, 'way,fārer, 'wrong,doer ['rɒŋ,dʊə].
(ii) Stress-neutral -er may be added to a number of geographical names to indicate a person originating from the place referred to; for example:

‚Ber'līner, 'borderer, 'Brītisher, 'easterner, 'Ham‚burger, 'Hīghlander, 'Īcelander, 'Löndoner, 'Lōwlander, 'Midlander, 'Newfound‚lander, ‚New 'Yorker, ‚New 'Zealander, 'northerner, 'söutherner, 'westerner.

-ery
a'dultery², ‚ar'tillery².

'baptistery, 'brāvery, 'brewery, 'brībery, buf'fōōnery.

ca'jōlery, 'cannery, 'cĕmetery², 'chäncellery^c, 'chäncery², chi'cānery [ʃɪ-], con'fectionery, 'cookery, 'creamery, 'crockery.

'deanery, dë'bauchery, di'stillery, 'drāpery, 'drōllery, 'drudgery, 'druggery, 'dÿsentery^c.

ëf'fröntery².

'fīnery, 'fīshery, 'flummery², 'fōōlery, 'foppery, 'forgery, 'frippery².

'greenery, 'gunnery.

'hatchery, 'house‚wīfery.

'īmagery.

'jewellery, 'jobbery, 'joinery.

'knāvery ['neɪvərɪ].

'lāmasery², 'lottery.

ma'chīnery [mə'ʃiːnərɪ], 'mid‚wīfery^c, 'mockery, 'mockery, 'mŏnastery².

'nāpery, 'nunnery, 'nursery.

'ŏrangery.

per'fūmery (see note (iv) below), phÿ'lactery², 'piggery, ‚pol'trōōnery, 'pōpery, 'pottery, 'prūdery.

'quackery.

'raillery², rë'fīnery, 'rockery, 'rōguery ['rəugərɪ], 'rookery, 'rōpery.

'săvagery, 'scēnery, 'scullery², 'shrubbery, 'slāvery, 'snobbery, 'surgery².

'tannery, 'thiēvery, 'trācery, 'trickery, 'trumpery².

Notes:
(i) The following words are made up of a stem ending in **-er** plus the (stress-neutral) suffix -y: 'buttery, dë'līvery, di'scövery, ëm'broidery, 'flattery, 'īron‚möngery, 'mästery, rë'covery, 'rēdi'scövery, ‚up'hōlstery.
(ii) The following words are made up of a stem plus the suffix **-er** plus the (stress-neutral) suffix -y: 'archery, 'butchery ['bʊ-], 'colliery, 'häber-‚dăshery, 'lĕchery, 'millinery, 'presbytery, 'robbery.
(iii) The following words are made up of a bound stem ending in **-er** plus the (pre-stressed 2) suffix -y: 'mīsery, pe'rīphery, 'sorcery, 'trĕachery.

(iv)   The word per'fümery is based on the verb stem per'füme rather than the noun stem 'per,füme.
(v)   The following words are best treated as simple roots: 'artery, 'battery, 'cĕlery, 'ĕmery, 'gallery, 'lĭvery, 'psaltery ['sɔːltərɪ].
(vi)   Adjective-forming -y attaches to a number of stems ending in -er, e.g. 'flowery, 'lĕathery, 'peppery, 'powdery, 'silvery, 'thundery.

-ine

'ăda'man,tīne, 'Ālĕ'xän,drīne, 'alka,līne, 'al,pīne, ,am'phĕta,mīne², 'ăni,līne, 'ăquama'rïne⁴, 'ăqui,līne, 'Argen,tīneᶜ (adj.), 'ăsi,nīne, 'auber,gïneᶜ ['əubə,ʒiːn], 'Ăven,tīne³.

bĕ'guïne⁴ [-'giːn], 'bĕne'dic,tïneᶜ, 'benze,drïne², 'ben,zïne², 'bō,vīne, 'bōwline⁵, 'brĭgan,tïneᶜ, 'brillian,tïneᶜ, 'brō,mïne², ,Bÿ'zan,tīne.

'căla,mīne³, 'cā,nīne, 'car,bīne³, 'car,mīne, 'Căro,līne¹ˑ³, 'Cătherine⁵, 'cĕlan,dīne³, 'chlo,rïne² ['klɔː-], ,clan'dĕstine⁵, 'cŏlum,bīne³, 'compline⁵, 'concū,bīne³, 'crĭnoline⁵, 'crÿstal,līneᶜ, cui'sïne⁴ [kwɪ'ziːn].

'del,phīne, 'den,tīne², 'dĕstine⁵, dĕ'termine⁵, 'dīa'man,tīne, 'dĭscipline⁵, di'vīneᶜ, 'doctrine⁵.

'ĕglan,tīne³, 'ĕlĕ'phan,tīne, 'endo,crīne, 'engine⁵, 'ĕ,quīne, ĕ'xămine⁵.

'fămine⁵, 'fē,līne, 'fĕminine⁵, 'fīgu'rïne⁴, 'Flŏren,tīneᶜ.

'găber'dïne⁴ (or 'găber,dïneᶜ), 'gĕla,tīne² (or 'gĕlatine⁵), 'gĕnūine⁵, 'glÿce,rïne² (or 'glÿcerine⁵), 'grĕna'dïne⁴ (or 'grĕna,dïneᶜ), 'guillo,tïneᶜ (or 'guillo'tïne⁴) ['gɪlə,tiːn].

'hĕrōine⁵.

il'lümine⁵, i'măgineᶜ, 'inter'nē,cīne, ,in'testine⁵, 'īo,dïne² (or 'īodine⁵).

'jasmine⁵, 'jessamine⁵, 'Jō'han,nīne.

'lăby'rin,thīne, la'cus,trīne, la'trïne⁴, Lĕ'van,tīne, 'lĭber,tïneᶜ (or 'lĭber'tïne⁴), 'lĭmou'sïne⁴ ['lɪmə'ziːn].

ma'chïne⁴ [mə'ʃiːn], 'măga'zïne⁴ (Brit.) (or 'măga,zïneᶜ (Amer.)), 'marga'rïne⁴ (Brit.) (or 'margarine⁵ (Amer.)) [-dʒə-], ma'rïne⁴ᶜ (adj.), 'măscūline⁵, 'mĕdicine⁵, 'mĕla,mīne², 'mezza,nïneᶜ, 'mor,phïne², 'moüsse'līne⁴.

'necta'rïne⁴ (or 'necta,rïneᶜ), 'nĭco,tīne², 'nītro'glÿcerine⁵ (or -,rïne²).

'ōpa,līne, 'ō,vīne.

'păla,tīne, 'Păle,stīne³, 'Pau,līne (='relating to the apostle Paul'), ,Pau'līne⁴ (or 'Pau,līneᶜ) (girl's name), 'pĕregrine⁵, 'Pĕ,trīne, 'phĭli,stīne¹ˑ³, 'pis,cīne, 'Plasti,cïneᶜ (or 'Plasti'cïne⁴), 'por,cīne, 'porcū,pīne³, 'prä,līneᶜ, ,prē'dĕstine⁵, 'pris,tïneᶜ (or 'pris,tīne), 'psitta,cīne.

'quaran,tïneᶜ ['kwɒ-], 'quĭ,nīne².

'ră,pīne³, ra'vīne⁴, 'rĕ,xïne²ᶜ, ,roü'tïne⁴.

'saccharine⁵, 'sā‚līne, 'sanguine⁵ [-gwɪn], ‚sar'dïne⁴, 'sătur‚nïneᶜ, 'serpen-‚tïneᶜ, 'strych‚nïne² ['strɪk-]. 'subma'rïne⁴ (Brit.) (or 'subma‚rïneᶜ (Amer.)), 'sü‚pīne.

'tambou'rïne⁴, 'tange'rïne⁴, 'tau‚rīne, ‚ter'rïne⁴, 'trampo‚lïneᶜ, ‚trans-'pon‚tīne, ‚trī'den‚tīne, 'tur‚bīne³, 'turpen‚tīne³.

'ultrama'rïne⁴, 'ūrine⁵, 'ūte‚rīne.

'vac‚cïne², 'Vălen‚tīne³, 'văse‚lïne², 'vul‚pīne.

'wolve‚rïneᶜ ['wul-].

Notes:

(i) The following verbs are of the form prefix+stem: com'bīne, con'fïne, dë'clīne, dë'fïne, ën'shrīne, ën'twīne, in'clīne, o'pīne, ‚out'shīne, rë'clīne, rë'fïne, ‚rë'līne, rë'pīne, 'under'līne, 'under'mīne.

(ii) The following are compounds: 'cō‚sīne, 'mōōn‚shīne, 'out‚līne, 'stream‚līne, 'sun‚shīne, 'wood‚bīne.

-ism

'absen'teeism, 'abso‚lü‚tism, ‚ag'nŏsti‚cism, 'albi‚nism², 'alco‚hŏ‚lism, 'al‚trü‚ism², A'mĕrica‚nism, a'năchro‚nism² [-krə-], 'ănar‚chism² [-‚kɪzm], 'ăneu‚rism², 'Anglica‚nism, 'angli‚cism², 'ăni‚mism², ‚an'tăgo‚nism², 'anthropo'mor‚phismᶜ, 'anti-'sĕmi‚tism, 'ăpho‚rism², 'ar‚chā‚ism² [-‚keɪ-], as'cĕti‚cism, a'stigma‚tism², 'ăta‚vism², 'āthë‚ism².

'bap‚tism², 'barba‚rism², bë'hāviou‚rism, 'Bud‚dhism ['bu‚dɪzm].

'Calvi‚nism, 'canniba‚lism, 'căpita‚lism, 'cătë‚chism [-‚kɪzm], Ca'thŏli‚cismᶜ, 'caute‚rism², 'charlata‚nism ['ʃɑ:-], 'char‚tism², 'chauvi‚nism² ['ʃəu-], 'classi‚cism, col'lecti‚vism, 'commū‚nism. con'serva‚tism², crë'ātio‚nism, 'crĕti‚nism, 'crīti‚cism, 'cū‚bism, 'cỹni‚cism.

'Dalto‚nism ['dɔ:l-], 'Darwi‚nism, dë'fea‚tism, 'dē‚ism², 'dēmo‚nism, 'dĕspo‚tism, dë'termi‚nism, 'dīlët'tan‚tism, 'dogma‚tism², 'dūa‚lism, 'dỹna‚mism².

'ĕgō‚ism, 'ĕgo‚tism², 'embo‚lism², ë'mōtiona‚lism, ëm'pïri‚cism², 'euphë‚mism², 'euphū‚ism², ë'vange‚lism, 'ĕ‚xor‚cism², ex'pansio‚nism, ex'trē‚mism.

fa'năti‚cism, 'fă‚scism² [-‚ʃɪzm], 'fāta‚lism, 'fāvouri‚tism, 'fĕmi‚nism², 'fĕti‚shism, 'feuda‚lism, 'forma‚lism, 'funda'menta‚lism, 'fūtū‚rism.

'galli‚cism, 'galva‚nism², 'grădūa‚lism.

'heathe‚nism, 'hē‚brā‚ism², 'hēdo‚nism² (or 'hĕ-), 'hĕrō‚ism, 'Hindü‚ism, 'hŏ‚lism², 'hōōliga‚nism, 'hūma‚nism, 'hypno‚tism².

‚ī'dēa‚lism, im'pēria‚lism, im'pressio‚nism, in'cendia‚rism, 'indi'vīdūa‚lism, in'fanti‚lismᶜ, 'intel'lectūa‚lism, 'inter'nătiona‚lism, 'Īri‚shism, 'īso-'mor‚phismᶜ.

'Jăcobi‚nism, 'Janse‚nism, 'jingō‚ism², 'journa‚lism ['dʒɜ:-], 'Jü‚dā‚ism.

'Lăti,nism, 'lēga,lism, 'lĭbera,lism, 'lōca,lism, 'lўri,cism.

'magne,tism, 'manne,rism, 'măso,chism² [-,kızm], ma'tēria,lism, 'mĕch-a,nism² [-kə-], 'Mende,lism, 'mesmerism², më'tăbo,lism, 'Mĕtho,dism, 'mĭlita,rism, 'mŏder,nism, ,Mō'hammeda,nism, 'mō,nism², 'mŏnothë,ismᶜ, 'Mormo,nism, 'mўsti,cism.

'narcis,sism², 'nătiona,lism, 'nătura,lism ['nætrə-], në'ŏlo,gism², 'nĕpo,tism², 'nīhi,lism², 'nŏmina,lism.

ob'jecti,vism, 'ob,scū'ran,tismᶜ, 'ō,nă,nism², 'oppor,tū,nism, 'opti,mism², 'orga,nism², 'ŏstra,cism².

'păci,fism², 'pāga,nism, 'panthë,ism², 'păralle,lism (or 'păral,lĕ,lism), 'părasi,tism, pa'rōchia,lism [-kı-], 'pătrio,tism (or 'pā-), 'paupe,rism, per'fec-tio,nism, 'pessi,mism², 'Phări,sā,ism, 'phĭlisti,nism, 'pīë,tism², 'plāgia,rism², 'Plāto,nism², 'plüra,lism, 'pŏlythë,ismᶜ, 'pŏsiti,vism, 'pragma,tism², 'Presby'tēria,nism, 'prīa,pism², 'prŏbabi,lism, pro'fessiona,lism, 'prŏsely,tism, 'Prŏtëstan,tism, 'pūgi,lism², 'pū,rism, 'pūrita,nism.

'quīë,tism.

'rācia,lism, 'rădica,lism, 'rătiona,lism, 'rēa,lism, rë'cĭdi,vism², 'rĕlati,vism, rë'pūblica,nism, rë'vīsio,nism, 'rheuma,tism², 'rhōta,cism², 'rītūa,lism, 'Rōma,nism, ro'manti,cism, 'rowdy,ism.

'sā,dism², 'Sāta,nism, 'scepti,cism ['skep-], scho'lăsti,cism [skə-], 'Scot-ti,cism², 'sĕcūla,rism, ,sen'sātiona,lism, 'sĕpara,tism, 'sĕ,xism, 'sōcia,lism, 'sŏlë,cism², 'sŏlip,sism², ,som'nambū,lism², 'sō,phism², 'spĕcia,lism, 'spĭri,tism, 'spĭritūa,lism, 'spŏōne,rism, 'stŏi,cism, sur'rēa,lism², 'syllo,gism², 'symbo,lism, 'synchro,nism² [-krə-], 'syncrë,tism², 'sўner,gism.

'Täō,ism (or 'Tāō-), 'tërro,rism, 'thē,ism², 'Thō,mism² ['təʊ-], 'Tōry,ism, 'tōte,mism, 'toü,rism, tra'dītiona,lism, 'tran,scen'denta,lism, 'trība,lism, 'trü,ism.

'ultra'monta,nism, 'ūnio,nism, 'ūni'versa,lism.

'vanda,lism, 'vĕgë'tāria,nism, ,ven'trīlo,quism², 'vōca,lism, 'vōō,dōō,ism, 'vulga,rism.

'witti,cism².

-ist

'abso,lü,tist, 'ăgri'cultū,ristᶜ, 'alchë,mist² [-kı-], 'altrü,ist², A'mĕrica,nist, 'Ăna'bap,tistᶜ, 'ănar,chist² [-,kıst], a'năto,mist², 'ăni,mist², ,an'tăgo,nist², 'anthro'pŏlo,gist², 'anti-'vīvi'sectio,nist, 'āo,rist², a'pŏlo,gist², 'Ăra,bist, 'arche'ŏlo,gist² [-kı-], 'ar,tist, 'āthë,ist².

'Bap,tist², bë'hăviou,rist, 'bĭga,mist, ,bī'ŏlo,gist², 'bŏta,nist², 'Bud,dhist ['bʊ,dıst].

'Calvi,nist, 'căpita,list, 'căsū,ist², 'cătë,chist² [-,kıst], 'cel,list ['tʃe,lıst], 'cen,trist, 'char,tist, 'chauvi,nist² ['ʃəʊ-], 'chë,mist², 'classi,cist, 'cŏlo,nist, 'commū,nist, con'for,mist, 'conser'vātionist, 'cŏpy,ist, 'cū,bist, 'cў,clist.

dë'fea,tist, 'dē,ist², 'den,tist², dë'termi,nist, 'dīa,rist, di'plōma,tist², 'drăma,tist², 'drug,gist, 'dūa,list, 'dūel,list.

ë'cŏno,mist², 'ĕgō,ist, 'ĕgo,tist², ë'mōtiona,list, ën'cȳclo'pē,dist, 'eucha,rist [-kə-], ë'vange,list, 'ĕ,xor,cist², ëx'pansionist, ëx'trē,mist.

'fă,scist² [-,ʃıst], 'fāta,list, 'fĕdera,list, 'fĕmi,nist², 'fĕti,shist, 'flau,tist², 'flŏ,rist², 'forma,list, ,fū'nambū,list², 'funda'menta,list, 'fūtū,rist.

'gēnë'ălo,gist², 'Germa,nist, 'grădūa,list.

'har,pist, 'hē,brā,ist, 'hēdo,nist² (or 'hĕ-), 'Helle,nist, 'herba,list, 'hūma,nist, 'hūmo,rist, 'hypno,tist².

,ī'dēa,list, 'īde'ŏlo,gist², il'lüsio,nist, im'pēria,list, im'pressio,nist, 'indi'vī-dūa,list, 'inter'nătiona,list.

'Janse,nist, 'jingō,ist², 'journa,list ['dʒɜ:-], 'jü,rist².

'lēga,list, 'lin,guist² [-,gwıst], 'lobby,ist, 'lōca,list, 'lüte,nist².

ma'chĭ,nist [-'ʃi:-], 'măni,cū,rist, 'măso,chist² [-kıst], ma'tēria,list, 'mĕcha-,nist² [-kə-], 'mĕdal,list, 'mētëo'rŏlo,gist², 'Mĕtho,dist, 'mĭlita,rist, 'mĭnima,list, 'mŏder,nist, 'mō,nist², 'mŏnothë,istᶜ, 'mŏra,list, 'mōto,rist.

'nătiona,list, 'nătura,list ['nætrə-], 'nātū,rist, 'nĕpo,tist², 'nīhi,list², 'nŏmina-,list, 'noncon'for,mist, 'nŏve,list, 'nū,dist.

'obscū'ran,tistᶜ, 'ŏcū,list², 'oppor'tū,nistᶜ, 'opti,mist², 'orga,nist.

'păci,fist², 'pal,mist ['pɑ:-], 'panthë,ist², 'pā,pist², 'păro,dist, pa'thŏlo,gist², per'fectio,nist, 'pessi,mist², phi'lanthro,pist², phi'lŏlo,gist², 'phўsi,cist, 'phўsi'ŏlogist², 'pїa,nist², 'pїĕ,tist², 'plāgia,rist², 'Plāto,nist², 'plüra,list, po'lўga,mist², po'lўpho,nist², 'pŏlythĕ,istᶜ, 'pŏpū,list², 'pŏsiti,vist, 'pragma,tist², 'prŏbabi,list, 'prŏpa'gan,dist, pro'tăgo,nist², 'psal,mist ['sɑ:,mıst], psë'phŏlo,gist² [sı-], ,psў'chїa,trist² [,saı'kaı-], ,psў'chŏlo,gist² [,saı'kɒ-], 'pŭbli,cist, 'pūgi,list², 'pū,rist.

'quїĕ,tist.

'răcia,list, 'rătiona,list, 'rēa,list, rë'cĭdi,vist², rë'līgio,nist, rë'ser,vist, rë'vīsio,nist, rë'vīva,list, 'rїgo,rist, 'rītūa,list, 'Rōma,nist, 'roya,list.

'să,crist², 'sā,dist², 'Sāta,nist, 'săti,rist, 'scїen,tist², 'sĕcūla,rist, 'sĕmina,rist, ,sen'sātiona,list, 'sensūa,list, 'sĕpara,tist, 'sĕ,xist, 'Shintō,ist, 'sōcia,list, ,som'nambū,list², 'sŏ,phist², 'spĕcia,list, 'spїritūa,list, 'stoc,kist, 'strătë,gist, 'stў,list, 'suffra,gist, 'sū,fist, sur'rēa,list², 'symbo,list, 'sympho,nist, 'syn-crĕ,tist², 'sўstema,tistᶜ.

'Tāŏ,ist (or 'Tāŏ,ist), 'tăxi,der,mistᶜ (or 'tăxi'der,mistᶜ), të'lĕgra,phistᶜ, të'lĕpho,nistᶜ, 'tĕrro,rist, 'thē,ist², 'thēo,rist, 'thĕra,pist, 'Thŏ,mist² ['təʊ-], to'bacco,nist², 'toü,rist, tra'dītiona,list, 'Trap,pist², 'trība,list, 'tympa,nist, 'tў,pist.

'ūnio,nist, 'ūni'versa,list.

,ven'trїlo,quist², 'vїo'lĭ,nist, 'vōca,list.

ˈYorˌkist.

ˌzoˈŏloˌgist [ˌzuːˈɒləˌdʒɪst].

ite

ˈăcoˌnīte⁶, ˈammoˌnīte¹,³, ˈanchoˌrīte⁶ [-kə-], ˈanthraˌcīte³, ˈĂphroˈdītëᶜ, ˈappëˌtīte⁶, ˈapposite⁶, ˈarchiˈmanˌdrīteᶜ [ˈɑːkɪ-], ˈĂrëˈŏpaˌgīte².

ˈbākeˌlīte³ [ˈbeɪkəˌlaɪt], ˈbauˌxīte³, ˈbĕnëˈdīcitëᶜ, ˈBethlëˌhĕˌmīte, ˌbīˈparˌtīteᶜ.

ˈcalˌcīte³, ˈCānaaˌnīte [ˈkeɪnəˌnaɪt], ˈCarmeˌlīte, ˈchlōˌrīte³ [ˈklɔː-], ˈcoaˌlīte³, ˈcomposite⁶, ˈconˌtrīte⁶ (or conˈtrīteᶜ), ˈcorˌdīte³, ˌcosˈmŏpoˌlīte⁶.

ˈdĕfinite⁶, ˈdīsˌūˈnīte⁵ (prefix is not part of the SP), ˈDŏloˌmīte³,⁶, ˈdўnaˌmīte³.

ˈĕboˌnīte³, ëˈlīteᶜ, ˈĕrëˌmīte⁶, ˈĕruˌdīte⁶, ˈexpëˌdīte⁴, ëxˈquĭsiteᶜ (or ˈexquisite⁶), ˈextraˌdīte⁴.

ˈfāvourite⁶, ˈfĭˌnīte⁶, ˈflüoˌrīte³.

ˈgĕligˌnīte³, ˈgrănite⁶, ˈgrăˌphīte³.

ˈHăˌmīte, ˈhēmaˌtīte³, ˌherˈmăphroˌdīte⁶, ˈhĕteroˌclīteᶜ, ˈHusˌsīte, ˈhўpocrite⁶.

igˈnīte⁵, ˈimpoˈlīteᶜ, inˈdĕfinite⁶, inˈdīte⁵, ˈinfinite⁶, inˈvīte⁵, ˈIshmaeˌlīte, ˈIsraeˌlīte.

ˈJăcoˌbīte, ˈJĕbūˌsīte.

ˈLēˌvīte, ˈligˌnīte³, ˈLudˌdīte.

ˈmălaˌchīte³ [-ˌkaɪt], ˈmarcaˌsīte³, ˈmargueˈrīteᶜ [ˈmɑːɡəˈriːt], ˈMăroˌnīte², ˈMennoˌnīte², ˈmētëoˌrīteᶜ, ˈMīnoˌrīte², ˈMōaˌbīte, moˈnŏphyˌsīte⁶, ˈmultiˈparˌtīte³, ˈMŭscoˌvīte².

ˈNăzaˌrīte², ˈnĭˌtrīte³.

ˈŏoˌlīte³ [ˈəʊəˌlaɪt], ˈopposite⁶.

ˈpăraˌsīte⁶, ˈperquisite⁶, pëˈtīteᶜ, ˈphosˌphīte³, ˈplĕbiˌscīte⁶ (or -scite), poˈlīteᶜ, ˌprē-ˈRăphaeˌlīte, ˌprēˈrĕquisite⁶, ˈprĕterite⁶, ˈpўˌrīte³.

ˈquartˌzīte³ [ˈkwɔːtˌsaɪt].

ˈRĕchaˌbīte [ˈrekə-], rëˈconˌdīteᶜ (or ˈrĕconˌdīteᶜ), ˈrĕquisite⁶, rëˈquĭte⁵, ˈrĕsˌpīte⁶ (or ˈrĕspite⁶), ˈrēˌūˈnīte⁵ (prefix is not part of the SP).

ˈsătelˌlīte⁶, ˈSēˌmīte², ˈShĭˌīte, ˈsŏdoˌmīte, ˈstălacˌtīte⁶, ˈstălagˌmīte⁶, ˈsulˌphīte³, ˈsўbaˌrīte⁶.

ˈterˌmīte⁶, thëˈŏdoˌlīte⁶, ˌtŏˈxŏphiˌlīte⁶, ˌtrīˈparˌtīteᶜ.

ˌūˈnīte⁵.

vëˈnītëᶜ.

Notes:

(i) The following are of the form prefix+stem: dëˈspīte, ëxˈcīte, inˈcīte, rëˈcīte.

(ii) The following are compounds: ˈbackˌbīte, ˈhўpoˈchlōˌrīte [-ˈklɔː-], ˈhўpoˈphosˌphīte, ˈhўpoˈsulˌphīte.

-ize/-ise

ac'clīma,tīze, 'actūa,līze, 'adver,tīze², 'ăgonīze, ag'gran,dīze^c (or 'aggran-
,dīze²), 'allēgo,rīze, 'alphabë,tīze, a'mĕrica,nīze, a'mor,tīze^c, a'naēsthë,tīze²,
a'nălo,gīze, a'năthëma,tīze, a'năto,mīze, 'angli,cīze², 'ănima,līze, ,an'tăgo-
,nīze², 'anthropo'mor,phīze^c, a'pŏlo,gīze, a'pŏsta,tīze², a'pŏstro,phīze²,
'appë,tīze², 'arbo,rīze², 'ar,chā,īze² [-,keı-], 'ăto,mīze, 'atti'tūdi,nīze²,
'autho,rīze².

,bap'tīze^c, 'băstar,dīze, 'bĕstia,līze, 'bŏta,nīze, 'bowdler,īze², 'brüta,līze,
'burglar,īze (Amer.).

'căna,līze^c, 'căno,nīze, 'căpita,līze, 'carbo,nīze, 'carbū,rīze², 'cătë,chīze²
[-,kaız], 'cătëgo,rīze, 'cauter,īze², 'centra,līze, 'chăracter,īze ['kæ-], 'chrĭs-
tia,nīze ['krıs-], 'cĭca,trīze², 'circūla,rīze, 'cĭvi,līze, 'cog,nīze, 'cŏlo,nīze,
'cosmo'pŏlita,nīze, 'crĭti,cīze, 'crўstal,līze.

,dē'carbo,nīze, ,dē'centra,līze, ,dē'hūma,nīze, ,dē'magne,tīze, 'dēma'tēria-
,līze, ,dē'mĭlita,rīze, dë'mōbi,līze (or ,dē-), dë'mŏcra,tīze^c, ,dē'mora,līze,
,dē'nătiona,līze, dë'ōdo,rīze, dë'ŏxi,dīze, ,dē'persona,līze, ,dē'pōla,rīze,
'dĕpū,tīze, ,dē'sensi,tīze, ,dē'vīta,līze, 'diph,thong,īze, dis'orga,nīze²,
'dogma,tīze², 'drăma,tīze².

ë'cŏno,mīze, 'ĕlĕ,gīze, ë'mōtiona,līze, 'empha,sīze², 'ĕner,gīze, ë'pĭto,mīze,
'ēqua,līze, 'ĕty'mŏlo,gīze, 'eulo,gīze, 'euphë,mīze², ë'vange,līze,
'ĕ,xor,cīze, ëx'tempo,rīze², ,ex'terna,līze (or ëx-).

'facto,rīze, fa'mĭlia,rīze, 'fĕdera,līze, 'ferti,līze, 'feuda,līze, 'forma,līze,
'fossi,līze, 'fractio,nīze, 'frăter,nīze.

'galli,cīze, 'galva,nīze², 'gĕnera,līze, 'germa,nīze, 'gorman,dīze², 'graē,cīze²,
gram'măti,cīze.

'harmo,nīze, 'heathen,īze, 'hē,brā,īze, 'hellen,īze, 'hĭspa,nīze², 'hūma,nīze,
'hўbri,dīze, 'hypno,tīze², ,hў'pŏthë,sīze², ,hў'pŏsta,sīze², ,hў'pŏsta,tīze².

'īco,nīze, ,ı̄'dēa,līze, 'īdo,līze, im'mōbi,līze, im'morta,līze, 'immū,nīze^c,
'indi'vīdūa,līze, 'intel'lectūa,līze, 'īo,dīze², 'īo,nīze, i'tălia,nīze, i'tăli,cīze,
'īte,mīze.

'jargo,nīze, 'jeopar,dīze, 'jü,dā,īze².

'lābia,līze, 'lāi,cīze², 'lăti,nīze, 'lēga,līze, lë'gĭti,mīze, 'lībera,līze, 'lōca,līze.

ma'căda,mīze, 'magne,tīze, 'marty,rīze, ma'tēria,līze, 'măxi,mīze²,
'mĕcha,nīze² ['mekə-], 'mĕdi'ēva,līze, 'mĕmo,rīze, 'mercer,īze²,
'mĕsmer,īze², më'tăbo,līze², 'mĭlita,rīze, 'mĭni,mīze², 'mōbi,līze, 'mŏder,nīze,
mo'nŏpo,līze, 'mŏra,līze, 'mōto,rīze.

'narco,tīze, 'năsa,līze, 'nătiona,līze, 'nătura,līze ['nætrə-], 'neutra,līze,
'norma,līze.

'ōdo,rīze, 'orga,nīze², 'ōri'enta,līze, 'ŏstra,cīze², 'ŏxi,dīze, 'ŏxyge,nīze.

'păga,nīze, 'pălata,līze, 'părasi,tīze, pa'renthë,sīze², par'tĭcūla,rīze,
'pästeu,rīze^c, 'pătro,nīze², 'pauper,īze, 'pēna,līze, 'persona,līze, pha'rynga-

‚līze [-ˈrɪŋgə-] or phaˈryngea‚līze [-ˈrɪndʒə-], phiˈlŏso‚phīze, ˈplāgia‚rīze², ˈplătiˈtūdi‚nīze², ˈplüra‚līze, ˈpōla‚rīze, poˈlīti‚cīze², ˈpŏpūla‚rīze, ˈpragma‚tīze², ˈprŏpaˈgan‚dīze, ˈprŏsely‚tīze, ˈprŏtestan‚tīze, ‚psȳˈchŏlo‚gīze [‚saɪˈkɒ-], ˈpulve‚rīze², ˈpūrita‚nīze.

ˈquan‚tīze [ˈkwɒn-].

ˈrătiona‚līze, ˈrĕcog‚nīze², ˈrĕgūla‚rīze, rëˈorga‚nīze², rëˈpŭblica‚nīze, ‚rēˈvīta‚līze, ˈrĕvoˈlütio‚nīze, ˈrhapso‚dīze, ˈrhōta‚cīze², ˈrōma‚nīze, ˈrüra‚līze.

ˈsăti‚rīze, ˈscanda‚līze, ˈschēma‚tīze², ˈscotti‚cīze², ˈscrüti‚nīze, ˈsectio‚nīze, ˈsĕcūla‚rīze, ‚senˈsātiona‚līze, ˈsentiˈmenta‚līze, ˈsermo‚nīze, ˈsigna‚līze, ˈsōcia‚līze, ˈsŏlem‚nīze, soˈlīlo‚quīze, ˈspĕcia‚līze, ˈspīritūa‚līze, ˈstăbi‚līze², ˈstandar‚dīze, ˈstĕri‚līze, ˈstigma‚tīze², ˈstȳ‚līze, ˈsubsi‚dīze, ˈsumma‚rīze, ˈsyllo‚gīze, ˈsymbo‚līze, ˈsympa‚thīze, ˈsynchro‚nīze², ˈsyncrë‚tīze², ˈsynthë‚sīze², ˈsȳstema‚tīzeᶜ.

ˈtanta‚līze², ˈtempo‚rīze², ˈtĕrro‚rīze, thëˈŏlo‚gīze, ˈthēo‚rīze, ˈtōta‚līze, ˈtranquil‚līze, ˈtȳrann‚īze.

ˈūnio‚nīze, ˈūniˈversa‚līze, ˈurba‚nīze, ˈūti‚līze².

ˈvāpo‚rīze, ˈvēla‚rīze, ˈverba‚līze, ˈvicti‚mīze, ˈvīsūa‚līze, ˈvīta‚līze, ˈvōcaˈlīze, ˈvulca‚nīze², ˈvulga‚rīze.

ˈwester‚nīze, ˈwoma‚nīze [ˈwʊ-].

-ment

aˈbandonment, aˈbāsement, aˈbātement, aˈbridgement, aˈbutment, acˈcompaniment, acˈcomplishment, ‚acˈcoüche‚mentᶜ [‚æˈkuːʃ‚mɒŋ], acˈcoütrement⁴, aˈchiĕvement, acˈknowledgement [-ˈnɒlɪdʒ-], adˈjustment, adˈmŏnishment, aˈdornment, adˈvăncement, adˈvertisementᶜ, agˈgrandize-mentᶜ [-dɪz-], aˈgreement, aˈlīgnment [əˈlaɪn-], ˈăliment⁴, alˈlotment, alˈlürement, aˈmāzement, aˈmendment, aˈmüsement, anˈnouncement, anˈnulment, aˈpartment, apˈpeasement, apˈpointment, apˈportionment, ˈargūment, ˈarmament⁴, arˈraignment [-ˈreɪn-], arˈrāngement, ˈascerˈtain-ment, asˈsessment, asˈsignment [-ˈsaɪn-], asˈsortment, asˈtŏnishment, aˈtōnement, atˈtachment, atˈtainment, ‚augˈment² (verb), ˈaug‚mentᶜ (noun).

ˈbănishment, ˈbattlement, ˈbetterment, bëˈwilderment, ˈblandishment, ‚bomˈbardment.

‚canˈtonmentᶜ [-ˈtuːn-], cëˈmentᶜ, ˈchăstisementᶜ, comˈmändment, comˈmencement, ˈcom‚mentᶜ, comˈmitment, comˈpartmentᶜ, ˈcomplë‚ment³ (verb), ˈcomplëment⁴ (noun), ˈcompli‚ment³ (verb), ˈcompliment⁴ (noun), conˈcealment, ˈcondiment⁴, conˈfīnement, conˈsignment [-ˈsaɪn-], conˈtentment.

ˈdĕcrëment⁴, dëˈfīlement, ‚déˈnoue‚mentᶜ [‚deɪˈnuː‚mɒŋ] or ˈdé‚noue‚mentᶜ [ˈdeɪ‚nuː‚mɒŋ], dëˈpartmentᶜ, dëˈportmentᶜ, dëˈrāngement, dëˈtachment, ˈdĕtriment⁴, dëˈvĕlopment, ˈdĕvilment, disˈāblement, ˈdisaˈgreement, ˈdis-apˈpointment, disˈarmament⁴, ˈdisarˈrāngement, disˈcernment, ˈdisconˈtent-ment, disˈcöuragement, ˈdisënˈchăntment, ˈdisënˈdowment, ˈdisënˈgāgement, 'disës'tăblishment, dis'fĭgurement, dis'franchisement^c, 'disin'terment, dis'memberment, dis'păragement, dis'plăcement, 'dŏcū‚ment³ (verb), 'dŏcūment⁴ (noun).

'ĕlĕment⁴, ë'lōpement, ëm'bankment^c, ëm'bărrassment, ëm'bellishment, ëm'bezzlement, ëm'bitterment, ëm'blāzonment, ëm'bŏdiment, ë'mŏlūment⁴, ëm'ployment, ë'nactment, ën'campment, ën'chäntment, ën'cöuragement, ën'dearment, ën'dorsement, ën'dowment, ën'forcement, ën'franchisement^c, ën'gāgement, ën'jambment^c, ën'joyment, ën'largement, ën'lightenment [-'laɪtn-], ën'listment, ën'nŏblement, ën'richment, ën'rōlment, ën'tanglement, 'enter'tainment, ën'tīcement, ën'vĕlopment, ën'vīronment, ë'quipment, ë'scāpement, ë'scarpment^c, ë'stăblishment, ë'strāngement, ëx'cîtement, 'excrĕment⁴, ëx'pĕri‚ment³ (verb), ëx'pĕriment⁴ (noun).

fer'ment² (verb), 'fer‚ment^c (noun), 'fĭlament⁴, 'firmament⁴, ‚ful'filment [‚fʊl-], 'fundament⁴.

'garnishment, 'gövernment.

ha'bīliment⁴, 'hărassment (Brit.) or ha'rassment (Amer.), 'hĕrë'dītament⁴.

im'peachment, im'pĕdiment⁴, 'implë‚ment³ (verb), 'implĕment⁴ (noun), im'pŏverishment, im'prĭsonment, im'provement [-'pruːv-], in'cītement, 'incrë‚ment³ (verb), 'incrĕment⁴ (noun), in'dictment [-'daɪt-], in'dūcement, in'stalment [-'stɔːl-], 'instrument⁴, in'tĕgūment⁴, in'terment, in'ternment, in'vestment, in'volvement.

la'ment^c, 'lĭgament⁴, 'lĭnëament^c, 'lĭniment⁴.

'mălad'justment, 'mănagement, 'mĕasūrement, 'mĕdicament^c (or më'dĭcament⁴), 'merriment, ‚mis'gövernment, mis'judgement, mis'mănagement, 'mŏnūment⁴, 'mūniment⁴.

'nöurishment, 'nūtriment⁴.

'ornament⁴.

'parliament⁴ ['pɑːləmənt], 'pĕdiment⁴, 'prēar'rāngement, prë'dĭcament⁴, prë'ferment, ‚prē'payment, prë'sentiment⁴, pro'nouncement, 'pŭnishment, 'puzzlement.

‚rap'proche‚ment^c [‚ræ'prɒʃ‚mɒŋ], 'răvishment, 'rēap'pointment, 'rēar'rāngement, 'rēas'sessment, 'rēas'signment [-'saɪn-], 'rēcom'mitment, 'rēë'nactment, 'rē-ën'listment, rë'fīnement, rë'freshment, 'rĕgi‚ment³ (verb), 'rĕgiment⁴ (noun), 'rēim'bursement, 'rēin'forcement ['riːɪn-], 'rēin'stātement ['riːɪn-], ‚rē'payment, rë'plācement, rë'quīrement, rë'sentment, ‚rē'settlement, rë'tīrement, rë'trenchment, rë'vetment, 'rūdiment⁴.

'săcrament⁴, 'sĕdiment⁴, ‚seg'ment² (verb), 'segment⁴ (noun), 'sentiment⁴, 'settlement, 'supplë‚ment³ (verb), 'supplĕment⁴ (noun).

'temperament^c, 'tĕnĕment⁴, 'tĕstament⁴, ‚tor'ment² (verb), 'tor‚ment^c (noun), 'tournament⁴ ['tɜː-].

'under'stātement, 'unĕm'ployment, ‚un'settlement.

'wönderment, 'wörriment.

Note:
The adjective 'vēhement ['vɪəmənt] consists of stem+suffix **-ent**.

-or, -our
(Words with parenthesised **u** are spelt with **u** in British English and without it in American English.)

ac'cĕle,rātor, ac'cūmū,lātor, 'actor, ad'mĭni,strātor, ag'gressor², 'ăgi,tātor, 'alli,gātorᶜ, ,am'bassador², 'an,cestorᶜ, 'anchor² ['æŋkə], ,an'tērior⁴, 'appli,cātorᶜ, 'arbi,trātor, 'ardo(u)r³, 'armo(u)r³, ,ar'tĭcū,lātor, as'sessor, 'auditor, 'author².

'băchelor², bë'hāvio(u)r³, 'bĕnĕ,factorᶜ, ,bī'sector.

'calcū,lātor, 'cando(u)r³, 'can,torᶜ, 'captor², 'cästor², 'censor², 'chäncellorᶜ, 'clămo(u)r³, 'clango(u)r³, ,cō'adjutor², col'lector, 'cŏlo(u)r³, com'mūni,cātor, com'pĕtitor², com'pŏsitor², com'pressor, 'con,dorᶜ, con'ductor, con'fessor, con'nector, 'conqueror [-kə-], ,con'quĭsta,dorᶜ, con'spĭrator², con'strictor, con'tractor, cor'rector, cor'rĕgi,dorᶜ, 'cŏrri,dorᶜ, 'councillor, 'counsellor, crĕ'ātor, 'crĕditor, 'culti,vātor, ,cū'rātor², 'cursor².

'debtor['detə], 'dĕco,rātor, dë'fector, dë'flector, dë'meano(u)r³, 'dĕmon,strātor, dë'nŏmi,nātor, dë'pŏsitor, dë'structor², dë'tector, 'dĕto,nātor, dë'tractor, ,dic'tātor (Brit.) or 'dic,tātor (Amer.), di'rector (or ,dī'rector), dis'cŏlo(u)r (*dis-* is not part of the SP), dis'fāvo(u)r, dis'hŏno(u)r [dɪs'ɒnə], di'vīsor², 'doctor², 'dŏlo(u)r³, 'dōnor², 'dŭpli,cātor.

'ĕditor, 'ĕdū,cātor, ë'jector, ë'lector, 'ĕlĕ,vātor, 'emperor², ën'dĕavo(u)r³, ë'quātor², ë'rector, 'ĕrror³.

'factor², 'fāvo(u)r³, 'fervo(u)r³, 'flāvo(u)r³.

'gĕner,ātor, 'glădi,ātor, 'glămo(u)r³, 'gŏvernor, 'guăran,torᶜ.

'harbo(u)r³, 'hŏno(u)r³ ['ɒnə], 'hŏrror³, 'hūmo(u)r³.

'illus,trātor, 'ĭmi,tātor, im'postor², in'cīsor², 'incū,bātor, 'indi,cātor, in'fērior⁴, in'hĕritor, i'nīti,ātor, in'jector, 'inno,vātor, in'quĭsitor², in'spector, in'structor, 'inter'cessor², in'tērior⁴, 'inter'lŏcūtor², in'tĕrro,gātor, in'ventor, in'vestor.

'jănitor², 'jūnior⁴, 'jūror².

'lābo(u)r³, 'Lăbra,dorᶜ, 'languor³, 'lector², 'lessor² (or 'les,sorᶜ), 'lictor², 'lĭquor³.

'mājor⁴, 'mălĕ,factorᶜ, 'mănor³, 'măta,dorᶜ, 'mēdi,ātor, 'mentor², 'mĕta,phorᶜ (or 'mĕtaphor³), 'mētëor², 'mīnor⁴, 'mĭrror², 'misdë'meano(u)r³, 'mŏnitor², ,mon'sĭ,gnorᶜ [-,njɔ:], 'mōtor².

nar'rātor, 'neighbo(u)r² ['neɪbə], 'nūmer,ātor.

ob'jector, ob'structor, 'ōdo(u)r³, op'pressor, 'ŏratorᶜ, 'ōvi'pŏsitor².

'pallor³, 'parlo(u)r³, 'pästor², pe'rambū,lātor, 'phosphor³, 'pĭca,dorᶜ, pos'sessor, ,pŏs'tērior⁴, prë'centor², prë'ceptor², prë'cursor², 'prĕdator², 'prēdë,cessor^c, prë'pŏsitor^2, 'prĕsti'dĭgi,tātor, prë'vări,cātor, 'prīor^{2,4}, 'proctor^2, pro'fessor, pro'gĕnitor^2, pro'jector, 'prŏmul,gātor, pro'prīetor^2, pro'spector^2 (or 'pros,pector), pro'tector, pro'tractor, ,pul'sātor, pur'veyor.

'rādi,ātor, 'ranco(u)r^3, 'rāzor^2, rë'actor, 'rēal,tor^c, 'rector^2, rë'flector, rë'frīger,ātor, 'rĕspi,rātor, rë'tractor, 'rĭgo(u)r^3, ,rō'tātor, 'rōtor^2, 'rümo(u)r^3.

'sailor, 'sāvio(u)r^2, 'sāvo(u)r^3, 'scissor^2, ,scrü'tātor^c, 'sculptor^2, 'sector^2, 'sĕnator, 'sēnior^4, 'sensor, 'servitor^2, sï'gnor^c (or 'sï,gnor^c) [-njɔ:], so'lĭcitor^2, ,spec'tātor^2, 'splendo(u)r^3, 'sponsor^2, 'squalor^3 ['skwɒlə], 'stüpor^3, suc'cessor^2, 'succo(u)r^3, 'suitor ['su:tə] or ['sju:tə], ,sü'pērior^4, sur'veyor, sur'vīvor.

'tailor^2, 'tĕnor^{2,3}, 'tensor^2, 'tĕrror^3, ,tes'tātor^2, 'tŏrĕa,dor^c, ,tor'mentor, 'torpor^3, 'tōta,lĭ,zātor^c, 'tractor^2, 'traitor^2, ,trans'gressor, ,trans'lātor, 'trĕmor^3, 'trĭcolo(u)r^3, 'troüba,dour^c [-,dɔ:], 'Tūdor^c, 'tümo(u)r^3, 'tūtor^2.

,ul'tērior^4.

'vălo(u)r^3, 'vāpo(u)r^3, 'vector^2, 'vendor, ,vī'brātor (or 'vī,brātor (Amer.)), 'victor^2, 'vĭgo(u)r^3, 'vīo,lātor, 'vĭsitor, 'vīsor^2.

'warrior^2 ['wɒrɪə].

Notes:
(i) The following are best treated as simple roots: ,ä'moür, 'camphor, 'dĕ,cor (or ['deɪ-]), 'hector.
(ii) The following are best treated as being of the form prefix+root: 'dĕ,toür, ën'ämour, 'păra,moür.

-ory (excluding words in **-atory**)
(Words with parenthesised secondary stress marks have pronunciations ending in [-ərɪ] or [-rɪ] in British English, but [-ɔ:ri] in American English.)

ac'cessory^2, ad'mŏni,tory^2, ad'vīsory, 'audi,tory^2.

'cătĕ,gory^2, com'pulsory^2, con'sistory, 'contra'dictory, con'trĭbū,tory^c, 'cursory^2.

dë'pŏsi,tory, dë'rīsory, 'dĕsul,tory^c, di'rectory (or ,dī-), 'dormi,tory^2.

ëx'crētory, ëx'pŏsi,tory^2.

'factory^2, 'fūmi,tory^2.

'hĭstory^2.

il'lüsory^2, in'hĭbi,tory, 'inter'cessory^2, 'inter'lŏcū,tory^2, 'intro'ductory^2, 'inven,tory^c.

'mĕmory^2.

'offer,tory^c, ,ol'factory^2.

pe'remptory^2, per'functory^2, 'pillory^2, prë'cursory^2, prë'mŏni,tory^2, 'prīory, 'prŏmis,sory, 'prŏmon,tory^c, pro'vīsory (from root pro'vīsō).

'rectory, rë'fectory², rë'fractory, 'rĕper,tory°, rë'pŏsi,tory², rë'sponsory.

'sătis'factory², 'sensory, 'stătū,tory, 'süper,vīsory, sup'plētory², sup'pŏsi,tory², su'spensory.

'tĕrri,tory², 'thēory², tra'jectory², 'transi,tory².

'un,sătis'factory².

'vălë'dictory², 'victory, 'vŏmi,tory.

Note:
The following are best regarded as simple roots: 'chĭcory, 'hickory, 'īvory.

-ose

'ädi,pōse, 'anchy,lōse [-kɪ-].

'belli,cōse.

'cellū,lōse³, 'cōma,tōse.

'dex,trōse³, 'dīag,nōse°.

'fron,dōse, 'fruc,tōse.

'glü,cōse³, 'grandi'ōse° (or 'grandi,ōse).

jo'cōse².

'lăchry,mōse [-krɪ-], 'lac,tōse³.

'mal,tōse³ ['mɔ:l-], 'mĕta'mor,phōse°, mo'rōse².

'ōti,ōse.

'pec,tōse³, 'plü,mōse.

'sücrōse³.

'tūbe,rōse ['tju:bə,rəuz].

'vări,cōse, ver'bōse² (or ,ver-), 'vĭs,cōse³.

Notes:
(i) The following are of the form prefix+root: com'pōse, 'counter'pōse, dë'pōse, di'sclōse, di'spōse, ën'clōse, ëx'pōse, ,fore'clōse, im'pōse, 'inter'pōse, op'pōse, ,pōst'pōse, 'prēdi'spōse, ,prē'pōse, 'prēsup'pōse, pro'pōse, rë'pōse, 'süperim'pōse, 'süper'pōse, sup'pōse, ,trans'pōse.
(ii) The following are compounds: 'dog,rōse, 'över,dōse, 'prim,rōse.
(iii) The following is best treated as a simple root: 'purpose ['pɜ:pəs].

-ous

(Excluding words in which **-ous** is added directly to a monosyllabic root, where the stress has to be on the root syllable; some words listed below may end up being pronounced in two syllables by reason of coalescences, e.g. **captious** ['kæpʃəs].)

ab'stēmious[2], a'cĭdūlous[2], 'ācri'mōnious[2], a'dulterous[2], 'ad,vän'tāgeous[2], 'ad,ven'tītious[2], ad'ventūrous, ,al'būminous[2], 'ambi'dextrous[2], ,am'bĭgūous[2], ,am'bītious[2], 'āmorous[2], a'morphous[2] (or ,ā-), ,am'phībious[2], a'nălogous (root is a'nalogy), ,an'drŏgynous[2], a'nŏmalous, a'nŏnymous[2], ,an'tŏnymous[c], 'anxious[2], 'äqueous[2] (or 'ā-), 'ardūous[2], as'sīdūous[2], 'ătra'bīlious[2], a'trōcious[2], ,au'dācious[2], ,au'spīcious[2], ,au'tŏnomous, 'äva'rīcious[2].

'barbarous[2], 'beautëous ['bju:tɪəs], 'bībūlous[2], 'bīgamous, 'bīlious[2], bi'tūminous[2], 'blasphëmous[c], 'boisterous[2], 'bumptious[2].

ca'cŏphonous, ca'dăverous, ca'lămitous, ,cal'cārëous[2], ca'lumnious[2], 'cancerous, ,can'tankerous[2], ca'pācious[2], ca'prĭcious[2], 'captious[2], 'carbo'nīferous[2], 'cārious[2], ,car'nīvorous[c], 'carti'lăginous[2], 'cautious[2], 'căvernous, ,cen'sōrious[2], 'cërë'mōnious[2], 'chĭvalrous[c] ['ʃɪ-], cir'cūitous[c], 'clămorous, 'clangorous, com'mōdious[2], com'pendious[2], 'congrūous[2], co'nīferous[2], 'con,san'guīnëous[2] [-'gwɪn-], 'consci'entious[2] ['kɒnʃɪ'enʃəs], 'conscious[2], con'spīcūous[2], con'tāgious[2], con'tempo'rānëous[2], con'temptūous[2], con'tentious[2], con'tĭgūous[2], con'tīnūous, 'contū'mācious[2], 'cōpious[2], ,cō'terminous[2], cou'rāgeous[2], 'côurtëous[2], 'cövetous, 'crăpūlous[2], 'crĕdūlous[2], crë'tāceous[2], 'crĕtinous, 'cūrious[2], ,cū'tānëous[2].

'dāngerous, dë'cĭdūous[2], 'dĕcorous[2], 'dĕlë'tērious[2], dë'līcious[2], dë'līrious[2], dë'sīrous, 'dēvious[2], 'dexterous[2], ,dī'äphanous[2], ,dī'chŏtomous [-'kɒ-], 'disad,vän'tāgeous[2], di'sästrous, 'discon'tĭnūous, di'scôurtëous[2], 'dīsin'gēnūous[2], 'dispū'tātious[2], 'dŏlorous, 'dūbious[2], 'dūtëous[2].

'effi'cācious[2], ë'grēgious[2], ë'normous[2], 'envious[2], ë'pŏnymous[2], ër'rōnëous[2], ,eu'phōnious[2], ë'xĭgūous[2], 'expë'dītious[2], ëx'tempo'rānëous[2], ëx'trānëous[2].

'făbūlous[2], fa'cētious[2], 'factious[2], ,fac'tītious[2], fal'lācious[2], 'fāri'nāceous[2], ,fas'tĭdious[2], 'fătūous[2], fë'līcitous, fë'lōnious[2], fe'rōcious[2], fis'sīparous[2], ,flir'tātious[2], ,for'tūitous[2], 'fractious[2], 'frĭvolous[2], 'fūrious[2].

'gărrulous[2], 'gāsëous[2] (or 'găs-), gë'lătinous[c], 'gĕnerous[2], 'glămorous, 'glōrious[2], 'glŭtinous[2], 'gluttonous, 'gorgeous[2], 'grācious[2], gra'mĭnëous[2], gra'tūitous, grë'gārious[2].

,har'mōnious[2], 'hăzardous, ,her'bāceous[2], ,her'bĭvorous[c], 'hĕtero'gēnëous[2], 'hīdëous[2], hi'lārious, 'hŏmo'gēnëous[2], hor'rendous[2], 'hūmorous.

'ignëous[2], 'igno'mĭnious[2], il'lŭstrious[2], 'impë'cūnious[2], im'pērious[2], im'pervious[2], im'pĕtūous[2], 'impious[2], 'in,au'spīcious[2], in'cĕstūous[2], in'congrūous[2], 'incon'spīcūous[2], in'crĕdūlous[2], in'dĕcorous[2], in'dĭgenous[2], in'dŭstrious[2], 'in,effi'cācious[2], 'infamous[2] (negative in- is here, exceptionally, part of the SP), in'fectious[2], 'infë'līcitous, in'gēnious[2], in'gēnūous[2], in'glōrious[2], i'nĭquitous, 'in,jü'dĭcious[2], in'jūrious[2], in'nŏcūous[2], 'in,sec'tīvorous[c], in'sīdious[2], 'instan'tānëous[2], in'vīdious[2].

,jü'dĭcious[2].

la'bōrious[2], 'languorous [-gərəs], la'scīvious[2], 'lĕcherous, lë'gūminous[2], 'lībellous, li'bīdinous[2], 'lĭ'centious[2], 'lignëous[2], li'tĭgious[2], 'lon'gēvous[2], lo'quācious[2], ,lü'brĭcious[2], 'lūdicrous[2], ,lü'gūbrious[2], 'lūminous[2], 'lŭscious[2], ,lü'xūrious[2] [,lʌk'ʃuəriəs] or [-g'ʒʊ-].

‚mag‛nănimous², ma‛līcious², ‚māl‛ōdorous, ‛marvellous, mël‛līfluous², më‛lōdious², ‚men‛dācious², ‛mercūrous, ‛mërë‛trīcious², ‛mëri‛tōrious², më‛tīcūlous², mi‛răcūlous², ‛miscel‛lānëous², ‛mischievous [‛mɪstʃɪvəs], mo‛mentous‛ (or ‚mō-), mo‛nŏgamous², mo‛nŏtonous², ‛mountainous, ‛multi‛fārious², ‛multi‛tūdinous², ‛murderous, ‛mūtinous, my‛stērious².

‛nācrëous², ‛nauseous² [‛nɔːʃəs], ‛nĕbūlous, në‛cessitous, në‛fārious², no‛tōrious², ‛nŏxious² [‛nɒkʃəs], ‛nūmerous², ‚nū‛trītious².

o‛blīvious², ob‛nŏxious², ob‛sēquious², ob‛strĕperous², ‛obvious², ‛ōdious², ‛ōdo‛rīferous², ‛ōdorous, of‛fīcious², ‛ōlë‛ăginous², ‛ōminous², ‚om‛nīvorous‛, ‛ōnerous² (or ‛ōnerous²), op‛prōbrious², ‛ossëous², ‛ŏsten‛tātious² (or -‚ten-), ‚out‛rāgeous², ‚ō‛vīparous².

‛păchy‛dermatous² [‛pækɪ-], ‛parsi‛mōnious², ‛pendūlous², pë‛nūrious², per‛fīdious², ‛pĕrilous, per‛jūrious², per‛nīcious², ‛perspi‛cācious², per‛spīcūous², ‛perti‛nācious², ‛pes‛tīferous², ‛pītëous², ‛plăti‛tūdinous², ‛plentëous², ‛poisonous, ‛ponderous², ‛pŏpūlous², ‚por‛tentous‛, ‛pŏsthūmous² [‛pɒstjəməs], prë‛cārious², ‛prĕcious², prë‛cīpitous², prë‛cōcious², prë‛pŏsterous², ‚prĕs‛tīgious², prë‛sumptūous², prë‛tentious², ‛prēvious², pro‛dīgious², pro‛mīscūous², pro‛pītious², ‛prŏsperous, ‚pseu-‛dŏnymous‛ [‚sju:-], ‚pug‛nācious², ‚punc‛tīlious², ‛pūsil‛lănimous².

‛quĕrulous².

‚ram‛pāgeous², ‛rancorous, ra‛pācious², ‛raptūrous, ‛răvenous², rë‛bellious², rë‛līgious², ‛rĕsinous, ri‛dīcūlous‛, ‛righteous² [‛raɪtʃəs], ‛rīgorous, ‛rīotous, ‛rüinous, ‚rum‛bŭstious².

‛săcri‛legious² [-‛lɪdʒəs], sa‛gācious², sa‛lācious², sa‛lübrious², ‛sancti‛mōni-ous², ‚san‛guīnëous² [-‛gwɪn-], ‛scandalous, ‛scrŏfūlous², ‛scrumptious², ‛scrüpūlous², së‛bāceous², së‛dītious², ‛sĕdūlous², ‛sensūous², ‚sen‛tenti-ous², ‛sērious², ‛sīmul‛tānëous² (or ‛sī- (Amer.)), ‛sīnūous², ‛slănderous, so‛līcitous², ‛sŏnorous² (or so‛nōrous²), ‛spācious², ‛spĕcious², ‛spīritous, ‚spon‛tānëous², ‛spūrious², ‛stertorous², ‛strĕnūous², ‛stūdious², ‚stū‛pendous², ‚sub‛conscious², ‛sub‚cū‛tānëous², ‛sulphūrous, ‛sumptūous², ‛süper‛cīlious², ‚sü‛perflüous², ‛süper‛stītious², sup‛pŏsi‛tītious², ‛sŭrrep-‛tītious², su‛spīcious-, ‛synchronous² [-krə-], sy‛nŏnymous‛.

‛tēdious², ‛tĕmer‛ārious², ‚tem‛pestūous², të‛nācious², ‚ten‛dentious², ‛tĕnūous², ‛thunderous, ‛tīmorous², ‛tortūous², ‛tortūrous, ‛traitorous, ‛trēacherous, trë‛mendous², ‛trĕmūlous², ‚tū‛bercūlous², ‚tū‛multūous², ‛tyrannous.

‚ū‛bīquitous², ‛ulcerous, ‚um‛brāgeous², ‚ū‛nănimous², ‛un‚cĕrë‛mōnious², ‚un‛conscious², ‛unctūous², ‚un‛grācious², ‚un‛scrüpūlous², ‚up‛roarious², ‚ū‛xōrious².

‛văcūous², ‚vain‛glōrious², ‛vălorous, ‛vāporous, ‛vĕnomous, ve‛rācious², ‛verminous, ‚ver‛tīginous², vi‛cārious², ‛vīcious², ‛vic‛tōrious², ‛vīgorous, ‛villainous, ‛virtūous, vi‛vācious², vi‛vīparous², vo‛cīferous² (or ‚vō-), vo‛lūminous², vo‛luptūous², vo‛rācious².

-ure

ad'mixtūre, ad'ventūre², 'äpertūre', 'archi,tectūre [-kɪ-], 'āzūre².

'bordūre², 'brōchūre² ['brəʊʃə].

'captūre², 'censūre², 'clōsūre, ,coif'fūre' [,kwæ'fjʊə], com'pōsūre, con'jectūre², 'creatūre', 'cultūre².

dë'bentūre², 'dentūre², dë'partūre, di'sclōsūre, di'scömfitūre, di'splĕasūre.

'em,bou,chure ['ɒm,bu,ʃʊə] (or 'em,bou'chure), ëm'brāsūre², ën'clōsūre, ën'raptūre², ë'rāsūre, ëx'penditūre², ëx'pōsūre.

'failūre, 'featūre², 'fissūre², 'fixtūre, ,fōre'clōsūre, 'forfeitūre, 'fractūre², 'furnitūre², 'fūtūre².

'gĕstūre².

'hāchure² ['hæʃə].

im'pŏstūre², in'clōsūre, in'dentūre², in'vestitūre².

'junctūre².

'lectūre², 'leisūre² ['leʒə] (Brit.) or ['li:ʒə] (Amer.).

'mănū'factūre², 'mĕasūre², 'mīsad'ventūre², 'mixtūre, 'moistūre.

'nātūre², 'nurtūre².

'ordūre², 'ōvertūre'.

'pästūre², 'perad'ventūre², 'pictūre², 'plĕasūre, 'portraitūre, 'pŏstūre², 'prē,fectūre, 'pressūre, 'prīmo'gĕnitūre², pro'cēdūre, 'punctūre².

'raptūre², ,rē'captūre², 'ruptūre².

'scriptūre², 'sculptūre², 'sēizūre, 'stătūre², 'strictūre², 'structūre², 'sütūre².

'tempera'tūre', 'tĕnūre², 'textūre², 'tinctūre², 'tonsūre², 'tortūre², 'trĕasūre².

'ventūre², 'verdūre², 'vĕstūre², 'vultūre².

Notes:
  (i)   The following are best treated as simple roots: 'cönjure, dë'mūre,
        'fĭgure (Brit.) ['fɪgə] or 'fĭgūre (Amer.) ['fɪgjə], 'injure, ma'nūre,
        ma'tūre, 'perjure, së'cūre.
  (ii) The following are of the form prefix+stem: ab'jure, ad'jure, al'lūre,
        as'sure [ə'ʃɔ:], con'fĭgure, dis'fĭgure, ën'dūre, ën'sure [ɪn'ʃɔ:],
        im'mūre, 'im'pūre, 'insë'cūre, in'sure [ɪn'ʃɔ:], i'nūre, ob'scūre,
        ,prē'fĭgure, 'prĕmatūre (or 'prēma'tūre), pro'cūre, 'rëas'sure ['rɪə'ʃɔ:],
        ,trans'fĭgure, ,un'sure [,ʌn'ʃɔ:].
  (iii) The following are best regarded as compounds: 'ăcū,punctūre,
        'cȳno,sūre [-,sjʊə], 'ĕpi,cūre, 'măni,cūre, 'pĕdi,cūre, 'phōtogra,vūre,
        'sīnë,cūre, 'sub,structūre, 'süper,structūre; also all words ending in
        -,cultūre.

-ute

'abso͵lute (corresponding adverb may be pronounced 'abso'lütely[c]), a'cüte[2], a'stüte[2], at'tribüte[c] (verb), 'attri͵büte (noun).

'consti͵tüte, con'trï͵büte[c] (or 'contri͵büte), 'convo͵lüte.

'desti͵tüte, ͵dï'lüte[2] (verb), ͵dï'lüte[2] or 'dï͵lüte[c] (adj.), 'disso͵lute, dis'trï͵büte[c] (or 'dïstri͵büte).

ë'lectro͵cüte, 'ëxë͵cüte.

'hir͵süte[c].

'insti͵tüte, 'invo͵lüte, ir'rĕso͵lüte.

͵mï'nüte[2] (adj.), 'mïnute[c] (noun) ['mɪnɪt].

'păra͵chüte [-͵ʃuːt], 'persë͵cüte, pol'lüte[2], 'prŏsë͵cüte, 'prŏsti͵tüte.

͵rē'constitüte, 'rēdis'trï͵büte[c] (or ͵rē'dïstri͵büte), 'rĕso͵lüte.

sa'lüte[2], 'stătüte[c], 'substi͵tüte.

'trï͵büte[c].

-y
(Words of three or more syllables, excluding those where the suffix is clearly one of the following: **-acy**, **-ancy** (**-ant**+**-cy**), **-ary**, **-atory**, **-cy**, **-ency** (**-ent**+**-cy**), **-ery**, **-fy**, **-ify** (**-efy**), **-ity** (**-ety**), **-ly**, **-mony**, **-ory**, **-ry**, **-ty**.)

a'cădemy[3], 'ăgony[3], a'grŏnomy[4], 'alchemy[3], a'nălogy[4], 'ănarchy[3], a'nătomy[3], a'nŏmaly[3], ͵an'thŏlogy[4], 'anthro'pŏlogy[4], 'anthro'pŏphagy[4], an'tïpathy[4], ͵an'tŏnymy[4], 'ăpathy[4], a'pŏlogy[4], 'ăpo͵plĕxy[5], a'pŏstasy[3], 'ap͵pen'dectomy[4], 'archae'ŏlogy[4] [-kɪ-], 'archery[2], 'armo(u)ry[2], 'ăssyri'ŏlogy[4], a'strŏlogy[4], a'strŏnomy[4], ͵ā'symmetry[4], 'ătrophy[3], 'audi'ŏlogy[4], 'audi'ŏmetry[4], 'augüry[2], 'auto͵bï'ŏgraphy[4], ͵au'tŏnomy[4], 'au͵topsy[5].

'bac͵tēri'ŏlogy[4], 'bărony[2], 'băstardy[2], 'bïbli'ŏgraphy[4], 'bïgamy[4], 'billŏwy, 'bï'ŏgraphy[4], ͵bï'ŏlogy[4], 'bï͵opsy[5], 'blăsphëmy[c], 'bosomy ['buzəmɪ], 'bŏtany[3], 'Brittany[3], 'buggery[2], 'Burgundy[3], 'butchery[2] ['bu-], 'buttery[2].

ca'cŏphony[4], cal'lïgraphy[4], 'călumny[3], 'campa'nŏlogy[4], 'carpentry[2], ͵car'tŏgraphy[4], 'carto͵mancy[5], 'căta͵lepsy[5], 'centüry[3], ͵chres'tŏmathy[4] [͵kres-], ͵chris'tŏlogy[4] [͵krɪs-], chro'nŏlogy[4] [krə-], 'clĕrisy[3], 'colliery[2], 'cŏlony[3], 'contro͵versy[5c] (or con'trŏversy[3]), 'con͵tümely[c], ͵cos'mŏgony[4], ͵cos'mŏlogy[4], 'cŏurtesy[3], 'crïmi'nŏlogy[4], 'crotchety, 'crȳstal'lŏgraphy[4], 'cŭstody[3].

dë'lïvery[2], dë'mŏgraphy[4], 'dēmo'nŏlogy[4], 'dĕstiny[3], 'deute'rŏnomy[4], ͵dï'ăchrony[4] [-krənɪ], 'dïa͵lec'tŏlogy[4], 'dïa͵thermy[5], ͵dï'chŏtomy[4] [-'kɒ-], 'difficulty[2], di'scŏvery[2], ͵dŏ'xŏlogy[4], 'drăma͵turgy[5].

ë'cŏlogy[4], ë'cŏnomy[4], 'ecstasy[3], 'effigy[3], 'Ēgyp'tŏlogy[4], 'ĕlĕgy[3], 'embassy[3], 'embry'ŏlogy[4], 'empathy[4], 'ĕnergy[3], ën'quïry[2], 'ento'mŏlogy[4], ën'treaty[2], 'entropy[3], ë'pïgraphy[4], 'ĕpi͵lepsy[5], ë'pïphany[4], ë'pïste'mŏlogy[4], 'ĕquerry[c], 'ĕscha'tŏlogy[4] [-kə-], ͵eth'nŏgraphy[4], ͵eth'nŏlogy[4], ë'thŏlogy[4], 'ēti'ŏlogy[4], 'ĕty'mŏlogy[4], 'eulogy[4], 'euphony[4], ëx'pïry[2].

'fămily³, 'fantasy³, 'fěathery, 'fělony², 'flattery², 'flowery, 'frīary².

'gălaxy³, ˌgas'trŏnomy⁴, 'gēnë'ālogy⁴, gë'ŏdesy⁴, gë'ŏgraphy⁴, gë'ŏlogy⁴, gë'ŏmetry⁴, 'gluttony², 'gossipy, gra'phŏlogy⁴ (or ˌgrä-), 'gȳnae'cŏlogy ['gaɪnɪ-].

'hăberˌdăshery², 'hăgi'ŏlogy⁴, 'harmony³, 'hĕathery, 'hĕresy³, 'herpë'tŏlogy⁴, 'hĕteroˌdŏxy⁵, 'hīerˌarchy⁵, ˌhĭs'tŏlogy⁴, 'hĭstori'ŏgraphy⁴, 'hŏmily³, 'hōmoe'ŏpathy⁴ ['həʊmɪ-], ho'mŏphony⁴, ˌhȳ'pertrophy⁴, hy'pŏcrisy⁴, ˌhȳ'pŏnymy⁴, 'hȳster'ectomy⁴.

'ichthy'ŏlogy⁴ ['ɪkθɪ-], 'īco'nŏgraphy⁴, 'īdë'ŏlogy⁴, 'īdio'syncrasy⁴, ˌī'dŏlatry⁴, 'ĭgnominyᶜ, 'industry³, 'infamy³, 'injury², in'quīry², 'ironˌmŏngery², 'īrony.

'jĕopardy³, 'jĕalousy².

'larceny³, 'lĕathery, 'lĕchery², 'lĕprosy³, 'lĕthargy³, 'lĭtany³, li'thŏgraphy⁴, 'lĭturgy³, lo'bŏtomy⁴, 'lŭxŭry³, ˌlȳ'canthropy⁴.

'mălady³, 'māri'ŏlatry⁴, 'mästery², 'mātriˌarchy⁵, 'mĕlancholyᶜ [-kəlɪ] (or -ˌchŏly [-ˌkɒlɪ]), 'mĕlody³, 'mĕmory³, 'mĕtalˌlurgy⁵ (or më'tăllurgyᶜ), 'mĕtëo'rŏlogy⁴, 'mĕtho'dŏlogy⁴, më'tŏnymy⁴, ˌmī'crŏscopy⁴, 'mĭner'ălogy⁴, 'mĭnistry², mi'scellany³, 'mĭsery⁴, 'mŏnarchy², 'mŏnody³, mo'nŏgamy⁴, mo'nŏpoly⁴, mo'nŏtony⁴, ˌmor'phŏlogy⁴, 'mūtiny³, 'muttony, 'mȳstery³, my'thŏlogy⁴.

në'crŏlogy⁴, 'nĕcroˌmancy⁵, ˌneu'rŏlogy⁴.

'ŏbloquy⁴, 'ōcea'nŏgraphy⁴ ['əʊʃə-], 'ŏliˌgarchy⁵ [-kɪ], ˌon'tŏgeny⁴, ˌon'tŏlogy⁴, 'oph,thal'mŏlogy⁴, 'orni'thŏlogy⁴, 'orthoˌdŏxy⁵, 'orthō,ĕpyᶜ, ˌor'thŏgraphy⁴, 'orthoˌprăxy⁵, 'ŏstë'ŏpathy⁴.

'pălë,on'tŏlogy⁴, 'pănoply³, 'pāpery, 'părasi'tŏlogy⁴, 'părody³, pa'thŏlogy⁴, 'pātriˌarchy⁵, 'pĕda'gŏgyᶜ, më'nŏlogy⁴, 'pĕnūry³, 'peppery, 'perfidy³, pe'rĭphery³, 'perjury², 'pharma'cŏlogy⁴, phë'nŏmë'nŏlogy⁴, phi'lanthropy⁴, phi'lătely⁴, phi'lŏlogy⁴, phi'lŏsophy⁴, pho'nŏlogy⁴, pho'tŏgraphy⁴, 'phrăsë'ŏlogy⁴, phrë'nŏlogy⁴, phy'lactery⁴, ˌphȳ'lŏgeny⁴, 'physi'ognomy⁴, 'phȳsi'ŏlogy⁴, 'pillory³, 'pleurisy³, 'pŏlyˌandry⁵, po'lȳgamy⁴, po'lȳphony⁴, ˌpor'nŏgraphy⁴, 'porphyry³, 'powdery, 'prīory², 'prŏdigy³, 'prŏgeny⁴, 'prŏsody³, ˌpsȳ'chīatry⁴ [ˌsaɪ'kaɪ-], ˌpsȳ'chŏlogy⁴ [ˌsaɪ'kɒ-], 'pȳroˌtechny⁵ [-ˌtek-].

'rackĕty, rë'cŏvery², 'rectory², 'rĕgistry², 'rĕmedy³, 'rhapsody³, 'rhīnoˌplăsty⁵, 'rickĕty.

'Săxony², ˌscă'tŏlogy⁴, 'scrŭtiny³, 'shĭvery, 'showery, 'silvery, 'sōci'ŏlogy⁴, 'sŏdomy², so'lĭloquy⁴, 'splintery, stë'nŏgraphy⁴, 'strătegy³, 'subsidy³, 'sugary ['ʃʊgərɪ], 'sȳcoˌphancy⁵, 'symmetry⁴, ˄sympathy⁴, 'symphony⁴, 'synchrony⁴ [-krə-], sy'nŏnymy⁴, 'sȳrupy, 'syzygy³.

'tăpestry³, 'Tartary², 'tau'tŏlogy⁴, 'tăxiˌdermy⁵, ˌta'xŏnomy⁴, ˌtech'nŏlogy⁴ [ˌtek-], të'lĕgraphy⁴, 'tēlë'ŏlogy⁴, të'lĕpathy⁴, të'lĕphony⁴, të'lĕscopy⁴, 'termi'nŏlogy⁴, ˌtë'trălogy⁴, 'tĕˌtrarchy⁵, 'thaumaˌturgy⁵, thë'ŏlogy⁴, thë'ŏphany⁴, thë'ŏsophy⁴, 'thĕrapy³, 'thrĕnody³, 'thundery, 'tonsil'lectomy⁴,

to'pŏgraphy⁴, to'pŏlogy⁴, 'trăchë'ŏtomy⁴, 'trăgedy³, 'trĕachery³, 'trĕasŭry²,
'trīgo'nŏmetry⁴, 'trīlogy⁴, 'tympany³, ˌtȳ'pŏgraphy⁴, ˌtȳ'pŏlogy⁴, 'tȳranny³.

ˌū'rŏlogy⁴, 'ūsŭry³.

'velvety, 'vĕnery³ (or 'vē-), 'victory², 'villainy².

'watery ['wɔ:-], 'willŏwy.

ˌzo'ŏlogy⁴ [ˌzu:'ɒlədʒɪ].

Stress in Compounds

5.1 Compounds with Initial Stress

Are compounds one word or two? The answer must be that they are *both* one word *and* two. They are combinations of words that may occur independently elsewhere, and hence must be two words; at the same time, they are combined in such a way that they form a single relatively close-knit whole with a number of characteristics that indicate rather clearly that they are one word. One of the most important of these characteristics is that they have many of the accentual and rhythmic features of single words. In English this means that they tend to have a main stress near the *beginning* of the combination, rather as single words have a tendency to bear penultimate or antepenultimate stress rather than final stress; phrase constructions, in which the individual words have much more independence, tend to have main stress on their *final* element.

Thus the noun phrase **black board** (='board which is black') normally has nuclear stress on the second element **board**: 'black `board; the only context in which this does not hold is when **black** has contrastive stress: **the 'black ,board, not the white one**. The relative independence of the two parts of the phrase **black board** is reflected in the ease with which each of the two elements of the phrase can be independently extended: we can have '**very 'black `board** (='board which is very black'), '**coal-,black `board** (='board which is coal-black'), and also '**black 'floor,board** (='floorboard which is black'), '**black 'wooden `board** (='wooden board which is black'), not to mention **very black wooden board**, etc.

The compound noun **blackboard** (='board for writing on with chalk'), on the other hand, takes nuclear stress on the first element **black**: 'black,board. In many examples, including this one, no extensions can be added independently to either of the two elements (it makes no sense to say, for instance, **very blackboard** or **black-woodenboard**), but only to the compound as a whole, as in **wooden blackboard**. We shall refer to the first element of a compound (**black** in this particular case) as the *compound initial*, and to the second (**board** in this example) as the *compound final*.

The elements of a compound need not be monosyllabic, or even words with a single stress. Where longer words are involved, the general principle is that the relative stress levels in each word are maintained, but that the nuclear stress of the whole expression falls on the compound initial. Thus when `ĕle,vātor is compounded with `ŏpe,rātor, the stress pattern might be represented as:

`ĕle,vātor `ŏpe,rātor

which could be analysed as:

`(`ĕle,vātor) ,(`ŏpe,rātor).

Compounds often form 'building blocks' out of which more complicated compounds can be constructed. Thus `black,board and `rubber may be compounded into:

`(`black,board) ,(`rubber)

which would be pronounced in a manner representable as:

`black,board `rubber

where **black** is the syllable with the strongest stress, and **rub** is slightly more stressed than **board**. Similarly the phrase **elevator operator training scheme** would have a structure something like:

`[`(`ele,vātor),(`ope,rātor)] ,[`(`training),(`scheme)]

which would result in a stress pattern like:

`ele,vātor ,ope,rātor `training ,scheme.

Notice that our notation appears to have run out of means of differentiating between stress levels: the two stresses of **operator** are now indicated as being of equal strength, rather than stronger followed by weaker as before. The notation could be refined so as to maintain the marking of different stress-levels, but this would in fact be misleading: the physical properties which signal stress in English (cf. Section 1.1) do not enable hearers, even trained phoneticians, to distinguish consistently more than three degrees of strength. The restriction on the notation thus reflects an important fact about the workings of English, and we shall continue with the notation as we have used it so far.

There is a considerable amount of variation in the way compounds are written: some, e.g. **training scheme**, are written as two separate words; others, e.g. **blackboard**, as a single word; yet others are hyphenated, e.g. **gold-digger**. Very frequently one and the same compound can be written in more than one fashion with no loss of acceptability: **ice cream**, **ice-cream**, and **icecream** are all to be found, as are **colour blind**, **colour-blind**, and **colourblind**; **match box**, **match-box**, and **matchbox**.

English uses a large number of compounds (mostly nouns and adjectives), with a wide variety of constituent elements. The compound noun ˈblackˌboard, for example, is of the form adjective+noun, as also are ˈredˌcoat (=‘person distinguished by wearing a red coat’) and ˈtightˌrope (=‘rope or wire on which a circus artist balances’). The majority of English compounds, however, are nouns of the structure noun+noun, as, for example, ˈfloorˌboard (=‘board for making floor’), ˈelevator ˈoperator (=‘person who operates an elevator’), ˈblackboard ˈrubber (=‘implement for rubbing a blackboard clean’). Note that although the compound final in these cases is less prominent *phonetically*, it is central from a *semantic* point of view: a floorboard is a type of board, not a type of floor, and an elevator operator is a kind of operator, not a kind of elevator.

5.2 Compounds with Final Stress

The discussion so far might be taken as implying that the distinction between phrases and compounds in English is clear-cut, with phrases (ˈblack ˈboard) taking final stress and compounds (ˈblackˌboard) taking initial stress.ˈ The situation, however, is greatly complicated by the existence of a number of constructions which are syntactically very like compounds (often indistinguishable from them) but which take *phrasal* stress-patterns. Thus, alongside ˈChristmas ˌcake (with the normal compound stress-pattern), we find ˈChristmas ˈpudding and ˈChristmas ˈpie (with the phrasal type of pattern), There is surely no syntactic reason for saying that **Christmas cake** is a compound whereas **Christmas pudding** and **Christmas pie** are straightforward noun phrases, and yet the stress-patterns are totally distinct. Again, with the range of names for thoroughfares, combinations with **Street** and (in the north of England) -**gate** (=‘street’ as in ˈLowˌgāte, ˈKirkˌgāte) are stressed on the initial element, whereas combinations with **Road**, **Avenue** and all other words denoting thoroughfares take final stress: ˈLondon ˌStreet as opposed to ˈLondon ˈRoad, ˈLondon ˈAvenue, ˈLondon ˈGardens, ˈLondon ˈClose, etc. Here also there can be no independent justification for saying that the construction types are different. We have little alternative but to recognise a second type of compound whose nuclear stress falls on the compound final, and whose stress pattern is therefore identical with the phrasal pattern.

This means that it is important to investigate whether there are any general principles governing which stress patterns are assigned to various construction-types; if both initial stress and final stress can be associated with certain constructions, as for instance in the case cited in the previous paragraph, we must if possible say which is normal and which exceptional. In Appendix 5.1 below we list the main constructions involved in English compounds, and show the stress-patterns associated with each. Before this, however, we must draw attention to a further complicating factor.

5.3 Contextually-Determined Stress-Shift

Just as the relative strengths of main and secondary stresses in certain words may be reversed in certain types of phonetic context (cf. Section 4.5 above), the same switch may take place in finally-stressed compounds in similar contexts; the end result of this is that a compound which in isolation takes stress on the compound final may in pronunciation actually be indistinguishable from initially-stressed compounds. Thus when the finally-stressed 'North 'Sea is combined with oil to form a larger finally-stressed compound, the pronunciation is not ˌNorth 'Sea 'oil (with Sea more strongly stressed than North as it is in isolation), but 'North ˌSea 'oil; this rhythmic pattern is not distinguishable from that of 'bike ˌshed 'door, even though the first element of this compound is the initially-stressed 'bike ˌshed. There seems to be a tendency for stronger stresses to alternate with weaker ones rather than to follow one another directly.

As exactly analogous shift takes place when a finally-stressed compound stands in a phrasal construction with a following noun. Colour names like 'sky-'blue are finally-stressed in isolation, and in contexts such as the cover of the book is 'sky-'blue, but show stress-shift in attributive position: The book has a 'sky-ˌblue 'cover. Many adverbial compounds are finally-stressed but show stress-shift when used adjectivally: We stopped in York 'over'night as opposed to Our 'over ˌnight stop in York.

The converse case (initial stress shifting to final stress) could only arise if an initially-stressed compound were to act as the second element in another initially-stressed compound; this is in fact a rather rare occurrence, principally because of the close-knit character of initially-stressed compounds to which we referred in Section 5.1 above. Even when they do occur, such compounds are often interpretable as if their middle element were in construction with the first rather than with the last; thus the example (given above at 5.1):

'eleˌvātor ˌopeˌrātor 'training ˌscheme

could be analysed as 'scheme for elevator operator training' just as easily as 'training scheme for elevator operators', and with little practical meaning-difference. From the phonetic viewpoint, the strongest stress comes first, which makes it highly likely that the later stresses will be post-nuclear (cf. example 4, Section 1.1), and therefore all rather weak, so that discrimination between the relative strengths of **operator**, **training** and **scheme** in the above example is not at all easy. The upshot of this is that stress-shift on rhythmic grounds within initially-stressed compounds is not a normal occurrence.

The only type of context in which stress-shift does occur in initially-stressed compounds is when contrastive stress is applied to the compound final, e.g. **He's an 'elevator 'operator, not an 'elevator me'chanic**. This kind of stress-shift can also, of course, operate within finally-stressed compounds, as in **She lives in `London ,Gardens, not `Norwich ,Gardens** (as opposed to **She lives in 'London `Gardens** without contrastive stress).

Where the majority of uses of a particular compound involve an explicit or implicit contrast with some other compound (or with one of its roots or stems used on its own), it often happens that the contrastive version of the stress-pattern becomes 'built-in' as the normal pattern. Thus **monosyllable** would be expected by our rules to take main stress on its final element: **'mono`syllable**. However, this word is preponderantly used in contrast with **disyllable**, **polysyllable**, etc., and hence the pattern `**mono,syllable**, which is the normal pronunciation of this word. Again **metalanguage** tends to occur in contrast with **language** and hence contrastively-stressed `**meta,language** has become the normal pattern. We refer to this phenomenon in this book as *built-in contrastive stress*, and it can also occur on words other than compounds (see e.g. remarks on the suffix **-ess** in Appendix 4.1).

5.4 Compounds Involving Bound Forms

Up to this point we have considered only those compounds in which free forms have been combined, i.e. elements which occur as words in their own right as well as occurring as parts of compounds. Thus in **blackboard**, the two parts **black** and **board** are quite normal words of English. There are, however, many other words which are clearly formed by the combination of two parts ('clearly', because each of the two parts normally recurs with similar meaning in other combinations), but where one or both of the parts never occurs on its own as a separate word. For example, **fishmonger** is clearly a combination of the free form **fish** and the bound form **-monger** (meaning something like 'person who sells or deals in X'); even though **monger** never occurs as a separate word, it does recur with a similar meaning in a number of other combinations such as **ironmonger**, **gossip-monger**. On these grounds we can call **fishmonger**, etc., compounds. Further justification is provided by the stress pattern of such words (`**fish,monger**), which is very much like that of the initially-stressed compounds we discussed in 5.1.

Incidentally, it must be emphasised that, just as absolute borderlines cannot be drawn between *compounds* and *phrases* (cf. the existence of phrase-like finally-stressed compounds as discussed in 5.2), so they cannot be drawn between *compounds* and *root+affix combinations*. Thus, while ˈblackˌboard is clearly a compound, and ˈfarmer is equally clearly of the form root+suffix (since -**er** does not occur as a word on its own with the same meaning, and does not bear its own stress), words like ˈmilkman have features of both types of structure. For example, the written sequence -**man** here is obviously relatable to the free form **man** (and to this extent **milkman** might be taken as compound-like), and yet shares the property of being unstressed with the suffix -**er** of **farmer** (and to this extent **milkman** might be taken as a combination of root+suffix, as we have done above, at p. 86).

Besides the 'monger' type of compound dealt with above, there are two main types of compounds involving bound forms:

1 A fairly systematic set of compounds whose compound initials are 'prepositional' or 'adverbial' and which are mainly of Latin or Greek origin, such as **intergalactic** (an adjective meaning 'between galaxies') or **pseudo-scientific** (an adjective meaning 'appearing scientific, though failing to be truly scientific'). In these cases the compound-finals are usually free forms, and the range of words which can occur in this position is so large that there is no point in attempting to list them.

The compound initials, on the other hand, are much more restricted in number. Appendix 5.2 includes all those in current use in English (there may be others in the vocabulary of certain specialised technical fields). With this type of compound, the word tends to be treated in two separate parts as far as such matters as secondary stress (cf. Section 3.2 above) and 'strong initial syllable' stress (cf. Section 7.2.3 below) are concerned.

For example, the **o** of **pseudo-scientific** is lengthened (as if it were word-final, cf. Section 2.2), and hence unreduced (cf. Section 7.1): the pronunciation is [ˈsjuːˌdəʊˈsaɪənˈtɪfɪk]. By contrast the **o** of **pseudo-nym** (a compound of type 2 – see below) is reduced, indicating that this word is treated as a single whole: [ˈsjuːdəˌnɪm]. The hyphen in **pseudo-scientific** is a marker of the divisibility of the word.

Again, in type 1 compounds rhythmic secondary stress is assigned in the compound final separately rather than in the word as a whole. In **monocotyledon**, for example, main stress falls on the strong syllable -**lē**-, and then, since -**co**- (two syllables back) is weak, rhythmic secondary stress would be expected on the syllable -**no**-; actually, however, secondary stress falls on -**co**-, which is where it falls in the word

cotyledon. As with **pseudo-scientific**, the second **o** of **mono-** is lengthened and protected from reduction; though this time the written form contains no hyphen to mark divisibility. One consequence of this is that, in compounds of type 1, main stress never falls on the second syllable of the compound initial: **pseudo-** is always ['sju:ˌdəʊ-] and never [ˌsju:'dɒ-] (as in the type 2 compound **pseudonymous**); **mono-** is always ['mɒˌnəʊ-] and never [mə'nɒ-] (as in type 2 **monotony**). Notice that some elements, including **pseudo-** and **mono-**, occur in both types of compound.

Finally, the strong initial syllable rule (Section 7.2.3 below) operates in these type 1 compound finals, even though the syllable is not the first syllable of the word as a whole: thus **post-Edwardian** shows the same non-reduction of **-Ed-** as does **Edwardian** although this is not the initial syllable of the whole compound word.

2   A set of compounds in which both elements are likely to be of Greek origin, and in which both elements tend to be bound forms. These words may consist of compound initial and compound final exclusively, e.g. **telegram**, **thermostat**, **pseudonym**, or they may incorporate one or more suffixes in addition, e.g. **thermostatic**, **pseudonymous**, **democratisation**. The os of **pseudonym**, **thermostat** and **thermostatic** reduce, indicating that the compound is treated as a single word rather than as two (in contrast to type 1 compounds – see above). The reasons for considering **telegram**, etc., as being compounds rather than of the form stem+suffix are given in Section 4.3.4 above.

Where the compound final is monosyllabic, the compound initial receives main stress and the compound final takes secondary stress: ˈmĭcroˌphōne, ˈorthoˌdox. If the secondary stress falls on a weak syllable, it prevents the reduction which would occur in a non-compound word of similar syllabic structure. Compare, for instance, ˈteleˌgram ['telɪˌgræm] with the simple root ˈmarjoram ['mɑːdʒərəm]. This principle of stress-assignment also applies to disyllabic compound finals ending in **-el**, **-er**, **-le**, **-re**, **-sm**, e.g. ˈĕpiˌcȳcle, ˈorthoˌcentre, ˈprōtoˌplasm.

In other cases, main stress and secondary stress are assigned by the rules of Section 3 (where the SP contains no suffixes) or Section 4 (where the SP does contain suffixes), applied to the word as a whole without reference to the division between compound initial and compound final. This may result in a stress pattern which is completely different from that applied to related words. Thus, adding **-ic** to ˈthermoˌstat produces ˈthermoˈstătic, while adding **-y** to ˈmĭcroˌscōpe produces ˌmĭˈcrŏscopy. Similar stress patterns, including some with stress on the final syllable of the compound initial, may arise where there are no suffixes, as in ˈhȳpoˈchondria, aˈnăphora, ˌhȳˈperbolë.

Table 5.1 Normal Stress-Placements for Compounds Involving Bound Elements

Type of compound	Monosyllabic compound final	Disyllabic compound final where second syllable is (or ends with) -el, -er, -le, -re, -sm	Other compound finals
1	Main: 1st syllable of compound initial Secondary: Compound final e.g. ˈsüper͵man	Main: 1st syllable of compound initial Secondary: 1st syllable of compound final e.g. ˈorthō͵centre	Main: Rules of Section 3 or Section 4 operating on compound final Secondary: As above, *plus* 1st syllable of compound initial e.g. ˈprē͵cogˈnītion pseudō-ˈscienˈtific ˈmōnōˈcōtyˈlēdon
2	Main: 1st syllable of compound initial Secondary: compound final e.g. ˈpseudo͵nym ˈmōno͵lōgue	Main: 1st syllable of compound initial Secondary: Compound final e.g. ˈcāta͵plasm ˈmōno͵cycle	Main: } Rules of Section 3 or Secondary: } Section 4 operating *on the word as a whole* e.g. ˈhydroˈchlōric auˈtōcracy ˈsüperˈēroˈgātion

The normal stress-assignment patterns for these two types of compounds are summarised in Table 5.1, while the most commonly occurring compound initials of both types are listed in Appendix 5.2. Compound-final elements of type 2, unlike those of type 1, form a comparatively small set in current English, though items of specialised vocabulary in science, medicine, etc., all add enormously to the total. We will content ourselves with listing the commonest here (a dash following the element indicates that the compound final occurs commonly only with a further suffix after it: more details of such combinations may be found in Appendix 4.1):

-anthrope	-grade	-metre	-scope
-arch	-gram	-morph	-soph-
-chrome	-graph	-nome	-sphere
-chron-	-latr-	-nym	-stat
-crat	-lept-	-path	-therap-
-culture	-litre	-phag-	-therm
-derm	-log(ue)	-phan-	-tom-
-dox	-loqu-	-phile	-trope
-flex	-mach-	-phobe	-type
-gam-	-mant-	-phone	-urge
-gen(e)	-metr-	-pod	-vore
-gog(ue)			

Exercises

1   State whether the following noun+noun compounds are initially-stressed or finally-stressed. In the case of exceptions (or exceptions to the exceptions) say also which of the categories of Appendix 5.1 are involved (for instance the finally-stressed '**kitchen** '**sink** is in category a of the exceptions to the normal initially-stressed noun+noun compound, while '**Christmas** ,**present** is in category (iv) of words which might be expected to be category a exceptions, but actually are not).

(*a*) Alexandra Palace, (*b*) apple juice, (*c*) Bond Street, (*d*) flute sonata, (*e*) gallon can, (*f*) greyhound, (*g*) jam sandwich, (*h*) lawn mower, (*j*) love story, (*k*) North Road, (*l*) Pentland Hills, (*m*) spring fever, (*n*) tree snake, (*o*) water pot, (*p*) Winston Churchill, (*q*) wire wool.

2   State whether the following compound nouns are initially-stressed or finally-stressed. In each case give the structure and category

involved, e.g. **tightrope** is of structure 2 (adj.+noun) and of category b(i).

(*a*) bighead, (*b*) cut-off, (*c*) driftwood, (*d*) four-poster, (*e*) hard-liner, (*f*) hothouse, (*g*) killjoy, (*h*) mare's-nest, (*j*) paleface, (*k*) pullover, (*l*) screech-owl, (*m*) six-wheeler, (*n*) windfall.

3 Repeat the procedure of Exercises 1 and 2 for the following compound adjectives:

(*a*) barrel-chested, (*b*) bed-ridden, (*c*) broken-hearted, (*d*) chromium-plated, (*e*) fireproof, (*f*) grass-covered, (*g*) leaf-green, (*h*) many-sided, (j) red-haired, (*k*) slate-coloured, (*l*) trouble-free, (*m*) water-tight.

4 Do the same for the following compound verbs:

(*a*) cross-fertilise, (*b*) feather-bed, (*c*) off-load, (*d*) pussy-foot, (*e*) spoonfeed, (*f*) upgrade.

Further Reading

Where full bibliographical details of a work are not given, they may be found in the 'Further Reading' for Section 1. See pp. 14–16 above.)

5.1 and 5.2 Initially-Stressed and Finally-Stressed Compounds

Kingdon on 'English-type Compounds', *Groundwork*, pp. 145–95, is of primary relevance here. It should be noted that he uses the term 'single-stressed' where we have 'initially-stressed' and the term 'double-stressed' where we have 'finally-stressed'. H. Sweet, *New English Grammar Part 1* (London: Oxford University Press, 1891), pp. 286-97 gives a very full account of the different types of compounds in English. Again, his terminology differs from ours – 'uneven stress' where we have 'initial stress' and 'even stress' where we have 'final stress'.

Chomsky and Halle (*Sound Pattern*, pp. 15–22) do not appear to consider the possibility of compounds with final stress, but this omission is rectified in Halle and Keyser, *English Stress*, pp. 21–3, where the compound stress rule is recognised as having two distinct parts.

5.3 Contextually-Determined Stress-Shift

Chomsky and Halle (*Sound Pattern*, p. 117) touch on this question without going into great detail. For more exemplification, see Gimson, *Introduction*, p. 285, and also D. T. Langendoen, 'Some problems in the description of English accentuation', in Goyvaerts and Pullum, *Essays* (pp. 205–18), pp. 207–8.

5.4   Compounds Involving Bound Forms

These are referred to by Chomsky and Halle (*Sound Pattern*, pp. 100–6) as 'complex nouns and adjectives'. Our type 1 compounds are there analysed as consisting of a prefix followed by a noun or an adjective, whereas our type 2 compounds are taken to be of the form prefix followed by stem (see our remarks in the 'Further Reading' section for Section 4). Kingdon's section on 'Greek-type compounds' (*Groundwork*, pp. 120–45) is also recommended reading in this connection. Guierre (*Essai*, pp. 737–64) deals at some length with our type 2 compounds, which he calls 'composés quasi-morphématiques'.

Appendix 5.1   Construction-Type and Stress-Type

We attempt here to state the main regularities which can be discerned in the assignment of initial or final stress to compounds. Our major classification will be in terms of the parts of speech involved in the compound. The following symbols are used:

*Initial stress is an alternative possibility in all contexts.
†Rhythmic stress-shift is possible.
[Noun₁] The thing named by Noun₁.

1   $Noun_1 + Noun_2 = Noun$. This is by far the most frequent type of compound, and in the majority of cases such compounds are *initially-stressed*. The main exceptions fall into the following categories:

   (a)   [Noun₁] is a location or a time, and [Noun₂] is at or near [Noun₁]: *finally-stressed (rhythmic stress-shift not usual).*

Examples: ([Noun₁] is a location) 'kitchen 'sink, 'garden 'seat, 'Channel 'ferry, 'lawn 'tennis, 'town 'crier. ([Noun₁] is a time or season) 'morning 'paper, 'summer 'weather, 'Christmas 'Day, 'Easter 'holiday, 'night 'watchman.

Exceptions: (i)   (Noun₂ is a generic term denoting time) 'summer ‚time, 'Whitsun‚tide, 'night ‚shift.
   (ii)   (Noun₂ is a generic term denoting some kind of animal) 'sea‚gull, 'marsh ‚warbler, 'water ‚buffalo, 'hedge ‚sparrow.
   (iii)   ([Noun₂] is automatically assumed to be a part of [Noun₁]) 'sea‚shore, 'river ‚bank, 'mountain ‚top.
   (iv)   (Combinations with **present** and **cake**) 'Christmas ‚present 'Eccles ‚cake, 'birthday ‚cake and the analogous 'Easter ‚egg.
   (v)   'table ‚tennis, 'window ‚seat.

Note: 'car ‚ferry, 'news‚paper, 'Boxing ‚Day are initially-stressed because [Noun₁] is not a location or a time in these instances.

   (b)   [Noun₁] is a material, and [Noun₂] is made of [Noun₁]: *finally-stressed (rhythmic stress-shift not usual).*

Examples: 'cotton 'dress, 'iron 'railings, 'gravel 'path, 'paper 'napkin, 'china 'doll, 'ginger 'beer, *'orange 'squash, 'meat 'pie.

Exceptions: (i) (combinations with **cake, juice** and **milk**) 'chocolate ,cake, 'orange ,juice, 'coconut ,milk.
(ii) 'butter ,mountain, 'dung,hill, 'snow,man, 'water,fall (perhaps butter, dung, snow, and water are not counted as recognised building materials).

Note: This type of finally-stressed compound parallels the stressing of adj. + noun combinations like 'wooden 'box, 'woollen 'jumper.

(c) Noun$_2$ is a geographical term, the name of a type of thoroughfare, etc., and Noun$_1$ (often a proper noun) is the name applied to the [Noun$_2$] under consideration; the whole compound itself often forms a proper noun: *finally-stressed (rhythmic stress-shift possible).*

Examples: (Noun$_2$ is a geographical term) 'Thames 'valley, 'Nile 'delta, 'Ilkley 'Moor.
(Noun$_2$ is a type of thoroughfare) 'Shaftesbury 'Avenue, 'Grosvenor 'Square, 'Pennine 'Way.

Exceptions: (Thoroughfare names ending in **Street** or **-gate**) 'Oxford ,Street, 'Downing ,Street, 'Mickle,gate.

(d) Noun$_1$ and Noun$_2$ form the two parts of the proper name of a particular person, place, or thing: *finally-stressed (rhythmic stress-shift not usual).*

Examples: 'William 'Smith, 'Mary 'Brown, ,Vic'toria 'Station, 'Ash 'Wednesday, 'Emperor Con'certo (ctr. 'piano con,certo, which is not the designation of one particular piece of music).

(e) Noun$_1$ specifies the value of [Noun$_2$]: *finally-stressed (rhythmic stress-shift not usual).*

Examples: 'pound 'note, 'dollar 'bill, 'ton 'weight, '10 ,p 'piece.

(f) Noun$_1$ is semantically central and Noun$_2$ specifies it further (the opposite way round from the normal noun + noun compound): *finally-stressed (rhythmic stress-shift not usual).*

Examples: 'knight 'bachelor (a type of knight, not a type of bachelor), 'queen 'mother, 'herb 'robert, 'River 'Thames, 'Loch 'Ness.

(g) Miscellaneous cases: *'arm'chair, †'armour 'plate, *'baby 'doll, *'bargain 'basement, 'bay 'window (and all combinations with **window**), 'canon 'law, 'carrier 'pigeon, *'channel 'swimmer, 'club 'foot, 'com,bine 'harvester, 'company com'mander, 'county ¸council (and all combinations with **council**), 'creature 'comforts, 'demon 'bowler, 'dialect ge'ography, 'drum 'major, 'ebb 'tide (and all combinations with **tide**='state of the sea'), 'fairy 'godmother, 'fairy 'queen, 'fellow 'citizen (and all combinations with **fellow**), †'Field 'Marshal, 'gentleman 'farmer, 'God 'speed, †'ground 'floor, 'hand-'ball (offence in soccer, ctr. 'hand,ball, name of a ball game), 'hare 'lip, *'ice 'cream, †'india 'rubber, 'jack-'tar, 'landscape 'gardener, †'Lord 'Mayor, †'lump 'sum, †'Major 'General, 'master-'builder, 'master 'mariner, 'office 'party, *'part-'owner, †'plate 'glass, 'poke 'bonnet, 'port 'wine, 'pto,maine 'poisoning (ctr. 'food-,poisoning, etc.), 'queen 'bee, †'rock 'bottom, 'roller 'towel, 'self-de'ception (and all combinations with **self-**), *'stage 'manager, 'star 'player, 'sugar 'candy, †'top 'hat, 'town 'clerk, 'town 'hall, 'town 'planning, †'trade 'union, 'twin 'brother, 'twin 'sister, †'wing com'mander, 'works 'outing.

2   Adj.+Noun=Noun. Adjective followed by noun normally forms a full noun phrase, with *final stress*. This may sometimes be transformed into a more close-knit compound noun, which is usually signalled by *initial stress*; this happens in the following types of circumstance:

   (a)   The compound means 'person or thing characterised by having [noun] that is [adj.]'.

Examples: 'faint,heart ('person with a 'faint 'heart (metaphorically)')
'free,stone ('peach with a 'free 'stone (i.e. one which doesn't stick to the flesh of the fruit)')
'high,brow ('person with a 'high 'brow (metaphorically), (i.e. person of a very intellectual outlook)')
'red,skin ('member of a race with 'red 'skin')

   (b)   The compound means 'person or thing whose characteristics are (i) more narrowly specified than or (ii) related metaphorically to what might be expected from the phrase adj.+noun'.

Examples: (i)   'tight,rope (is a 'tight 'rope, but one used specifically by balancing acts in circuses)
   (ii)   'funny-bone (is a bone, but not a 'funny'bone)
'tall,boy (is not even a boy, let alone a 'tall 'boy, but is a piece of furniture – a high chest of drawers)

3   Adj.+Noun=Adj. An adj.+noun noun phrase may sometimes be transformed without derivational affixes into a compound adjective, also usually signalled by *initial stress*.

Examples: 'narrow-,gauge (a narrow-gauge railway is a railway with a 'narrow 'gauge)
'old-,time (old-time dancing is dancing as it used to be done in 'old 'times: note the loss of the plural suffix in the compound adjective)

4   (Noun₁+-'s)+Noun₂=Noun. This combination normally forms a full noun phrase, with *final stress*. This, as in type 2 above, may sometimes be transformed into a more close-knit compound noun, which is usually signalled by *initial stress*; the meaning of such compounds is relatable to that of the corresponding full noun phrases, but usually involves some metaphorical or other extension (cf. type 2(b)).

Examples: 'bulls,eye (not 'the eye of a bull', which would be a 'bull's 'eye, but 'the central circle on a target' (which looks rather like a bull's eye)
'crows,nest
'doll's ,house (not 'the house belonging to a specific doll' but 'a house whose scale is commensurate with the size of dolls')

5 (Numeral+Noun)+-**er**=Noun. The compound means 'person or thing characterised by [Numeral][Noun]': *finally-stressed (rhythmic stress-shift not usual).*

Examples: 'four-'seater
'six-'footer
'ten-'pounder

6 (Adj.+Noun)+-**er**=Noun. The compound means 'person or thing associated with [adj.][noun]'; stressing is normally the same as that of the (adj.+noun) part on its own (i.e. -**er** is stress-neutral in this combination).

Examples: 'flat-,racer (cf. 'flat ,race)
'hot-'gospeller (cf. 'hot 'gospel)
'wild,fowler (cf. 'wild,fowl)

Exceptions: 'free,booter (no related phrase without -**er** exists)

7 Verb+Noun=Noun. *Initially-stressed.*

Examples: 'bake,house
'cut-,throat
'grind,stone
'pick,pocket

8 Noun+Verb=Noun. *Initially-stressed.*

Examples: 'sun,rise
'wind,break

9 (Noun$_1$+Noun$_2$)+-**ed**=Adj. The compound means 'having [Noun$_2$] of (or like) [Noun$_1$]': *finally-stressed (rhythmic stress-shift frequent).*
Examples: †'eagle-'eyed
†'wasp-'waisted
†'pig-'headed

Exceptions: All compounds with -**coloured** and -**shaped**:
'pear-,shaped
'rose-,coloured

10 (Numeral+Noun)+-**ed**=Adj. The compound means 'having [Numeral] [Noun]': *finally-stressed (rhythmic stress-shift frequent).*

Examples: †'two-'faced
†'four-'legged [-'legɪd]

11 (Adj.+Noun)+-**ed**=Adj. The compound means 'having [Adj.][Noun]': *finally-stressed (rhythmic stress-shift frequent).*

Examples: †'absent-'minded
†'blue-'eyed (note the loss of the plural suffix as compared with the phrase 'blue 'eyes)
'heavy-'hearted

12 Noun+Adj.=Adj. Two distinct patterns must be recognised.
    (a) The compound adjective means '[Adj.] to the extent of [Noun]' or 'as

[Adj.] as [Noun]'. *Finally-stressed (rhythmic stress-shift possible in some cases).*

Examples: †'blood-'red
'dirt 'cheap
†'knee-'high
'stone 'deaf

   (b)   The compound adjective means '[Adj.] with respect to [Noun]'. *Initially-stressed.*

Examples: 'air,tight
'care,free
'love,sick
'sea,worthy
'work,shy

Exceptions: †'rent-'free (and all compounds with **-free** except 'care,free)
'word-'perfect

13   Noun+(Verb+-ed)=Adj. The meaning of the compound is '[Verb]ed by [Noun]': *initially-stressed.*

Examples: 'hen,pecked
'moth-,eaten
'snow,bound
'weather,beaten

Exceptions: †'armour-'plated (and all compounds with **-plated**)
†'hand-'made (and all compounds with **-made**)

14   Noun+Verb=Verb. *Initially-stressed.*

Examples: 'baby,sit
'keel,haul
'man,handle

15   Noun₁+Noun₂=Verb (derived from a compound noun without the addition of a suffix): stressing follows that of the compound noun.

Examples: 'jack-,knife
'muck,rake
'side,step
'stone'wall

16   Adverb+Verb=Verb. *Finally-stressed (rhythmic stress-shift not usual).*

Examples: 'cross-e'xamine
'ill-'treat

Exception: *'back,fire

Note: The first element of 'back,bite is probably the *noun* **back**, not the adverb **back**; this word is best taken as belonging to type 14 above.

The remaining types of compound involve minor lexical types, such as prepositions and particles. These prefix-like elements are dealt with in more detail in Appendix 5.2.

17   Prep.+Noun=Adverb. *Finally-stressed (rhythmic stress-shift not usual).*

Examples:	'down'stream
	'in'doors
	'off'hand
	'over'seas

Exceptions:	a'mid,ships
	be'fore,hand
	be'hind,hand
	be'tween ,whiles
	*'over,board

18   Prep.+Noun=Adj. (derived from adverb, cf. type 17, often with loss of final -s). *Initially-stressed.*

Examples:	'down,stream
	'in,door (with loss of -s)
	'off,hand
	'over,seas (without loss of -s)
	'with-it

| *Exceptions:* | †'cross-'country (adj. and noun are finally-stressed as well as the adverb) |
| | 'up-'market |

19   Verb+Particle=Noun. ('Phrasal verb' becoming a noun without the addition of a suffix.) *Initially-stressed.*

| *Examples:* | 'write-,up (from phrasal verb **'write 'up**) |
| | 'set,back (from phrasal verb **'set 'back**) |

Note: As phrasal verbs, these combinations may be separated (e.g. 'I 'wrote the experiment 'up'), but as nouns they cannot (e.g. 'my 'write-,up of the experiment' but *not* 'my write of the experiment up').

20   Particle+Verb=Noun ('Phrasal verb' becoming a noun without the addition of a suffix, but with the two elements reversed). *Initially-stressed.*

| *Examples:* | 'down,fall (from phrasal verb **'fall 'down**) |
| | 'in,come (from phrasal verb **'come 'in**) |

21   Particle⎫
     Adverb⎬+Verb+-**er**=Noun. *Initially-stressed.*

Examples:	'by,stander
	'fore,runner
	'out,rider

22   Noun+Prep.=Adj. Restricted to the preposition **like**. *Initially-stressed.*

| *Examples:* | 'child,like |
| | 'workman,like |

Appendix 5.2 Bound Compound-Initials and their Accentual Properties

The indications 1 and 2 refer to the types of compounds designated by those numbers in the text of Section 5.4 above. The following additional symbols are used:

* There is an alternative pronunciation which follows the rules given.

† Rhythmic stress-shift may occur: **'after,noon 'tea** has **af-** more strongly stressed than **-noon** (cf. **'after'noon** in isolation, in which this relationship is reversed).

§ This exception may be accounted for in terms of 'built-in contrastive stress': **'mono,syllable**, for example, is in the overwhelming majority of its occurrences explicitly or implicitly contrasted with **disyllable, polysyllable,** etc., and the contrastive stress resulting in those instances has become part of the usual stress-pattern of the word.

allo- Type 2 compounds only.

Examples: 'allo,trōpe
               al'lōpathy

Note: The following words beginning with **allo-** consist of the prefix **al-** plus a stem beginning with **lo-**: 'allo,cāte, 'allo'cātion, 'allo'cūtion, al'lot, al'lotment.

ambi- Type 2 compounds only.

Examples: ,am'bīvalent
               'ambi'dextrous

amphi- Type 2 compounds only.

Examples: 'amphi,pod
               ,am'phībian

Exception: §'amphi,thēatre

ana- Type 2 compounds only.

Examples: 'āna,lŏg(ue)
               'àna'glypta
               a'nǎphora
               a'nǎtomy

ant-

1 *Examples:* ,ant'ǎcid
               ,ant'arctic

2 *Examples:* ,an'tǎgo,nīze
               'anto,nym

ante-

1 *Examples:* 'antë,chāmber
               'antë'nātal

'antë͵pĕn'ultimate (pronunciation 'antëpë'nultimate also occurs)

2 *Examples:* 'antë'cēdent
'antë͵tȳpe

Exception: *'antë'dāte

Notes: (i) ͵an'tenna, 'ante͵lōpe are simple roots.
(ii) 'ant͵eater is a compound beginning with the free element **ant**.

anti-

1 *Examples:* 'anti-͵nŏvel
'anti-͵freeze
'anti-'clĕrical
'anti-͵person'nel

Exceptions: 'anti-'knock ⎫
'anti-'tank ⎬ (Compound-final takes main stress in spite of being monosyllabic)
'anti-'trust ⎭
§'anti͵bŏdy
§'anti-͵hērō

2 *Examples:* 'anti͵clīne
͵An'tīpo͵dēs
͵an'tīci'pātion (secondary stress by **-ate**)
or 'antici'pātion (rhythmic secondary stress)

Notes: (i) The words 'antic, ͵an'tïque, ͵an'tïquity, 'antiquary, 'anti͵quāted, 'anti'quārian do not contain prefixes.
(ii) The name of the chemical element 'antimony follows the stress-pattern for the pre-stressed 2 suffix **-mony** (see Appendix 4.2), although it is not easy to see why the word should be analysed as stem+suffix.
(iii) **anti₁**- is usually ['æn͵taɪ-] in American English.

apo- Type 2 compounds only.

Examples: 'ăpo͵gee
'ăpo'stŏlic
a'pŏca͵lypse

Exceptions: a'pŏstate (or -͵tāte) ⎫
a'pŏthëo͵sīze ⎬ (pre-stressed 2 suffix in each case)
a'postle [ə'pɒsl] (in spite of monosyllabic final)

arch- Type 1 compounds only. Pronounced [a:tʃ-], except in †͵ar'chāngel [͵ɑ:'keɪndʒəl].

Examples: ͵arch'bĭshop
͵arch'ĕnemy
'arch͵dūke

Exceptions: *͵arch'fiēnd
*͵arch'priĕst

arche-, archi-   Type 2 compounds only. Pronounced [ɑ:kɪ-].

Examples: ʼarchëˌtÿpe
ʼarchiˌtect
ʼarchëˋŏlogy (or ʼarchae-, pronounced identically)
ʼarchiˋpĕlaˌgo

Exception: *§ʼarchiˋphōˌnēme

auto-

1   *Examples:*   ʼauˌtō-ˌchānger
ʼauˌtō-sugˋgestion
†ʼauˌtō-ˋdīˌdact

Exception: §ʼauˌtō-ˌpīlot

2   *Examples:*   ʼautoˌgräph (or -ˌgrăph)
ʼautoˌbīˋŏgraphy
ʼautoˋmātion
ˌauˋtŏnomous

Exception: ʼautomoˌbïle

Note: ʼauˌtō-daˋfe [-ˋfeɪ] is a foreign phrase rather than a compound.

cata-   Type 2 compounds only.

Examples: ʼcătaˌlŏg(ue)
ʼcătaˌclysm
ʼcătaˋtōnia
caˋtăstrophë

Notes: (i)   The sequence **cata-** is part of the stem in ʼCătaˌlan, ʼCătaˋlonia, ʼcătamaˋran.
(ii)   caˋtarrh is best treated as a simple root.

centi-   Type 2 compounds only.

Examples: ʼcentiˌgrāde
ʼcentiˌmētre (Amer. -ˌmēter)
ˌcenˋtillion

Exception: ʼcentiˌsĕcond

circum-

1   *Examples:*   ʼcircumˌcircle
ʼcircumloˋcūtion
ʼcircumˋvalˌlāte

2   *Examples:*   ʼcircumˌcīse
ʼcircumˌstance (sometimes pronounced [-stəns] as if it ended
in the suffix **-ance**)
ʼcircumˋscription
cirˋcumference

Exception: 'circum'vent (as if **circum-** were a stress-repellent prefix. See Section 6)

contra-, contre-, contro- Two distinct elements must be recognised:

A **contra\-. contre-.** Compound-initial of type 1.

Examples: 'contra-,bāss
'contra-bas'sōōn
'contre,temps ['kɒntrə,tɒŋ]
'contra-'indi,cāte

B **contra_B-, contro-.** Prefix: stress-repellent in verbs (see Appendix 6.1).

Notes: (i) con'tract, 'con,tract are clearly of the form prefix **con-**+root; con'träst, 'con,träst may possibly be of this form.

(ii) con'trāry, 'contrary, con'tral,tō are certainly related in meaning to the **contra-** prefix, but are stressed as if they were simple roots.

counter- Two distinct elements must be recognised:

A Compound-initial of type 1.

Examples: 'counter,bläst
'counter-,claim (noun, verb)
'counter,sink (verb)
'counter-,těnor
'counter-in'surgency
'counter-pro'ductive

Exceptions: §'counter-at,tack (noun, verb)
§'counter-,měasūre
*§'counter-of,fensive
§'counter-pro,pōsal
§'counter-,subject

B Prefix: stress-repellent in verbs (see Appendix 6.1).

deca- Type 2 compounds only.

Examples: 'děca,lŏgue
'děca'hēdron
dë'cathlon

Exception: §'děca,syllable

deci- Type 2 compounds only.

Examples: 'děci,mētre (Amer. -,mēter)
,dě'cillion

Note: In 'děcimal, 'děci,māte, the sequence **deci-** is part of the stem.

demi- Type 1 compounds only.

Examples: 'děmi,god
'děmi,tasse

ˈdĕmi-rëˈliēf
ˈdĕmi-ˈsĕmi-ˈquāver

di-   Two distinct elements must be recognised:

A   Meaning ˈtwoˈ: compound initial.

1   Always pronounced [daɪ].

Examples: ˈdī͵pōle
͵dīˈŏ͵xīde

Exception: §ˈdī͵syllable

2   Usually pronounced [daɪ], but sometimes [dɪ].

Examples: ˈdī͵gräph (or -͵gräph)
ˈdīph͵thong
͵dīˈglossia
͵dīˈcĕphalous

B   Prefix: stress-repellent in verbs and adjectives (see Appendix 6.1).

dia-   Type 2 compounds only.

Examples: ˈdīa͵dem
ˈdīa͵gram
ˈdīagˈnōsis
͵dīˈăphonous

Exception: ˈdīaˈbē͵tēs (regular if pronounced [ˈdaɪəˈbiːtɪs] with weak final
syllable)

dys-   Type 2 compounds only.

Examples: ͵dysˈpepsia
ˈdy̆strophy

Exception: ˈdy̆sentery

ecto-   Type 2 compounds only.

Examples: ˈecto͵morph
ˈecto͵plasm

endo-   Type 2 compounds only.

Examples: ˈendo͵crīne (or -͵crīne)
ˈen͵dōˈcentric
͵enˈdŏgamy

epi-

1   *Examples:*   ˈĕpiˈdermis
ˈĕpiˈdīa͵scōpe

*Exception:*ˈ§ˈĕpiphë͵nŏmenon

2   *Examples:*   ˈĕpi͵thet   ˈĕpi͵lepsy
ˈĕpi͵cy̆cle   ëˈpīscopal
ˈĕpiˈdĕmic   ëˈpīstëˈmŏlogy

Exception: e'pistle [ɪ'pɪsl]

equi-

1 *Examples:* 'ĕqui'dīstant
'ĕquipo'tential
'ĕqui'vālency (= 'the state of having equal valencies')

2 *Examples:* 'ĕqui,nox
'ĕqui'lībrium
ĕ'quīvocal
ĕ'quīvalence (= 'being of equal value')

extra-

1 *Examples:* 'extra-cur'rīcūlar
'extra-'sensory

2 *Examples:* 'extra,dīte   'extrapo'sītion
'extra,vert (or 'extro-)   ĕx'trăpo,lāte

Exception: 'extra'pōse (as if it were a stress-neutral prefix)

hemi- Type 2 compounds only.

Examples: 'hĕmi,sphēre
'hĕmi'plēgia

Exception: 'hĕmi-'dĕmi-'sĕmi'quāver

hetero- Type 2 compounds only.

Examples: 'hĕtero,clīte
'hĕtero'sĕxūal
'hĕte'rŏgynous

hexa- Type 2 compounds only.

Examples: 'hĕxa,teuch
,hĕ'xăgonal

holo- Type 2 compounds only.

Examples: 'hŏlo,caust
'hŏlo'phrastic
ho'lŏgraphy (or ,hŏ-)

homo- Type 2 compounds only.

Examples: 'hŏmo,nym
'hŏmo'gēnĕous (or 'hō-)
ho'mŏphonous

hydro-

1 *Examples:* 'hȳdro,foil
'hȳ,drō'carbon
'hȳ,drō-ĕ'lectric

2   *Examples:*   'hȳdro‚scōpe   'hȳdro‵chlŏric
              'hȳdro‵phōbia   ‚hȳ‵drŏmeter

hyper-

1   *Examples:*   'hȳper‚spāce
              'hȳpercor‵rect
              'hȳper-‵sensitive

   Exception: §'hȳper‚market

2   *Examples:*   'hȳper‵tŏnic
              ‚hȳ‵perbolë
              ‚hȳ‵pertrophy

hypo-

1   *Examples:*   'hȳ‚pō‵sul‚phīte
              'hȳ‚pō‵tension

2   *Examples:*   'hȳpo‚caust
              'hȳpo‵thermia (or 'hy‚pō-)
              ‚hȳ‵pŏthësis

Note: 'hȳpo‚crīte, hy‵pŏcrisy with **y** short rather than long.

infra-   Compound-initials of anomalous accentual properties.

Examples: 'infra‵dig
           'infra-‵red
           'infra‵sŏnic
           §'infra-‚structūre

inter-   Two distinct elements must be recognised.

A   Compound-initial of type 1.

Examples: 'inter-‚stāte
           'interdë'nŏmi‵nātional
           'inter-ga‵lactic

B   Prefix: stress-repellent in verbs (see Appendix 6.1).

intra-   Type 1 compounds only.

Examples: 'intra‵cellūlar
           'intra-‵ūte‚rīne
           'intra‵vēnous

Note: ‚in'tractable, ‚in'transitive consist of **in**ᴮ – followed by a stem beginning with **tra**-.

iso-   Type 2 compounds only.

Examples: 'īso‚bar   ‚ī'sŏsce‚lēs
           'īso‚tōpe   ‚ī'sŏchronous
           'īso‵mětric

kilo-

1 *Examples:*   'kī͵lō͵hertz (or 'kīlo-)
               'kī͵lō͵vōlt

   Exception: §'kī͵lō-͵calorie

2 *Examples:*   'kīlo͵gram
               'kīlo'mĕtric
               'kīlo͵mĕtre
               or ki'lŏmetre (as if the ending were -**meter**ₐ. See Appendix
                             4.2)

macro-

1 *Example:*   'mă͵crō-'ēco'nŏmics (or -'ēco-)

   Exception: §'mă͵crō-͵clīmate

2 *Examples:*   'măcro͵cosm
               'măcro'scŏpic

mega-   Type 2 compounds only.

Examples: 'mĕga͵phōne
            'mĕga'līthic

meso-   Type 2 compounds only.

Examples: 'mĕso͵morph
            'mĕso'zōic

Note: 'mē͵son with long **e**.

meta-

1 *Examples:*   'mĕta͵centre
               'mĕta͵stāble
               'mĕta'măthë'mătics

   Exceptions: §'mĕta͵language
                §'mĕta͵thēory

2 *Examples:*   'mĕta͵phor (sometimes -phor, as if it ended in suffix -**or**)
               'mĕta'morphic
               më'tăbolism

micro-

1 *Examples:*   'mīcro͵dot
               'mī͵crō-͵fiche
               'mī͵crō͵bī'ŏlogy

   Exceptions: §'mī͵crō͵circuit   §'mī͵crō-͵phōto͵gräph
                §'mī͵crō͵clīmate   *§'mī͵crō-͵prŏcessor
                §'mī͵crō͵cŏpy   §'mī͵crō͵sĕcond
                *§'mī͵crō-͵orga͵nism   §'mī͵crō͵structūre

2   *Examples:*   'mīcro͵phōne
'Mīcro'nēsia
͵mī'crŏmēter

milli-, mill-   Type 2 compounds only.

Examples: 'milli͵gram
'milli͵pēde
mil'lĕnium

Exception: 'milli͵sĕcond (like a type 1 compound with 'built-in contrastive
stress')

mono-

1   *Examples:*   'mŏ͵nō-͵hull
'mŏ͵nō͵rail (or 'mŏno-)
'mŏ͵nō'cŏty'lēdon

Exceptions: §'mŏno͵dräma
§'mŏno͵syllable
§'mŏnothĕ͵ism

2   *Examples:*   'mŏno͵gram
'mŏno'līthic
mo'nŏpoly
mo'nŏtonous

multi-

1   *Examples:*   'multi-͵stäge
†'multi-'purpose
'multi-'millio'naire

2   *Examples:*   'multi͵plȳ
'multi'plīcity
͵mul'tīparous

Exception: 'multipli͵cand

neo-

1   *Examples:*   'nē͵ō͵nāte
'nē͵ō-'classical
'nē͵ō-co'lōnialism

2   *Examples:*   'nēo͵phȳte
'nēo'līthic
nĕ'ŏlogism

omni-

1   *Examples:*   'omni-di'rectional
'omni'prĕsent

2   *Examples:*   'omni͵bus (or -bus)
͵om'nīpotent
͵om'nīvorous

ortho-

1   *Examples:*   'or͵thō͵centre
'or͵thōchro'mătic

2   *Examples:*   'ortho͵dox
'ortho'grăphic
͵or'thōgonal

   Exception: 'or͵thō͵ĕpy (**-y** would have been expected to be pre-
stressed 2)

para-

1   *Examples:*   'păra-͵drop
'păra-'mĕdical
'păra'tÿ͵phoid

   Exception: §'păra͵language

2   *Examples:*   'păra͵dox   'păra'bŏlic
'păral͵lel   pa'rălysis

penta-, pente-   Type 2 compounds only.

Examples: 'penta͵teuch   ͵pen'tăthlon
'Pentë͵cost   ͵pen'tămeter
'penta'tŏnic

peri-   Type 2 compounds only.

Examples: 'pĕri͵stÿle
'pĕripa'tĕtic
pe'rīpheral

Exception: 'pĕri͵car'dītis (non-reduction of **-car-** indicates that the strong
initial syllable rule might have applied in the
compound final; cf. type 1)

phil-, philo-   Type 2 compounds only.

Examples: 'phĭlo͵mel
'phĭlan'thrŏpic
phi'lŏsopher

physio-   Type 2 compounds only.

Examples: 'phÿsio'thĕrapy
'phÿsi'ŏlogy

poly-

1   *Examples:*   'pŏlychro'mătic
'pŏly-͵un'sătū͵rāted

   Exceptions: §'pŏly͵syllable
§'pŏlythë͵ism

2 *Examples:*   'pŏly,glot
'pŏly,ester
'pŏly'stȳ,rēne
po'lȳsemy

post-   Three distinct elements must be recognised:

A   Free form meaning 'mail', and operating in compounds as any other noun would.

Examples: 'pōst ,office (noun+noun)
'pōst-'free (noun+adj.)

B   Bound compound initial.

1 *Examples:*   ,pōst-'doctoral
'pōst-im'pressio,nist
,pōst-'ŏperative

   Exception: ,pōst-'war (compound final takes main stress in spite of being monosyllabic)

2 *Example:*   'pōsthūmous ['pɒstjəməs] (trisyllabic shortening operating?)

C   Prefix: stress-repellent in verbs (see Appendix 6.1).

Note: In ,pŏs'tērior, ,pŏs'tĕrity, 'pŏstern, the sequence **post-**, although related in meaning to **post**ʙ- and **post**ᴄ-, is part of the stem.

pre-

Two distinct elements must be recognised:

A   Compound initial. Always pronounced [pri:-]

1 *Examples:*   ,prē-'Christian
'prē,fab
'prē,view (noun and verb)
'prē-,dī'gest

   Exceptions: ,prē-'cäst
,prē-'dāte
,prē-'heat   } (compound finals are stressed in spite of being
,prē-'judge   } monosyllabic)
,prē-'pay

2 *Examples:*   'prēhis'tŏric
'prēvo'călic

   Exception: 'prēdë,cessor

B   Prefix: stress-repellent in verbs (see Appendix 6.1). Usually pronounced [prɪ-] but may be [pri:-] or [pre-].

pro-   Two distinct elements must be recognised:

A   Compound-initial of type 1. Always pronounced [prəu-].

   Example: ,prō-'Brĭtish

B Prefix: stress-repellent in verbs (see Appendix 6.1). Usually pronounced [prə-] but may be [prəʊ-] or [prɒ-].

proto- Type 2 compounds only.

Examples: ˈprōtoˌcol
           ˈprōtoˈzōa
           proˈtăgoˌnist

Exception: ˈprōˌtō-ˌlanguage (like a type 1 compound with 'built-in contrastive stress')

pseudo-

1 *Examples:*   ˈpseuˌdō-ˈGeorgian
              ˈpseuˌdō-ˈscīenˈtific

   Exception: ˈpseuˌdō-ˌscīence

2 *Examples:*   ˈpseudoˌnym
              ˌpseuˈdŏnymous

psycho-

1 *Examples:*   ˈpsȳˌchō-aˈnălysis
              ˈpsȳˌchōˌlinˈguistics

   Exception: ˈpsȳˌchōˌdräma

2 *Examples:*   ˈpsȳchoˌpath
              ˈpsȳchoˈlógical
              ˌpsȳˈchŏlogy

quasi-. Type 1 compounds only. Pronounced [ˈkweɪˌsaɪ-] or [ˈkwɑːzɪ-].

Example: ˈquasi-ˌjüˈdīcial

retro- Two distinct elements must be recognised:

   A Compound initial: type 1 compounds only.

Examples: ˈrĕˌtrō-ˌchoir
           ˈrĕˌtrōˈactive

Exception: §ˈrĕˌtrō-ˌrocket

   B Prefix: stress-repellent in verbs (see Appendix 6.1).

semi- Type 1 compounds only.

Examples: ˈsĕmiˌcircle   ˈsĕmi-dĕˈtăched
           ˈsĕmi-ˈcōlon   ˈsĕmi-ˈprĕcious

Notes: (i) ˈsĕmiˌnar is probably best taken as a simple root (though note the non-reduction of the final syllable).

       (ii) In ˈsĕmiˌŏlogy, ˈsĕmiˈŏtic, ˈSĕˌmīte and Sëˈmītic, the sequence **semi-** is part of the stem.

sub- Two distinct elements must be recognised:

   A Compound initial: type 1 compounds only. Always pronounced [sʌb-].

Examples: 'sub,cläss   ,sub-'trŏpical
              'sub,let (noun and verb)   'subter'rānëan
              ,sub'ĕdit

Exceptions: ,sub'lease (verb)   §'sub-,section
               §'sub-com,mittee   §'sub-,spē,ciēs
               §'sub'con,tractor   §'sub-,stātion
               §'sub,cultūre   §'sub-,strātum
               §'sub-dë,partment   §'sub-,structūre
               §'sub-,dĕ,pot [-,pɔu]   §'sub-,sy̆stem
               §'sub-,dis,trict   §'sub-,tŏtal
               §'sub-,fămily   §'sub-,ūnit
               §'sub-,hĕading   §'sub-va,rı̄ety
               §'sub-,roü,tïne

B   Prefix: stress-repellent (see Appendix 6.1). Usually pronounced [səb-] but sometimes [sʌb-].

super-   Two distinct elements need to be recognised.

A   Compound initial.

1   *Examples:*   'süper,charge   'süperim'pōse
                   'süper,star   'süpera'bundant

    Exceptions: 'süper'add   §'süper-,hīgh,way
                   †'süper-'cool   §'süper,market
                   †'süper'heat   §'süper-,strātum
                   §'süper,ē,gō   §'süper,structūre
                   §'süper-,hĕ,rō

2   *Examples:*   'süper,vīse
                   'süper'nūmerary

B   Prefix: stress-repellent (see Appendix 6.1).

supra-   Type 1 compounds only.

Examples: 'süpra,lap'sārian
               'süpra,seg'mental

syl-, sym-, syn-

    The basic form of this compound initial is **syn-**; **syl-** occurs before stems beginning with **l**, and **sym-** before stems beginning with the labials **b, m, p, ph**. These elements occur in type 2 compounds only.

Examples: 'syn,drōme   syl'lăbic
               'syn,tax   sym'pōsium
               'syllo,gism   sy'nŏnymous
               'sympathy   'synco'pātion
               'synchro,nīze   'sympa'thĕtic

Exceptions: 'sy̆na,gogue ⎱(disyllabic stems, but the rhythm is like many
               'sy̆no,nym   ⎰regular cases)

Note: 'symbol, 'symptom, 'sӯnod with reduced final syllable in each case are probably best taken as being simple roots, though the pronunciation 'sӯ,nod is compatible with being a type 2 compound.

tele-

1   *Examples:*   'tĕlë,com
                   'tĕlë,printer
                   'tĕlëcom'mūni'cātion

    Exception: §'tĕlë,phō,tō

2   *Examples:*   'tĕlë,phōne   'tĕlë'grăphic
                   'tĕlë,vīse   tĕ'lĕpho,nist

    Exception: *'tĕlë,vīsion

tetra-   Type 2 compounds only.

Examples: 'tĕtra,chord
                'tĕtra'hēdron
                tĕ'trălogy

theo-   Type 2 compounds only.

Examples: 'thēo'lōgian
                thĕ'ŏcracy

thermo-

1   *Examples:*   'ther,mō,dӯ'nămic
                   'ther,mō'nūclĕar
                   'ther,mō,cöuple

2   *Examples:*   'thermo,stat
                   'thermo'stătic
                   ther'mŏmeter

trans-   Two distinct elements need to be distinguished.

  A   Compound initial: type 1 compounds only.

Examples: 'trans-'conti'nental
                'transat'lantic

  B   Prefix: stress-repellent in verbs (see Appendix 6.1).

ultra-   Type 1 compounds only.

Examples: 'ultra-con'servative
                'ultrama'rīne
                'ultra-'vīolet

Exceptions: 'ultra-'high
                 'ultra-'short

vice-   Type 1 compounds only.

Examples: 'vīce,roy
                †,vīce-'prĕsident

Exception: *'vīce-'reine [-'reɪn]

Prefixes and Stress

6.1 Stress-Neutral Prefixes

Certain prefixes, like stress-neutral suffixes (cf. Section 4.1), are automatically discounted when the place of main stress is being calculated: main stress cannot possibly fall on them. They are not part of the stressable portion (SP) of the word (Section 2.1). Thus the word **imprŏper** might by the rules of Section 3 be expected to have antepenultimate stress (ˈimproper), but in fact stress can move back only as far as the penultimate syllable (imˈprŏper); the resulting stress-pattern is thus the same as for the corresponding non-negative word ˈprŏper. Again, the word **improbable** is stressed just as if it were **probable** – although -able when added to a root that cannot occur alone as a word ought to place stress *two* syllables back from the suffix (see Section 4.3.2), ˈimprobable is not the correct form, but im ˈprŏbable.

It is not that these prefixes cannot be stressed, but that they are irrelevant to the placement of main stress within the words as a whole. They may receive a stress in two sets of circumstances:

(a) They may receive nuclear stress (the most important stress in a sentence) if they are contrastively stressed; the following dialogue exemplifies this:

A   It's probable that Peter will win.
B   Really? I'd have thought that was very **im**probable [ˈɪmˌprɒbəbl].

(b) They may receive secondary stress if rhythmic considerations demand it: ˈimperˈturbable.

Stress-neutral prefixes typically attach themselves to free stems (i.e. stems which can occur without the prefix as words in their own right), and they tend to have meanings which do not vary greatly from one occurrence to another. Thus in our examples above, **im-** is attached to the stems **proper, probable, perturbable** (the first two of these occur frequently, and the third, although less frequent in occurrence, quite clearly means 'prone to be perturbed'), and in each case negates the meaning of the stem.

A further indication that these prefixes do not form part of the SP of words in which they occur is that their final consonant is not lost before a stem beginning with the identical consonant: **unnatural** is pronounced [ˌʌnˈnætrəl], **ex-service** is [ˌeksˈsɜːvɪs], **misspell** is [ˌmɪsˈspel].

They share this property with stress-neutral suffixes, e.g. **meanness** ['mi:nnəs]. The negative prefix **im-** (and its other forms **il-**, **in-**, **ir-**) is the only exception to this principle: **immature** ('not mature') is pronounced by most speakers as ['ɪmə'tjʊə], **immobile** as [ɪ'məʊˌbaɪl] (by Americans as [ɪ'məʊbl]), **illogical** as [ɪ'lɒdʒɪkl]. Some prefixes vary in stress-neutrality, and these also vary in their treatment of identical consonants: **dis-** for example is stress-neutral in **disservice** ([ˌdɪs'sɜ:vɪs] for most speakers) but not in **dissent** ([dɪ'sent] for all speakers). This is the basis for distinguishing **disₐ-** from **disв-** in the list below and in Appendix 6.1.

The following are the stress-neutral prefixes with their meanings (subscripts refer to the subdivisions of the prefixes in Appendix 6.1):

aₐ-	?locative	exₐ-	'formerly'
a_c-	negative	ilₐ-	negative
anв-	negative	imₐ-	negative
be-	?	inв-	negative
coₐ-	'together'	irₐ-	negative
deₐ-	'to get rid of' 'to get out of'	mal-	'badly'
disₐ-	reversive	mis-	'wrongly'
emₐ-	causative	reₐ-	'again'
enₐ-	causative	un-	negative

6.2 Stress-Repellent Prefixes

When the SP of a word contains no suffixes, main stress is normally placed according to the principles stated in Section 3. Certain words involving prefixes, however, behave somewhat differently: thus both **report** and **comprehend** ought to take main stress on the first syllable by the rules, but in fact take it on the final syllable. Rather than add words like this to the list of finally-stressed words which we have treated as exceptions and listed in Appendix 3.1, we can account for the final stress by saying that the prefixes **re-**, **com-**, **pre-**, etc., resist the placement of main stress upon them by the rules of Section 3 (and

Table 6.1

	report	comprehend
Rule 2 (Section 3)	'report	
Rule 3a (Section 3)		'comprehend
Stress-repellence of prefixes	re'port	com pre'hend
Resulting form	re'port	compre'hend

cause the stress to fall one syllable to the right within the SP of the word). Table 6.1 illustrates the working of this principle of 'stress-repellence'.

Like the stress-neutral prefixes (see 6.1 above), the stress-repellent prefixes may take secondary stress by the rhythmic principle, as in **'comprë'hend**, **'rĕcol'lect**. Again, they may receive contrastive stress as in:

I said 'comprehend', not 'reprehend'.

Unlike the stress-neutral prefixes, however, the stress-repellent prefixes accept stress *when it is placed by suffixes* (i.e. according to the principles stated in Section 4). Thus, in **'compli,cāte**, main stress is placed on the prefix **com-** because **-āte** is a pre-stressed 2 suffix (cf. pp. 60f. above). This difference is one of the main reasons for distinguishing the principles of Section 4 from those of Section 3. It also justifies the inclusion of stress-repellent prefixes within the SP of words, where stress-neutral prefixes are excluded from the SP.

A further difference between the two types of prefix is that stress-repellent prefixes are much more likely to occur with bound stems, and much less likely to have a constant meaning in all occurrences.

6.3　Prefixes and Noun-Verb Pairs

Some prefixes vary in stress-repellence depending on whether the word they appear in is a noun or a verb. Thus **re-** as in **report** is a prefix which in general repels stress in both types of word (**rë'port** (noun) – **rë'port** (verb)), whereas (non-negative) **in-** is one of the varying set: compare **in'crease** (verb), where the prefix is stress-repellent, with **'in,crease** (noun), where it is not stress-repellent.

Usually a prefix which forms a weak syllable (i.e. a syllable consisting either of a short vowel or of one or more consonants followed by a short vowel – see Section 2.2 above) will be stress-repellent in both verbs and nouns, whereas a prefix consisting of a strong syllable will be stress-repellent in verbs but not in nouns. However, several kinds of exceptions to this principle occur, and full information on each prefix is given in Appendix 6.1. One inviolable rule is that if stress falls on the stem in the noun member of a pair, it must also fall on the stem in the verb. The noun **com'mand**, for example, could not have a corresponding verb 'com,mand – the verb has to be **com'mand** like the noun.

In adjectives, prefixes are more likely to behave as they do in nouns than as they do in verbs; for example:

ab'stract (verb) – 'ab,stract (adj., noun)
,prŏ'strāte (verb) – 'prŏ,strate (adjective)

There are, however, a number of cases where prefixes are stress-repellent in adjectives but not in nouns; for instance:

a'dept (adjective) – 'ǎ,dept (noun).

When the prefix takes stress in a noun or an adjective, the vowel of the stem might if short be expected to show reduction due to lack of stress on the stem; this, however, rarely occurs. Table 6.2 illustrates this. This problem is further discussed in Section 7.2 below. A small number of verb-noun pairs where a 'prefix+stem' analysis hardly seems possible exhibit the stress-shift and non-reduction typical of words with prefixes; these are shown in Table 3.3 (p. 32). The vast majority of these end in **-ment**, and this is perhaps best handled as part of the accentual properties of this suffix (cf. Appendix 4.1).

A further peculiarity of stress-repellent prefixes is that they may show reduced vowels even when they form a strong initial syllable, e.g. **ad'mit**[əd'mɪt], **com'plain** [kəm'pleɪn], **ob'ject** [əb'dʒekt]. They do not show reduced vowels in strong initial syllables, however, when rhythmic secondary stress falls on them, e.g. **'comprë'hend** ['kɒmprɪ'hend], or when secondary stress arises from a suffix, e.g. **'ex,hor'tātion** ['eg,zɔ:'teɪʃn]. For a full discussion, see 7.2.3 below.

One final complicating factor in noun-verb pairs exhibiting stress-shift is that the verb (usually pronounced with stress on the stem, e.g. **im'port**) may be explicitly or implicitly contrasted with its opposite (**ex'port**); when this happens, contrastive stress may well be placed on the prefix, overriding the normal stress-pattern and making it indistinguishable from the noun **'im,port**. Thus an utterance like the following is quite normal:

We must 'import raw materials before we can 'export manufactured goods.

Table 6.2

	im_B+port (vb)	im_B+port (n.)	comfort (n.)
Rule 2 (section 3)	'import	'import	'comfort
Stress-repellence of prefix	' im'port		
Vowel reduction	[ɪ]	[ə]	[ə]
Predicted pronunciation	[ɪm'pɔ:t]	['ɪmpət] (incorrect)	['kʌmfət]
Actual pronunciation	[ɪm'pɔ:t]	['ɪm,pɔ:t]	['kʌmfət]

6.4 'Mixed' Prefixes

Just as with suffixes (cf. Section 4.4), some prefixes may have two or more different sets of accentual properties. We have already seen (Section 5.4) how some compound-forming elements may sometimes act as prefixes; where these appear in the list in Appendix 6.1, this fact is noted (e.g. for **inter-**). Other prefixes vary between being stress-neutral and stress-repellent (cf. **dis-**, mentioned in 6.1 above, p. 165). In these circumstances, as with suffixes, stress-neutral prefixes tend to be attached to free forms, whereas stress-repellent prefixes are analogous to pre-stressed suffixes in being more likely to be attached to bound forms.

Exercises

1   Using Table 6.1 as a model, show how we can account for the stress-patterns of the following words involving prefixes (the prefix to look up in Appendix 6.1 is shown in bold type in each case):

(*a*) **ac**cuse, (*b*) **ad**vent, (*c*) **ap**per**tain** (two prefixes **ap-** and **per-**), (*d*) **be**moan, (*e*) **col**lapse (verb), (*f*) **col**lapse (noun), (*g*) **com**press (verb), (*h*) **com**press (noun), (*j*) **de**throne, (*k*) **de**lay (verb), (*l*) **de**lay (noun), (*m*) **ex**chequer, (*n*) **inter**play, (*o*) **per**sist, (*p*) **pre**judge, (*q*) **pre**fect, (*r*) **sub**lime.

2   A stress-repellent prefix does not repel main stress when placed by a suffix. For each of the following prefixes (stress-repellent when occurring with verbs) find verbs which take main stress on the prefix because of the presence of a suffix. One example of each is given.

(*a*)   **con-**   e.g. ꞌcongre,gāte
(*b*)   **in-**   e.g. ꞌinfil,trāte
(*c*)   **per-**   e.g. ꞌperme,āte
(*d*)   **re-**   e.g. ꞌreso,nāte

Further Reading

(Where full bibliographical details of a work are not given, they may be found in the 'Further Reading' for Section 1. See pp. 14–16 above).

6.1 and 6.2   Stress-Neutral and Stress-Repellent Prefixes

Jespersen, *Modern English Grammar*, Part VI, pp. 464–533, gives a great deal of detail, especially historical, while Guierre, *Essai*, has a number of references to prefixes, the most important being pp. 358–63, 436–55, 704–9, and the word lists on pp. 810–15.

6.3 Prefixes and Noun-Verb Pairs

Chomsky and Halle (*Sound Pattern*, pp. 94–8) assume that the verb is primary and the noun derived in every case, but Ross ('Reanalysis', pp. 290–302) disputes this. The non-reduction of the stem vowel in those nouns and adjectives which take stress on the prefix is taken by Chomsky and Halle (pp. 36–8) to be evidence for the cyclic application of the stress rules. Guierre (*Essai*, pp. 391–416, 489–91) is also worth consulting.

Appendix 6.1 List of Prefixes and their Accentual Properties

a- Three distinct prefixes must be recognised.

A Adverb-forming **a-** (always short and pronounced [ə]): *stress-neutral*. This prefix always attaches itself to initially-stressed stems (usually monosyllabic) without suffixes, and therefore never actually takes secondary stress.

1 Stem is a free root.

Examples: 'drift – a'drift
'hĕad – a'hĕad
'way – a'way

2 Stem is not a free form (though it may be related to a free form).

Examples: a'fraid
a'gog

B Verb-forming **a-** (always short): *stress-repellent*. This prefix always attaches itself to initially-stressed stems (sometimes free, and usually monosyllabic), and is sometimes relatable to one of the prefixes **ab-** or **ad-**; suffixes may be attached, in which case the prefix may take secondary stress or suffix-placed main stress, and is then pronounced [æ].

Examples: a'bāse
a'līgn
a'vert
a'spīre – 'ăspi'rātion (secondary stress)
'ăspi,rāte (main stress placed by **-āte**)

C Negative **a-** (always long and therefore pronounced [eɪ]):

3 *Stress-neutral*. This prefix takes secondary stress, either by the rhythmic principle or by the strong initial syllable rule.

Examples: sym'mĕtrical – 'āsym'mĕtrical
'mŏral – ,ā'mŏral

Exception: 'thēist – 'ăthë,ist (built-in contrastive stress?)

The stem is not necessarily a free form.

Example: ,ā'lĕxia

ab-   *Stress-repellent in verbs.*

Examples: ab'duct (or ˌab'duct – cf. Section 7.2.3 below)
ab'sent (verb) – ctr. 'absent (adjective)
ab'stract (verb) – ctr. 'abˌstract (adj., noun)
'abdi'cātion (secondary stress placed by -ate)
'absoˌlüte (main stress placed by **-ute**)

Exceptions: a'brupt (adjective)
ab'strüse (adjective)
ab'surd (adjective)
a'būse (noun)

ac-   Historically viewed, this is the form of **ad-** which occurs before stems beginning with **c** or **qu**.

1   When the initial **c** of the stem is pronounced [s], the prefix forms a strong syllable and is *stress-repellent in verbs.*

Examples: ac'cent (or ˌac'cent) (verb) – 'acˌcent (or 'accent) (noun)

2   When the stem begins with **c** pronounced [k], or with **qu**, the prefix forms a weak syllable and is *stress-repellent in verbs and nouns.*

Examples: ac'cord (verb) – ac'cord (noun)
ac'count (verb) – ac'count (noun)
ac'claim (verb) – ac'claim (noun)
ac'quīre

In both cases the prefix may receive secondary stress or suffix-placed main stress. (This applies to all stress-repellent prefixes, and will not be further mentioned in the list below.)

Examples: 'accla'mātion (secondary stress by **-ate**)
'accident (main stress by **-ent**)

ad-   This prefix has alternative forms **ac-, af-, ag-, al-, an-, ap-, ar-, as-, at-,** which reflect assimilations typical of the Latin from which the relevant words were borrowed. *Stress-repellent in verbs and adjectives.*

1   When the initial of the stem is a consonant other than **d**, the prefix forms a strong syllable, which may, in spite of the strong initial syllable rule, remain unstressed in most varieties of English (see Section 7.2.3). In this case it is pronounced [əd]. When stressed, of course, it is pronounced [æd].

Examples: ad'mit (or ˌad'mit) (verb)
'adˌverb (noun)

Exception: ad'vīce (or ˌad'vīce) (noun) (cf. -ce, pp. 63f.)

2   When the initial of the stem is **d**, the **d** of the prefix is lost; when the initial of the stem is a vowel, the **d** of the prefix forms the initial consonant of the following syllable. In both cases, the initial syllable is weak, and the strong initial syllable rule could not apply.

Examples: ad'dict (verb) – 'adˌdict (noun) ([ˈæˌdɪkt])
a'dept (adj.) – 'ăˌdept (noun)

Exception: ad'dress (verb) – ad'dress (noun) (British – American English
has (regular) 'ad,dress)

af- The form of **ad-** which occurs before stems beginning with **f**. It forms a
weak syllable, pronounced [ə], and is *stress-repellent in verbs and nouns*.

Examples: af'fect (verb)
af'fair (noun)
af'frönt (verb) – af'frönt (noun)
'af,fec'tātion (secondary stress placed by -ate)

Exception: af'fix (verb) – 'af,fix (noun)

ag- The form of **ad-** which occurs before stems beginning with **g**. It forms a
weak syllable, pronounced [ə], and is *stress-repellent*.

Example: ag'grieve
'aggra,vāte (main stress placed by -ate)

al- The form of **ad-** which occurs before stems beginning with **l**. It forms a
weak syllable, pronounced [ə], and is *stress-repellent in verbs and nouns*.

Examples: al'lĕge
al'lūre (verb) – al'lūre (noun)
'allo,cāte (main stress placed by -ate)

Exceptions: al'loy (verb) – 'al,loy (noun)
al'lȳ (verb) – 'al,lȳ (noun)
(The past participle **allied** may take initial stress, and almost
always does when used as an adjective: **the 'Allied 'forces**)

Note: the word **alley**['ælɪ] is a simple root, and so does not exemplify the prefix
al-.

an- Two distinct prefixes must be recognised.
A   The form of **ad-** which occurs before stems beginning with **n**. It forms a
weak syllable, pronounced [ə], and is *stress-repellent in verbs*. In words other
than verbs it may receive stress, and is then pronounced [æ].

Examples: an'nounce
an'nex (verb) – 'an,nex (noun) (['æ,neks])

B   A form of the negative prefix **a₍c₎-**. *Stress-neutral*.

Example: 'hȳdröus – ,an'hȳdröus

ap- The form of **ad-** which occurs before stems beginning with **p**. It forms a
weak syllable, pronounced [ə], and is *stress-repellent in verbs and nouns*.

Examples: ap'peal (verb) – ap'peal (noun)
ap'proach (verb) – ap'proach (noun)

Notes: (a) 'apple is a simple root. (b) The abbreviation **appro** (from **approval**)
is stressed 'ap,prō, as if it were a simple root.

ar- The form of **ad-** which occurs before stems beginning with **r**. It forms a
weak syllable, pronounced [ə], and is *stress-repellent in verbs and nouns*.

Examples: ar'ray (verb) – ar'ray (noun)
ar'rest (verb) – ar'rest (noun)
'arrogant (main stress placed by -**ant**)

Notes (a) 'ar,rōw is a simple root.
(b) 'arrant probably consists of stem+suffix -**ant**.

as- The form of **ad-** which occurs before stems beginning with **s**. It forms a weak syllable, pronounced [ə], and is *stress-repellent in verbs and nouns.*

Examples: as'semble (verb)
as'sault (verb) – as'sault (noun)
'assīg'nātion (secondary stress placed by -**ate**)

Note: 'as,set could be a simple root, though the unreduced final syllable may indicate that its structure is prefix+stem, in which case it is an exception.

at- The form of **ad-** which occurs before stems beginning with **t**. It forms a weak syllable, pronounced [ə], and is *stress-repellent in verbs and nouns.*

Examples: at'tack (verb) – at'tack (noun)
at'tempt (verb) – at'tempt (noun)

Notes: (a) 'attar is a simple root
(b) 'attic is probably of the structure root+suffix

be- Usually verb-forming, though sometimes adverb-forming, as in **below**, **beside**. *Stress-neutral*, though unusual among stress-neutral prefixes in having no fixed meaning. This prefix always attaches itself to initially-stressed stems (usually monosyllabic) without suffixes, and therefore, like **a$_A$-**, never actually takes secondary stress.
　1　Stem is a free root.

Examples: 'calm ['kɑ:m] – bë'calm [bɪ'kɑ:m]
'friend – bë'friend [bɪ'frend]
'sīde – bë'sīde

　2　Stem is not a free form.

Examples: bë'draggle
bë'gin
bë'long

co- Two distinct prefixes must be recognised.
　A　*Stress-neutral*, always pronounced [kəʊ], usually meaning 'together'.

Examples: 'cō-ë'xist
,cō-'ŏpe,rāte
,cō-'wörker

Exceptions: 'cō,sine (built-in contrastive stress?)
*'cō,sēcant ⎫
*'cō,tangent ⎭ (for some speakers – same reason?)

　B　The form of **con-** which occurs before stems beginning with a vowel or **h**. Before a vowel it forms a strong syllable, pronounced [kəʊ]; before **h** it may

behave in the same way, or it may form a weak syllable, pronounced [kə].
Stress-repellent in verbs.

Examples: ‚cō'erce (verb)
‚cō'hēre (or co'hēre) (verb)
'cō‚hort (noun)
'cōin'cīde (verb, with two stress-repellent prefixes)
'cō-‚op (noun – abbreviation of **Co-operative Society**)

col- The form of **con-** which occurs before stems beginning with **l**. It forms a
weak syllable, pronounced [kə], and is *stress-repellent in verbs and nouns*.

Examples: col'lapse (verb) – col'lapse (noun)
col'lāte
'cŏlloquy (main stress placed by -**y**)

Exceptions: 'col‚lect (noun)
'col‚league (noun) (['kɒ‚li:g])

Notes: (a) 'collar, 'collie are simple roots.
(b) 'collier, 'colliery, and probably 'collëge are of the structure root+
suffix.

com- The form of **con-** which occurs before stems beginning with a bilabial
consonant (**p**, **b**, or **m**).
1   When the initial consonant of the stem is **p** or **b**, the prefix forms a strong
syllable, which may, in spite of the strong initial syllable rule, remain
unstressed in most varieties of English (see Section 7.2.3). In this case it is pronounced [kəm]. When stressed, of course, it is pronounced [kɒm]. *Stress-
repellent in verbs.*

Examples: com'bīne (verb) – 'com‚bīne (noun)
com'pound (verb) – 'com‚pound (adj., noun)
com'prīse (verb)
                        'com‚plex (adj., noun)
'compëtent (main stress placed by -**ent**)

Exceptions: *'com‚bat (verb – stressed as noun)
'com‚pere ['kɒm‚pɛə] (verb – stressed as noun)
com'plēte (adjective – stressed as verb)

Notes: (a) com'plaint is of the form com'plain (verb)+stress-neutral suffix
-**t**.
(b) 'cŏmpass, 'cŏmpany, 'compline, 'cŏmfort are simple roots.

2   When the initial consonant of the stem is **m**, the **m** of the prefix is lost; the
initial syllable is then weak, pronounced [kə]. *Stress-repellent in verbs
and nouns.*

Examples: com'mänd (verb) – com'mänd (noun)
com'mence (verb)
com'mūte (verb)
'com‚men'dātion (secondary stress placed by -**ate**)

Exceptions: 'commerce (noun) (or 'com,merce)
　　　　　　　　'com,mūne (noun)
　　　　　　　　'com,ment (verb and noun)

Note: 'common, 'commis,sar, 'commo,dore are simple roots.

con-   This prefix has alternative forms **co-, col-, com-, cor-**, which reflect assimilations typical of the Latin from which the relevant words were borrowed. *Stress-repellent in verbs.*

1   When the initial consonant of the stem is other than **n**, the prefix forms a strong syllable, which may, in spite of the strong initial syllable rule, remain unstressed in most varieties of English (see Section 7.2.3). In this case it is pronounced [kən] (or [kəŋ] if the stem begins with [k] or [g]). When stressed, of course, it is pronounced [kɒn] (or [kɒŋ] if the stem begins with [k] or [g]). *Stress-repellent in verbs.*

Examples: con'flict (or ,con'flict) (verb) – 'con,flict (noun)
　　　　　　　con'test (or ,con'test) (verb) – 'con,test (noun)
　　　　　　　'con,cāve (adjective)

Exceptions: (a)   con'cēit (noun)
　　　　　　　　　　con'cern
　　　　　　　　　　con'sent
　　　　　　　　　　con'tempt ⎬ (nouns stressed as corresponding verbs)
　　　　　　　　　　con'trōl
　　　　　　　　(b)   con'cīse
　　　　　　　　　　con'dīgn ⎬ (adjectives)
　　　　　　　　　　con'tent
　　　　　　　　(c)   *'con,tact (verb stressed as corresponding noun)

Note: 'cönjure, 'conquer ['kɒŋkə] are simple roots.

2   When the initial consonant of the stem is **n**, the **n** of the prefix is lost; the initial syllable is then weak. *Stress-repellent in verbs*, where it is pronounced [kə]. In words other than verbs it may be stressed, and is then pronounced [kɒ].

Examples: con'nect ⎱ (verbs)
　　　　　　　con'nīve ⎰
　　　　　　　'con,nāte ['kɒ,neɪt] ⎱ (adjectives)
　　　　　　　'con,nex ['kɒ,neks] ⎰
　　　　　　　'conno'tātion (secondary stress placed by **-ate**)

cor-   The form of **con** which occurs before stems beginning with **r**. It forms a weak syllable, pronounced [kə], and is *stress-repellent*.

Examples: cor'rōde
　　　　　　　cor'rupt (verb, adjective)
　　　　　　　'corre,lāte (main stress placed by **-ate**)

de-   Two distinct prefixes must be recognised.

A   Attached to free forms (usually nouns) to form verbs meaning 'to get rid of N' or 'to get out of N'. It is always pronounced long [di:], and is *stress-neutral*.

Examples: ˌdē'bug
ˌdē'train

B Attached to bound forms (or very occasionally to free forms) with no consistent meaning. It is always pronounced short [dɪ], ([de] when stressed) and is *stress-repellent in verbs, adjectives and nouns.*

Examples: dë'bāte (verb) – dë'bate (noun)
dë'feat (verb) – dë'feat (noun)
'dĕniˌgrāte (main stress placed by **-ate**)

Exceptions: Sometimes stressed in nouns, and then often lengthened.
dë'crease (verb) – 'dēˌcrease (noun)
dë'coy (verb) – *'dēˌcoy (noun)
dë'fect (verb) – 'dēˌfect (noun)
dë'sert (verb) – 'dĕsert (noun)
'dĕreˌlict (adj., noun)

Note: 'dĕlˌūge (noun, verb) works as a simple root.

di- Two distinct prefixes must be recognised.
A Meaning 'two'; its behaviour with regard to stress is more like a compound than a prefix (see Section 5.4.2).

Examples: ˌdī'glossia
'dīˌgraph

B Historically this is a form of **dis_B-**. It is pronounced long and forms a strong syllable: *stress-repellent in verbs and adjectives.*

Examples: ˌdī'gress (verb)
ˌdī'verse (adjective)
ˌdī'gest (verb) – 'dīˌgest (noun)

Exceptions: ˌdī'lūte (verb) – *'dīˌlūte (adjective)
dī'vīde (verb) – dī'vīde (noun)
*dī'rect [də'rekt] (verb, adjective)

dif- The form of **dis_B-** which occurs before stems beginning with **f**. *Stress-repellent.*

Examples: dif'fract
dif'fūse [dɪ'fju:z] (verb)
dif'fūse [dɪ'fju:s] (adjective)

Note: 'differ, 'difficult (or -ˌcult) are best taken as simple roots.

dis- Two patterns of stress-assignment must be distinguished.
A *Stress-neutral* when the stem is a free form.

Examples: 'dīsa'gree
ˌdis'grāce (verb, noun)
ˌdis'līke (verb, noun)

Exceptions: ˌdis'charge (verb) – 'disˌcharge (noun)
ˌdis'card (verb) – 'disˌcard (noun)
ˌdis'count (verb) – 'disˌcount (noun)

B   *Stress-repellent in verbs, adjectives and nouns* when the stem is not a free form. This prefix has the alternative forms **di-**, **dif-**.

Examples: ˌdisˈdain (verb, noun)
              ˌdisˈpūte (verb, noun)
              disˈsent (verb, noun)
              ˈdissident (main stress placed by suffix **-ent**)

Exceptions: ˈdisˌcord (noun)
              ˈdisˌcrete (adjective)
              ˌdisˈcourse [-ˈkɔːs] (verb) – ˈdisˌcourse (noun)
              ˈdisˌjoint (adj. – suffix **-t**?)

Notes: (a)   The following are best treated as simple roots: ˈdiscus, disˈcīple, ˈdisˌtäff, ˈdisˌtrict.
         (b)   The following are probably of the form root+suffix: ˈdiscipline, ˈdismal [ˈdɪzməl], ˈdistance, ˈdistant.

e-   The form of **ex**ᴮ- which occurs before stems beginning with a voiced consonant. It usually forms a weak syllable, pronounced [ɪ], but may on occasion be pronounced long [iː] for emphasis. *Stress-repellent in verbs, adjectives and nouns.*

Examples: ëˈject
              ëˈlect (verb) – ëˈlect (adj., noun)
              ëˈrupt
              ˈĕmiˌgrāte (main stress placed by **-ate**)

Exceptions: ˈēˌdict (noun – suffix **-t**?)
              ˈēˌgress

Notes: (a)   The following are simple roots: ˈēˌgō (or ˈĕˌgō), ˈēgret, ˈĕˌmïr (or ëˈmïr), ˈēˌmū, ëˈnough [ɪˈnʌf], ˈēˌpoch [-k], ˈēˌros, ˈēven, ˈĕver, ˈēvil.
         (b)   Although historically related to a form with prefix **e-**, ˈĕdit is best treated as a simple root.

ef-   The form of **ex**ᴮ- which occurs before stems beginning with **f**. It forms a weak syllable, pronounced [ɪ], and is *stress-repellent in verbs, adjectives and nouns.*

Examples: ëfˈfāce (verb)
              ëfˈfect (verb) – ëfˈfect (noun)
              ëfˈfēte (adjective)
              ˈefflüent (main stress placed by **-ent**)

Exception: ˈeffort

em-   The form of **en-** which occurs before stems beginning with **b** or **p**. As with **en-**, two distinct prefixes must be recognised:

A   Prefixed to free roots (occasionally to bound roots), with a causative meaning (ˈto put into N' or ˈto cause to be A'). *Stress-neutral.* Although it forms a strong initial syllable, it normally remains unstressed in most varieties of English (see Section 7.2.3).

Examples: em'balm [ɪm'bɑːm]
              em'bitter
              em'ploy

B   Prefixed to bound roots (usually Greek in origin); its original meaning, 'in', is not always clear in the resulting words. *Stress-repellent.*

Examples: 'empathy (main stress placed by **-y**)
              'emphasis (main stress placed by **-is**)

Notes: (a)   The following are simple roots: 'ember, 'emblem, 'embryō, 'em͵pīre.
      (b)   The following are of the form root+ suffix: 'emperor, 'empress.

en- This prefix has the alternative form **em-** which reflects assimilations typical of the French or Greek from which the relevant words were borrowed. Two distinct prefixes must be recognised:

A   Prefixed to free roots (occasionally to bound roots), usually with a causative meaning ('to put into N' or 'to cause to be A') rather similar to that of suffix **-en**ᶜ (see Appendix 4.1). *Stress-neutral* (as indicated by the fact that **ën'noble** has geminate [nn] in pronunciation). Although it forms a strong initial syllable, it normally remains unstressed in most varieties of English (see Section 7.2.3).

Examples: ën'camp
              ën'dūre
              ën'fran͵chīse
              ën'large
              ën'nōble (note geminate [n]:[ɪn'nəʊbl])
              ën'tränce (verb)

B   Prefixed to bound roots (usually Greek in origin); its original meaning, 'in', is not always clear in the resulting words. *Stress-repellent.*

Examples: ͵en'dĕmic (strong initial syllable rule applies)
              'ĕnergy (main stress placed by **-y**)

Notes: (a)   The following are simple roots: 'engine, 'en͵nui ['ɒ͵nwiː], 'ensign, 'enter, 'envy (verb and noun).
      (b)   The following are of the form root+suffix: 'engi'neer (rhythmic secondary stress), 'entrance (noun), 'entry.

ex- Two distinct prefixes must be recognised:
A   Attached to free forms, with the meaning 'formerly'.
1   *Stress-neutral* (actually behaves in some ways like the first element of a compound. See Section 5.4.2). It forms a strong syllable which always has secondary stress and is pronounced [eks].

Examples: ͵ex-'husband
              ͵ex-'service

Exception: 'ex-di'rectory is used to refer to telephone numbers that are 'not in the directory'; it thus expresses a meaning rather like 'out of' (cf. the most frequent meaning of **ex**ʙ- below).

B   Attached to bound forms (occasionally to free forms); its original mean-ing, 'out of', is not always clear in the resulting words. Its alternative forms **e-, ef-** reflect the situation in Latin, from which most of the relevant words are borrowed. *Stress-repellent in verbs, adjectives and nouns*. It always forms a strong syllable, which may, in spite of the strong initial syllable rule, remain unstressed in most varieties of English (see Section 7.2.3). There are two patterns of pronunciation:

2   When the stem begins with a vowel or **h**: if **ex-** is not stressed, it is pro-nounced [ɪgz]; if **ex-** is stressed, it may be pronounced either [egz] or [eks]. The [z] or [s] is attached to the following syllable in both cases.

Examples: ë'xact [ɪg'zækt] (verb, adjective)
ëx'haust [ɪg'zɔ:st] (verb, noun)
ë'xŏne,rāte [ɪg'zɒnə,reɪt]
'ĕxë'gēsis ['eksɪ'dʒi:sɪs] or ['egzɪ-] (rhythmic secondary stress)
'ĕxer,cīse ['eksə,saɪz] or ['egzə-] (main stress placed by **-īse**)

Exceptions: 'ĕ,xīle ['eg,zaɪl] or ['ek,saɪl] (verb, noun)
'ĕxit ['egzɪt] or ['eksɪt] (verb, noun)
'ĕxodus ['eksədəs]

3   When the stem begins with a consonant (not **h**): **ex-** is pronounced [ɪks] when unstressed and [eks] when stressed. The [s] may be attached to the following syllable if the consonants at the beginning of the stem allow it, and is lost when the stem begins with **c** pronounced [s].

Examples: ex'ceed [ɪk'si:d]
ex'chānge [ɪks'tʃeɪndʒ] (verb, noun)
ex'claim [ɪk'skleɪm]
ex'treme [ɪk'stri:m] (adjective, noun)
'expur,gāte ['ekspə,geɪt] (main stress placed by **-ate**)

Exceptions: ëx'cīse (verb) – 'ex,cīse (noun)
'ex,pert (adjective, noun)
ëx'ploit (verb) – 'ex,ploit (noun)
ëx'port (verb) – 'ex,port (noun)
ëx'tract (verb) – 'ex,tract (noun)

for-   1   *Stress-repellent*: pronounced [fə].

Examples: for'bid
for'lorn

2   *Stress-repellent in verbs*: pronounced [fɔ:].

Examples: ,for'beār (verb)
,for'gäther (verb)
'for,beār (noun) (='ancestor')

Note: The instances under 2 (with stress on **for-**) may well really be instances of **fore-**, structurally the first element of a compound (see Section 5).

il-   Two distinct suffixes must be recognised:

A Negative prefix: *stress-neutral.* The form of in_B- which occurs before a stem beginning with **l**. The **l** of the prefix is (unusually for a stress-neutral prefix) not pronounced, resulting in an unstressed weak syllable [ɪ].

Examples: il'līcit
                  il'lŏgical

B Non-negative prefix: *stress-repellent.* The form of in_C- which occurs before a stem beginning with **l**. The **l** of the prefix is not pronounced, resulting in a weak syllable [ɪ], which may be stressed by the suffix stress rule.

Examples: il'lūmine (or -'lü-)
                  'illu,strāte (main stress placed by -**ate**)

im-   Two distinct prefixes must be recognised:
A Negative prefix: *stress-neutral.* The form of in_B which occurs before a stem beginning with a bilabial consonant (**p**, **b**, or **m**). When the stem begins with **m**, the **m** of the prefix is (unusually for a stress-neutral prefix) not pronounced, resulting in a weak syllable [ɪ] which may receive rhythmic secondary stress. When the stem begins with **p** or **b**, the prefix forms a strong syllable, which freely receives stress by the strong initial syllable rule.

Examples: ,im'balance (or im'balance)
                  ,im'probable (or im-)
                  ,im'pure
                  im'moderate [ɪ'mɒdərət]
                  'imma'tūre ['ɪmə'tjuə]
Exceptions: 'im,passe ['ɪm,pæs] or ['æm-]
                   'impiöus
                   'impotent

B Non-negative prefix: *stress-repellent in verbs.* The form of in- which occurs before a stem beginning with a bilabial consonant (**p**, **b** or **m**). When the stem begins with **m**, the **m** of the prefix is not pronounced, resulting in a weak syllable [ɪ] which, in addition to being a candidate for rhythmic secondary stress, may have main or secondary stress placed on it by suffixes.

Examples: im'port (verb) – 'im,port (noun)
                  im'print (verb) – 'im,print (noun)
                  'immi'grātion (secondary stress placed by -**ate**)
                  'impro,vīse (main stress placed by -**ise**)

in-   Three distinct prefixes need to be recognised:
A The 'adverbial' prefix with constant meaning 'in', which is attached to free forms. Unlike in_B- and in_C-, it does not have variants **il**, **im**-, **ir**- before stems beginning with **l**, **p**, **b**, **m**, **r** (though phonetically the /n/ may optionally assimilate to a following plosive as regards place of articulation). Its stress behaviour is more like that of a compound-forming element (see Section 5 for details).

Examples: ,in'doors
                  'in,put ['ɪn,pʊt] or ['ɪm,pʊt]

B Negative prefix: *stress-neutral*. Usually attached to free forms. It has alternative forms **il-**, **im-**, **ir-** which reflect assimilations typical of the Latin from which the relevant words were borrowed.

Examples: ˌinˈclĕment
ˈincorˈrect
ˌinˈfirm   (A stress-repellent prefix would take main stress on
ˌinˈvĭsible   itself in each of these cases)

Exceptions: ˈinfinite (treated as if it were not the negative of ˈfīˌnīte, which it clearly is)
ˈinfamous (treated as if it were not the negative of ˈfāmŏus, which it probably isn't)
ˈinfiˌdel (or ˈinfidel)
ˈinˌgrāte

Note: The noun ˈinvalid could be taken as a simple root; the adjective ˌinˈvălid behaves exactly as the negative of ˈvălid might be expected to.

C Non-negative prefix, usually attached to bound forms. Its original meaning, ˈin' or ˈon', is not always clear in the resulting words. Like in$_B$-, it has alternative forms **il-**, **im-**, **ir-**. *Stress-repellent in verbs.*

Examples: inˈcrease (verb) – ˈinˌcrease (noun)
inˈcur
inˈhĭbit
inˈsert (verb) – ˈinˌsert (noun)
ˈinfilˌtrāte (main stress placed by **-ate**)

Exception: *ˈinˌfix (verb) – ˈinˌfix (noun)

Note: The following are best treated as simple roots: ˈinˌdex (noun, verb), ˈinjure, ˈinterval.

inter- Two distinct prefixes need to be recognised:
A ˈPrepositional' element, with a very clear and constant meaning ˈbetween' or ˈamong'; morphologically it is less integrated with the word than is **inter**$_B$-; it is often set off from the stem by a hyphen. *Stress-neutral.* It always bears secondary stress on its first syllable, even when the rhythmic principle would predict stress on its second syllable.

Examples: ˈinterdëˈnŏmiˈnātional
ˈinter-gaˈlactic
ˈinterˈplănetary (Amer.) -ˈplăneˌtary [-ˌterɪ]

B Genuine prefix, whose meaning is not simply statable in all cases. Morphologically it is very closely attached to the stem: it cannot be set off by a hyphen, and tends to occur with bound forms. *Stress-repellent in verbs.*

Examples: ˈinterˈvēne
ˈinterˈcept (verb) – ˈinterˌcept (noun)
ˈinterˌlüde
ˌinˈterpoˌlāte
ˌinˈtĕrroˌgāte

Exception: 'inter,view (verb as well as noun – as if it were a compound)

Notes: (i) 'inte,rest (verb and noun) has an alternative pronunciation ['ıntrəst] which makes it plausible to treat it as a simple root.

(ii) 'interval is probably a simple root.

(iii) in'terpret is not inter+pret, but a simple root, or possibly in_c+terpret.

(iv) ,in'terminable is certainly in_B+terminable, even though **terminable** does not occur alone.

ir- Two distinct prefixes need to be recognised:

A Negative prefix: *stress-neutral*. The form of **in_B-** which occurs before a stem beginning with **r**. The **r** of the prefix is (unusually for a stress-neutral prefix) not pronounced, resulting in a weak syllable [ı] which may receive rhythmic secondary stress.

Examples: ir'rătional
'ïrrë'trievable

B Non-negative prefix: *stress-repellent*. The form of **in_c-** which occurs before a stem beginning with **r**. The **r** of the prefix is not pronounced, resulting in a weak syllable [ı], which may be stressed by the suffix stress rule.

Examples: ir'rādi,āte
'ïrri,gāte

mal- *Stress-neutral*; takes secondary stress always.

Examples: 'mălad'just(ed)
'mal,for'mātion (strong initial syllable rule applies to -for-, indicating that **mal-** is not part of the SP, ctr. 'infor'mātion)
,măl'ōdorous

Exceptions: 'malcon,tent (noun) (built-in contrastive stress?)
'mălë,factor (more like a compound pattern)

Notes: (i) The following are best treated as simple roots: 'măla,prop, ma'lāria, ma'linger, ma'lign [mə'laın] (verb and adjective).

(ii) 'mălice is probably of the form root+suffix (cf. **justice**).

mis- *Stress-neutral*; takes secondary stress always.

Examples: ,mis-'spell [,mıs'spel] (double [s] indicates that **mis-** is not part of SP)
'mĩs,under'stand
,mis'rüle (verb and noun)
,mis'trust (verb and noun)

Exceptions: 'mis,crëant (takes stress from suffix, indicating **mis-** is stress-repellent in this case)
'mis,fit   ⎫ (indicating **mis-** behaves as stress-repellent in
*'mis,hap   ⎬ nouns for these three cases)
'mis,print (noun) ⎭
*'mis,carriage (built-in contrastive stress?)

Notes: (i) The following are simple roots: ʼmischief [ʼmɪstʃɪf], ʼmīser [-zə], miʼsère [mɪʼzɛə], ʼmister, ʼmis,tral, ʼmistle,toe [ʼmɪsl,təu]

(ii) The following are of the form root+suffix: ʼmiscelʼlāneous, misʼcellany, ʼmissal, ʼmis,sīle (Amer. ʼmissile), ʼmission, ʼmissive, ʼmistress, ʼmisty.

o- A form of **ob-**: *stress-repellent in verbs.*

Example: oʼmit

ob- *Stress-repellent in verbs and adjectives.*

Examples: obʼserve [əbʼzɜːv]
obʼscūre (verb and adjective)
obʼject (verb)
ʼobject or ʼob,ject (noun)

Note: ʼob,long, ʼobstacle are simple roots.

oc- The form of **ob-** appearing before stems beginning with **c**. *Stress-repellent.*

Examples: ocʼcur
ocʼcult
ʼoccident (main stress placed by suffix **-ent**)

Note: ʼoccū,pȳ is best treated as a simple root.

of- The form of **ob-** appearing before stems beginning with **f**. *Stress-repellent.*

Example: ofʼfend

Note: ʼoffer is a simple root.

op- The form of **ob-** appearing before stems beginning with **p**. *Stress-repellent.*

Examples: opʼpōse
opʼpress
ʼoppor,tūne

per- *Stress-repellent in verbs and adverbs.*

Examples: perʼcēive
perʼforce
perʼhaps
perʼmit (verb) – ʼper,mit (noun)
perʼvert (verb) – ʼper,vert (noun)
perʼfect (verb) – ʼperfëct (adjective) (or ʼper,fect)
ʼpermë,āte ⎱
ʼpersëʼcūtion ⎰(stress placed by suffix)

Note: The following are best treated as simple roots: ʼpĕregrine, ʼpĕril, ʼpersonʼnel.

pre- Two distinct prefixes need to be recognised:

A ʼPrepositionalʼ element, with a very clear and constant meaning ʼbefore(hand)ʼ; morphologically it is less integrated with the word than is **pre**ᵦ-: it is often set off from the stem by a hyphen. It always bears secondary stress and is pronounced ['pri:-]. *Stress-neutral*; behaves like a compound-forming element (see Section 5).

Examples: 'prē-ē'xist
,prē'pay
,prē'prandial

B   Genuine prefix, very closely integrated with the stem, tending to occur with bound forms. *Stress-repellent in verbs*, and usually pronounced [prɪ-]. It may take stress in nouns, and is then usually pronounced [pre-], but may be [pri:-], especially when followed by a stem beginning with a vowel.

Examples: prē'cēde (or ,prē-)
prē'fer
prē'scrībe
prē'sent (verb) – 'prĕsent (noun)
'prĕference (stress placed by suffix)
'prĕpa'rātion (secondary stress placed by suffix -**ate**)

Exception: 'prĕsage (verb as well as noun)

Notes: (i) The following are best treated as simple roots: 'prĕcipice, 'prĕcis ['preɪsɪ], 'prĕjudice, 'prĕmier, 'prĕmi'ère [-'ɛə], ,pres'tïge [-'ti:ʒ].
(ii) The following are of the form root+suffix: 'prĕcious, 'prĕdator, 'prēmium, 'prēvious.

pro-   Two distinct prefixes need to be recognised:
A   'Prepositional' element, with a very clear and constant meaning 'in favour of'; morphologically it is less integrated with the word than is **pro**ʙ-: it is often set off from the stem by a hyphen. It always bears secondary stress and is pronounced ['prəʊ-]. *Stress-neutral*; behaves like a compound-forming element (see Section 5).

Example: ,prō-'Brĭtish

B   Genuine prefix, very closely integrated with the stem, tending to occur with bound forms. The meaning of the prefix is not simply statable in all cases. *Stress-repellent in verbs*, and usually pronounced [prə]. It may take stress in nouns, and its pronunciation is then sometimes [prɒ-] and sometimes [prəʊ-].

Examples: pro'duce (verb) – 'prō,dūce (noun)
pro'gress (verb) – 'prō,gress (noun) (Brit.)
'prō,gress (noun) (Amer.)
pro'pel
pro'test (verb) – 'prō,test (noun)
'prŏminent ⎫
'prŏpa,gāte ⎬ (stress placed by suffix)
'prŏpa'gātion (secondary stress placed by suffix -**ate**)

Exception: 'prō,gram(me) (verb and noun)

Notes: (i) The following are best taken as simple roots: 'prŏblem, 'proffer, 'prŏfit (verb and noun), 'prŏmise (verb and noun), 'prŏphĕt, 'prŏper, 'prŏsper, 'prō,tēin.

(ii) The following are best taken as root+suffix: 'prŏbable, pro'bātion.

pur- *Stress-repellent in verbs*; usually pronounced [pə], though main stress may fall on it in nouns, when it is [pɜː].

Examples: pur'port (verb) – 'pur,port (noun)
pur'sūe
pur'vey

re- Two distinct prefixes need to be recognised:

A 'Adverbial' element with a very clear and constant meaning 'again'; morphologically it is less integrated with the word than is **re**ʙ-: it is often set off from the stem by a hyphen. *Stress-neutral*, and pronounced [riː-]; always bears secondary stress in verbs, though main stress may be shifted leftward on to it in nouns with monosyllabic stems.

Examples: 'reāp'pear
,rē'fill (verb) – 'rē,fill (noun)
,rē'play (verb) – 'rē,play (noun)
,rē'count (verb) (='count again', ctr. rë'count='narrate')
– 'rē,count (noun)
,rē'cŏver (verb) (='cover again' ctr. rë'cŏver='regain')

Note: The noun ,rē'birth does not take leftward stress shift because of the presence of the suffix **-th**.

B Genuine prefix, whose meaning is not simply statable. Morphologically it is very closely attached to the stem: it cannot be set off by a hyphen, and tends to occur with bound forms. *Stress-repellent in verbs, adjectives and nouns*, and pronounced [rɪ-] ([riː-] before stems beginning with a vowel). When stress is placed on the prefix by the suffix rule or the rhythmic principle, it is pronounced [re-].

Examples: rē'act
rë'būke (verb and noun)
rë'fer
rë'miss (adjective)
rë'päst (noun)
rë'port (verb and noun)
'rĕticent (stress placed by suffix)
'rĕcol'lect (two stress-neutral prefixes, and secondary stress placed by the rhythmic principle)

Exceptions: (a long list, but far short of the number of regular cases):
'rĕbel (noun) (ctr. rë'bel (verb))
'rē,bound (noun) (ctr. rë'bound (verb))
*'rē,call (noun) (ctr. rë'call (verb))
'rē,coil (noun) (ctr. rë'coil (verb))
'rĕcom,pense (verb and noun)
'rĕcon,cīle (verb)
'rē,cord (Brit.) ⎫
'rĕcord (Amer.) ⎬ (noun) (ctr. rë'cord (verb))

ˈrēˌflex (adjective and noun)
ˈrĕˌfūge (noun)
ˈrĕˌfūse [-ˌfju:s] (noun)
ˈrēˌgress (noun) (ctr. rëˈgress (verb))
ˈrēˌject (noun) (ctr. rëˈject (verb))
ˈrēˌlay (noun) (ctr. rëˈlay (verb))
*ˈrēˌmit (noun) (ctr. rëˈmit (verb))
*ˈrēˌsĕarch (noun) (ctr. rëˈsĕarch (verb))
ˈrēˌtail (verb and noun)

Notes: (i) The following are best regarded as simple roots: ˈrĕcipë, réˈgïme [rɪˈʒi:m] or [ˌreɪ-], ˈrĕgimen, ˈrĕgister, ˈrĕplica, ˈrĕquiem, ˈrĕsˌcūe, ˈrĕsin, ˈrĕspite, réˈsūmé [rɪˈzju:ˌmeɪ] or ˈréˌsūˌmé [ˈrĕˌzju,meɪ], ˈrĕtina, rëˈveillë (Brit.) [rɪˈvælɪ] or ˈrĕveillë (Amer.) [ˈrevəlɪ], ˈrĕvel.

(ii) The following are best regarded as being of the form root+ suffix: ˈrēal, ˈrēcent, ˈrēgal, ˈrēgent, ˈrēgion, ˈrĕgiment (noun), ˈrĕgiˌment (verb), ˈrĕgūˌlāte, ˈrĕlish, ˈrĕmedy, ˈrēnal, rëˈpŭblic, ˈrĕperˌtoire [-ˌtwɑ:].

se- Meaning 'aside (from)'; *stress-repellent.*

Examples: sëˈclude(d)
sëˈcūre (adjective and verb)
sëˈrēne
ˈsĕparate (adjective)⎫
ˈsĕpaˌrāte (verb)⎬(stress placed by suffix)
　　　　　　　　⎭

sub- Two distinct prefixes must be recognised:
　　A 'Prepositional' element, with a very clear and constant meaning 'under' or 'below'; morphologically it is less integrated with the word than is **sub**ᵦ-: it is often set off from the stem by a hyphen. *Stress-neutral,* always bearing secondary stress and pronounced [sʌb-]; contrastive stress may fall on this prefix, and in some cases may become 'built-in'. Unlike **sub**ᵦ- it does not have variant forms **suc-, suf-, sup-,** etc.

Examples: ˌsubˈhūman
ˌsubˈlet or (with contrastive stress) ˈsubˌlet
ˈsubˌtītle (with built-in contrastive stress)
ˌsubˈtrŏpical

　　B Genuine prefix, whose meaning is not simply statable in all cases. Morphologically it is very closely attached to the stem: it cannot be set off by a hyphen, and tends to occur with bound forms. *Stress-repellent,* and usually pronounced [səb-] (except in the English of northern England, cf. Section 7.2.3), though it may be stressed by suffixes, or receive secondary stress by the rhythmic principle.

Examples: subˈmit
subˈsist
subˈtract
ˈsubsëquent (stress placed by suffix)
ˈsubˌjecˈtīvity (secondary stress placed by **-ive**)

Exceptions: 'subjëct (or 'sub,ject) (noun, adjective) ctr. sub'ject (verb)
                'sub,script
                'subter,füge

Note: The following are best treated as simple roots: 'sŭbaltern, 'subtle
['sʌtl]

suc-   The form of **sub**ᴮ- which occurs before stems beginning with **c**. When the **c** of the stem is pronounced [s], the **c** of the prefix is separately pronounced [k] and the prefix is then pronounced [sək] (though northern English speakers may give it a full vowel, cf. Section 7.2.3). When the **c** of the stem is pronounced [k], the **c** of the prefix is dropped, and all speakers use the pronunciation [sə-]. *Stress-repellent.*

Examples: suc'cumb [sə'kʌm]
              suc'ceed [sək'si:d]
              suc'cinct [sək'sɪŋkt]

Note: 'succour (verb and noun), 'succo,tash are best treated as simple roots.

suf-   The form of **sub**ᴮ- which occurs before stems beginning with **f**. The **f** of the prefix is dropped, giving the pronunciation [sə-]. *Stress-repellent.*

Examples: suf'fīce
              suf'füse

Note: (i)   'suffer is best treated as a simple root.
        (ii) 'suffrage ['sʌfrɪdʒ], 'suffragan ['sʌfrəgən] are best treated as root+suffix(es).

sug-   The form of **sub**ᴮ- which occurs before stems beginning with **g**. *Stress-repellent.*

Example: sug'gest [sə'dʒest] (Brit.), [səg'dʒest] (Amer.)

sup-   The form of **sub**ᴮ- which occurs before stems beginning with **p**. The **p** of the prefix is dropped, giving the pronunciation [sə-]; where stress is placed on this prefix by suffixes, the pronunciation is [sʌ-]. *Stress-repellent.*

Examples: sup'plant
              sup'port (verb and noun)
              'suppli,cāte }(stress placed by suffix)
              'suppo'sītion }

Note: 'supple is best treated as a simple root.

super-   Two distinct prefixes must be recognised:
   A   'Prepositional' element, with a very clear and constant meaning 'above' or 'over'; morphologically it is less integrated with the word than is **super**ᴮ-: it is sometimes set off from the stem by a hyphen. *Stress-neutral.* It actually behaves like a compound-forming element (see Section 5); it always bears secondary stress on its first syllable, and is pronounced ['su:pə-] (or ['sju:pə-]. With a monosyllabic noun root, it may have main stress shifted on to it.

Examples: 'süpera'bundant
              'süper'nūmerary

'süper,man
'süper,tax
'süper,structūre (built-in contrastive stress)
'süper,vīse

B Genuine prefix, whose meaning is not simply statable in all cases. It tends to occur with bound forms. *Stress-repellent.*

Examples: 'süper'vēne
'süperin'tend

sur- Two distinct prefixes must be recognised:
A The form of **sub**ᵦ- that occurs with stems beginning with **r**. The **r** of the prefix is dropped, giving the pronunciation [sə-]; where stress is placed on this prefix by suffixes, the pronunciation is [sʌ-]. *Stress-repellent.*

Examples: sur'round
sur'render
'sŭrrogate (stress placed by suffix)

B A suffix related in meaning to **super-**, and occurring with stems beginning with letters other than **r**. The pronunciation is [sɜ:-] when stressed and [sə-] otherwise. *Stress-repellent in verbs.*

Examples: sur'vīve
sur'vey (verb) – 'sur,vey (noun)
'sur,nāme
'surtax

Exception: *sur'mīse (noun) (cf. sur'mīse (verb))

sus- Etymologically related to **sub-**, but with no very clear meaning. *Stress-repellent in verbs.*

Examples: su'spect (verb) – 'sus,pect (noun)
su'stain
'sŭstenance (stress placed by suffix)

trans- Two distinct prefixes need to be distinguished:
A 'Prepositional' element, with a very clear and constant meaning 'across'; morphologically it is less integrated with the word than is **trans**ᵦ-: it is often set off from the stem by a hyphen. Always bears secondary stress and is pronounced [trænz] or [trɑ:nz-] (or possibly with final [s] instead of [z]). *Stress-neutral.* It behaves like a compound-forming element (see Section 5).

Examples: 'trans-'conti'nental
'transat'lantic

B Genuine prefix, whose meaning is not simply statable in all cases. Morphologically it is very closely attached to the stem: it cannot be set off by a hyphen, and tends to occur with bound forms. *Stress-repellent in verbs*, and when unstressed may be pronounced [trənz-] or [trəns-] by some speakers.

Examples: ,tran'scend
,tran'scrībe

'tran,script (stress placed by suffix -**t**)
,trans'fer (verb) – 'transfer (noun)
,trans'plänt (verb) – 'trans,plänt (noun)

un- Negative prefix, *stress-neutral* and always pronounced with a full vowel. Usually attached to free forms.

Examples: ,un'ĕarth (verb)
,un'fair (adjective)
'uncon'cern (noun)
,un'cömfortable

Appendix 6.2   Stress-Shift across Parts of Speech for Words Involving Prefixes but No Suffixes

For the sake of complete coverage, a number of words are included in these lists which might be better treated as simple roots. There are two lists:

(a)   Words in which no stress-shift takes place
(b)   Words in which stress-shift does occur

The following symbols are used:

† Pronunciation may also show stress-shift: in such cases the verb takes stress on a later syllable than the noun.
§ Certain of the forms which are spelt alike are actually only tenuously, if at all, related in meaning.
‡ Verb ends in [-z], noun or adjective in [-s]: a suffix -s could be involved (cf. p. 97 above).

(a)   Words in which No Stress-Shift Takes Place

‡a'būse, †'ac,cent or 'accent, ac'claim, ac'cord, ac'count, †ad'dress (noun is 'ad,dress in Amer.), ad'vänce, af'frönt, al'lūre, ap'peal, ap'proach, ar'ray, ar'rest, as'sault, at'tack, at'tempt, at'tīre.

col'lapse, com'mänd, 'com,ment, †com'pact, com'pāre, com'plēte, con'cern, 'con,crēte, con'sent, con'serve, con'tent (='(be) satisfied, satisfaction'; the noun 'con,tent (='what is contained') is best regarded as derived from con'tain by the addition of the suffix -**t** (cf. p. 98 above)), con'trōl, cor'rect, cor'rupt.

dē'bāte, 'dēbit, dē'cay, dē'cease, dē'clīne, dē'coy, dē'cree, dē'feat, dē'fault, dē'lay, dē'līght, 'dē,lūge, dē'mänd, dē'pŏsit, dē'sign [-'zaɪn], dē'sīre, dē'spair, dē'spatch, dē'tail (Amer.) or 'dē,tail (Brit.), 'dē,toŭr, ‡dif'fūse, †,dī'lūte, †di'rect or ,dī'rect, †'dis,course [-,kɔ:s], dis'dain, dis'grāce, dis'guise [-'gaɪz], dis'gust, dis'līke, dis'may, dis'play, dis'pūte, dis'quīet, dis'sent, dis'trust, ‡dis'ūse, di'vīde, di'vorce.

ēf'fect, ē'lect, ēm'brāce, ēm'ploy, 'envy, ē'rect, ē'scāpe, †'es,say, ē'steem, §ē'xact, ēx'chānge, ‡ēx'cūse, ēx'haust, §ēx'press, 'ĕ,xīle, 'ĕ,xit.

'fore,cäst, 'forfeit.

†'in,fix, †in'trigue [-'tri:g].

mi'stāke, ,mis'trust, ‡mis'ūse.

ob'scūre, 'offer, 'out,fit, 'out,līne, 'out,rāge, 'ōver'work.

'prē,fix, †'prĕmise, 'prĕsage, prē'serve, 'prē,view, 'prŏ,cess (Brit.) or 'prŏ,cess (Amer.) (verb pro'cess (='walk in procession') is not semantically related), pro'fāne, 'prō,file, 'prŏfit, 'prŏmise, †'pros,pect, 'purchase, 'purpose.

rë'buff, rë'būke, †rë'call, †rë'cess, rë'crüit, rë'dress, rë'form, rë'gard, †rë'gress, rë'gret, rë'lapse, 'rē,lay, rë'lease, 'rĕlish, rë'mänd, rë'mark, †rë'mit, rë'move [rɪ'mu:v], rë'nown, rë'pair, rë'peal, rë'peat, rë'plȳ, rë'port, rë'pōse, rë'prieve, †'rĕpri,mänd, rë'prīse, rë'proach, rë'pulse, rë'pūte, rë'quest, 'res,cue, †rë'sēarch, rë'serve, rë'solve, rë'sort, rë'spect, rë'sult, 'rē,tail, rë'tort, rë'treat, rë'turn, 'rĕvel, rë'verse, rë'view, rë'vōke, rë'vōlt, rë'ward [rɪ'wɔ:d].

sup'port, †'sur,charge, sur'mīse, sur'prīse, sur'round.

(b) Words in which Stress-Shift Does Occur

Verb	Adjective	Noun
,ab'sent	'absent	–
ab'stract	'ab,stract or ab'stract	'ab,stract
,ac'cent or 'ac,cent	–	'ac,cent or 'accent
ad'dict	–	'ad,dict
ad'dress	–	{ad'dress (Brit.) / 'ad,dress (Amer.)
–	a'dept	'ă,dept
af'fix¹	–	'af,fix
al'loy	–	'al,loy
al'lȳ²	–	'al,lȳ
an'nex	–	'an,nex
col'lect	–	§'col,lect
com'bat or 'com,bat	–	'com,bat
com'bīne	–	'com,bīne
com'mūne	–	§'com,mūne
com'pact	com'pact	§'com,pact
com'pound	'com,pound	'com,pound
com'press	–	'com,press
con'cert	–	§'concert
con'cord	–	'con,cord
con'duct	–	'con,duct
con'fīne	–	'con,fīne
con'flict	–	'con,flict
con'script	–	'con,script
con'sort	–	'con,sort
con'struct	–	'con,struct

Verb	Adjective	Noun
con'test	–	'con,test
con'tract	–	'con,tract
con'träst	–	'con,träst
con'verse	§'con,verse	§'con,verse
con'vert	–	'con,vert
con'vict	–	'con,vict
dë'crease	–	'dē,crease
dë'fect	–	§'dē,fect
dë'file	–	§'dē,file
dë'sert	–	'dësert[3]
,dī'gest or di'gest	–	'dī,gest
dis'card	–	'dis,card
dis'charge	–	'dis,charge
dis'count	–	§'dis,count
ën'tail	–	'en,tail
ën'tränce	–	§'entrance
ën'vëlop	–	'enve,lōpe
ë'scort	–	'es,cort
ëx'cerpt	–	'ex,cerpt
ëx'cīse	–	'ex,cīse
ëx'ploit	–	'ex,ploit
ëx'port	–	'ex,port
ëx'tract	–	'ex,tract
frë'quent	'frëquent	–
im'pact	–	'im,pact
im'plänt	–	'im,plänt
im'port	–	'im,port
im'press	–	'im,press
im'print	–	'im,print
in'cense	–	§'in,cense
in'clīne	–	'in,clīne
in'crease	–	'in,crease
in'dent	–	'in,dent
in'fix or 'in,fix	–	'in,fix
in'lay	–	'in,lay
in'sert	–	'in,sert
in'set	'in,set	'in,set
–	in'stinct	'in,stinct
in'sult	–	'in,sult
'inter'cept	–	'inter,cept
'inter'chänge	–	'inter,chänge
'inter'lock	–	'inter,lock
–	in'vălid	§'invalid
–	'in,verse or in'verse	'in,verse
in'vert	'in,vert	'in,vert
in'vīte	–	'in,vīte[4]
–	,mī'nūte	§'mīnute

Verb	Adjective	Noun
ˌmisˈprint	–	ˈmisˌprint
obˈject	–	§ˈobˌject or ˈobjëct
ˌoffˈset	ˈoffˌset	ˈoffˌset
ˈōverˈdōse	–	ˈōverˌdōse
ˈōverˈlap	–	ˈōverˌlap
ˈōverˈlay	–	ˈōverˌlay
ˈōverˈload	–	ˈōverˌload
perˈfect	ˈperˌfect or ˈperfëct	–
perˈfūme	–	ˈperˌfūme
perˈmit	–	ˈperˌmit
perˈplex	–	ˈperˌplex
perˈvert	–	ˈperˌvert
prëˈsent	§ˈprësent	ˈprësent
proˈceed	–	§ˈprōˌceeds
proˈcess	–	{ ˈprōˌcess (Brit.) / ˈprŏˌcess (Amer.) }
proˈduce	–	ˈprŏˌdūce
proˈgress	–	{ ˈprōˌgress (Brit.) / ˈprŏˌgress (Amer.) }
proˈject	–	§ˈprŏˌject
proˈlapse	–	ˈprōˌlapse
proˈspect or ˈprosˌpect	–	§ˈprosˌpect
ˌprŏˈstrāte	ˈprŏˌstrāte	–
proˈtest	–	ˈprōˌtest
purˈport	–	ˈpurˌport
rëˈbel	ˈrëbel	ˈrëbel
ˌrēˈbound	–	ˈrēˌbound
ˌrēˈbuild [-ˈbɪld]	–	ˈrēˌbuild
ˌrēˈcharge	–	ˈrēˌcharge
rëˈcoil	–	ˈrēˌcoil
ˈrĕcomˈpense or ˈrĕcomˌpense	–	ˈrĕcomˌpense
rëˈcord	–	{ ˈrēˌcord (Brit.) / ˈrĕcord (Amer.) }
ˌrēˈcount	–	ˈrēˌcount
ˌrēˈfill	–	ˈrēˌfill
ˌrēˈfit	–	ˈrēˌfit
rëˈfund or ˌrēˈfund	–	ˈrēˌfund
rëˈfūse	–	§‡ˈrēˌfūse
ˌrēˈhash	–	ˈrēˌhash
rëˈject	–	ˈrēˌject
ˌrēˈload	–	ˈrēˌload
ˌrēˈmāke	–	ˈrēˌmāke
ˌrēˈpaint	–	ˈrēˌpaint
ˌrēˈplay	–	ˈrēˌplay
ˈrĕpriˈmänd or ˈrĕpriˌmänd	–	ˈrĕpriˌmänd

Verb	Adjective	Noun
ˌrēˈprint	–	ˈrēˌprint
ˌrēˈrun	–	ˈrēˌrun
rëˈsĕarch	–	ˈrēˌsĕarch or rëˈsĕarch
ˌrēˈtāke	–	ˈrēˌtāke
ˌrēˈtrĕad	–	ˈrēˌtrĕad
surˈvey	–	ˈsurˌvey⁵
suˈspect	ˈsusˌpect	ˈsusˌpect
ˌtränsˈfer or ˌtransˈfer	–	ˈtränsˌfer or ˈtransˌfer
ˌtränsˈform or ˌtransˈform	–	ˈtränsˌform or ˈtransˌform
ˌtränsˈplänt or ˌtransˈplänt	–	ˈtränsˌplänt or ˈtransˌplänt
traˈverse	–	ˈträˌverse
ˈunderˈlīne	–	ˈunderˌlīne
ˌupˈlift	–	ˈupˌlift
ˌupˈset	ˌupˈset	ˈupˌset

Notes

1 In addition to the basic verb **afˈfix** 'to attach (general sense)', there is a verb ˈafˌfix derived from the noun, meaning 'to attach an affix'.
2 The participial adjective ˌalˈlïed is often stressed ˈalˌlïed when attached directly to a noun, e.g. the ˈalˌlïed **forces**. See Section 5.3 for this type of stress-shift.
3 This is the noun meaning 'wasteland'. There is also a noun dëˈsert meaning 'what is deserved', involving the suffix -t.
4 Considered substandard by many speakers.
5 In addition to the basic verb surˈvey 'to look over' there is a verb ˈsurˌvey derived from the noun, meaning 'to conduct a survey'.

Vowel Quality Changes

The vowel quality changes which are most frequent in English can be exemplified by the three related words shown in (1), in which **ex-** is a prefix, **-plain/-plan-** is the root, and the remainder consists of suffixes:

(1) ëx'plain   ex'plănatory   'expla'nātion
     [eɪ]   [æ]   [ə]

The vowel of the root is shown in phonetic transcription in each word, and we can see two types of correspondence:

(a) 'Full' (**explain, explanatory**) v. 'reduced' (**explanation**)
(b) 'Long' (**explain**) v. 'short' (**explanatory**), within the 'full' category.

Sections 7.1 and 7.2 deal with the first type, and Sections 7.3 and 7.4 with the second.

7.1   Vowel Reduction in Relation to Secondary Stress

In the three words just cited, it will be noticed that the vowel of the root **-plain** has a full form in the words where main stress falls on it, and a reduced form [ə] where it is unstressed. Likewise the vowel of the prefix varies depending on its stress: secondary stress (as in **'expla'nātion**) gives a full vowel ([e] in this case) while lack of stress leads to a reduced vowel ([ɪ] in **ëx'plain** and **ëx'plănatory**).[1]

As a rough guide, we can say that vowel reduction will take place in syllables where the stress-assignment rules have assigned no stresses. Two examples are given in Figure 7.1. In the variety of English described in this book, and in many though not all others, there are two distinguishable reduced vowels, [ɪ] and [ə]. An approximate indication of when each is used was given in Table 1.2 above (p. 6), while Table 7.1 gives rather more detail.

In some cases vowel length is also enough to prevent reduction, quite independently of the assignment of main or secondary stress by the rules. Figure 7.2 illustrates this using the word pair **advocāte** (verb) ['ædvəkeɪt] and **advocate** (noun) ['ædvəkət]: the vowel of the final syllable does not receive stress by the rules in either case, but its full quality is maintained in the verb (where it is long) and lost in the noun

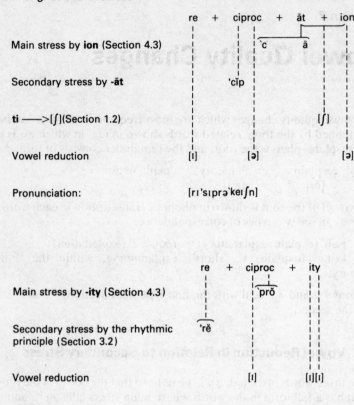

Figure 7.1

(where it is short). A long vowel in a syllable later in a word than main stress (as in the verb `**advocāte**`) may be rhythmically prominent, and this is the basis of the use of the mark , which we introduced earlier (Section 1.2), and which we shall use in these cases even though the long vowel is actually sufficient to rule out reduction. Thus the verb will be represented as `**advo,cāte**`, and transcribed as ['ædvə,keɪt].

We have also used the mark , to indicate non-reduced syllables of other kinds (including some which are not prominent rhythmically); for example the second syllable of 're,la`xation ['ri:,læk`seɪʃn]. Syllables marked in this way have been included under the cover term 'stressed' in, for example, Tables 1.1, 1.2, and 1.3 (pp. 5, 6 above). It must therefore be clearly understood that 'stressed' in this broader sense means strictly '*either* assigned a stress by the application of a rule

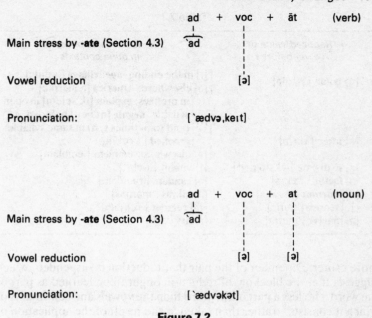

Figure 7.2

or rhythmically prominent *or* specially marked as not undergoing reduction'. The principles governing the blocking of reduction in certain syllables are discussed next.

7.2 Syllable Types Protected from Reducing

There are a number of different conditions under which syllables which have not been stressed by the rules may still resist reduction. We list these in the following paragraphs, beginning with the least systematic types.

1 If reduction would result in the loss of a distinction between a pair of words, it may be suspended in one or both of them. For example, the verbs **exercise** and **exorcise** would undergo stressing and reduction as shown in Figure 7.3, which would mean they were pronounced identically; in fact, however, **exorcise** maintains its second vowel unreduced, and this preserves the distinction between the two words. Another similar pair (though not of the same part of speech this time) is **confident** (adjective) and **confidant** 'person in whom someone confides'. The final syllable of the latter maintains its full vowel and the word is pronounced ['kɒnfɪ,dænt]. In general, it is in the less frequent,

Table 7.1

		Reduced value of vowel before **r**	Reduced value of vowel in other contexts
a	[ə] polar ['pəʊlə]		{ [ɪ] in the ending -*age*: **village** ['vɪlɪdʒ] [ə] elsewhere: **America** [ə'merɪkə]
e	[ə] after ['ɑ:ftə]		{ [ɪ] in prefixes: **explain** [ɪk'spleɪn] in open syllable: **negate** [nɪ'geɪt] before **d, g** (and sometimes **t, n**) in same syllable: **crooked** ['krʊkɪd] [ə] elsewhere: **emblem** ['embləm]
i	[ə] extirpate ['ekstə,peɪt]		[ɪ] **rabbit** ['ræbɪt]
o	[ə] factor ['fæktə]		[ə] **random** ['rændəm]
u	[ə] murmur [mɜ:mə]		[ə] **minus** ['maɪnəs]
ū	[jə] tenure ['tenjə]		[jə] **regular** ['regjələ]
y	[ə] martyr ['mɑ:tə]		[ɪ] **city** ['sɪtɪ]

more esoteric, member of the pair that reduction is suspended, which suggests that the blocking of reduction ought to be learned as part of the word – no less a part of the word than the vowels and consonants of which it consists – rather than taken as the result of the application of an additional rule to the word; if we adopt this suggestion, then we can account for ['ek,sɔː,saɪz] as shown in Figure 7.4. The vowel-pattern of **exercise**, of course, will be accounted for as in Figure 7.3.

It is not entirely clear why certain pairs of words are kept distinct in this way while others are allowed to merge in pronunciation, such as **dependent** (adjective) and **dependant** 'one who is financially dependent on another', which both end in reduced [-ənt].

2   An unstressed short vowel may sometimes retain its full quality even where no distinction would be lost if it were reduced. Thus, alongside regular **orator** ['ɒrətə] with obligatory reduction we have

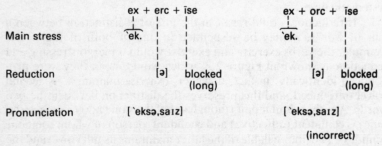

Figure 7.3

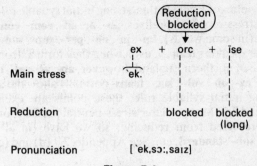

Figure 7.4

matador [ˈmætəˌdɔ:] with full vowel in the final syllable (although there is no word pronounced [ˈmætədə] with which it might be confused). There are also a number of words whose pronunciation varies between full and reduced vowel. Thus some people pronounce **corridor** [ˈkɒrɪˌdɔ:] while others say [ˈkɒrɪdə]. Although there are some endings which appear to favour this unexpected retention of full vowel quality (words ending in -**at**, for example, such as **ˈdɪploˌmăt**, **ˈforˌmăt** and **ˈhăbiˌtăt**), the only sure way is for the learner to memorise the pronunciation of such words, noting specifically that reduction of certain vowels is blocked. A number of these words are listed in Appendix 7.1(a).

3 The first of the systematically predictable cases of full-vowel retention that we shall consider is that of strong initial syllables. If the first syllable of the word has a long vowel, or if it has a short vowel followed by one or more consonants, then it does not undergo reduction. Figure 7.5 illustrates this.

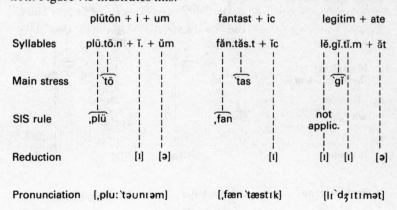

Figure 7.5

In most varieties of English, this 'strong initial syllable rule' does not apply to the stress-repellent prefixes, **ab-, ac, ad-, com-, con-, ec-, em-, en-, ex-, for-** (in some words), **im-, in-, ob-, per-, sub-, suc-, sug-, sur-** (and for some speakers **trans-**), even when they form a strong syllable. In the English of northern England, however, **ab-, ac-, ad-, com-, con-, ec-, em-, en-, ex-, ob-, sub-, suc-, trans-** normally allow the application of the strong initial syllable rule; these points are exemplified in Figures 7.6 and 7.7. Monosyllabic stress-neutral prefixes, on the other hand, are protected from reducing: so we have (in all varieties) ˌex-ˈservice, ˌsub-ˈstandard, etc. See Appendix 7.1 (d) and (e) for more details.

In most cases it can easily be seen whether an initial syllable is strong or weak. If the vowel is long, of course, the syllable is automatically strong, while if the vowel is short the consonants following it can usually be divided between syllables in only one way (see Section 2.2). The exception is where a short vowel if followed by **s** plus one or two consonants, and in this case the syllable boundary may fall either before the **s** (giving a *weak* initial syllable) or after the **s** (giving a *strong* initial syllable). For example, **prospective** is syllabified pro.spec.tiv(e), with a weak initial syllable accounting for the first reduced vowel in [prəˈspektɪv]; **prosperity**, on the other hand, is syllabified pros.pe.ri.ty, with a strong initial syllable accounting for the first full vowel in [ˌprɒsˈperɪtɪ]. Compare also **astronomy** [əˈstrɒnəmɪ] with weak initial syllable and **gastronomy** [ˌgæsˈtrɒnəmɪ] in which the initial syllable must be strong. The weak syllable tends to be favoured when there is a prefix of the same form; thus the **a-** of **astronomy** has the same form as the prefix **a-** of **ahead, astern**, etc., whereas there is no

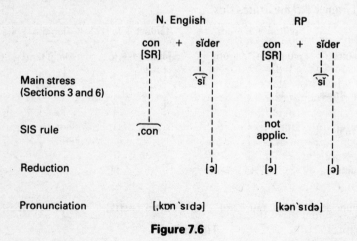

Figure 7.6

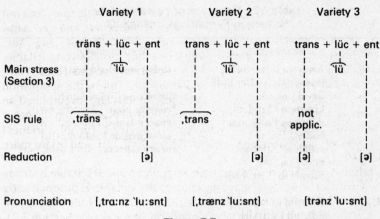

Figure 7.7

prefix **ga-** for the initial syllable of **gastronomy** to model itself on. The word **nasturtium** is unusual in permitting reduction of the initial syllable although there is no prefix **na-**; the British pronunciation of **moustache** [mə'stɑːʃ] is similarly unusual.

Disyllabic prefixes, of course, can always take secondary stress (usually on the first syllable) by the rhythmic principle (Section 3.2), and there is no difference between northern English varieties and the others in this respect. It is of some interest, however, to note that where the second syllable of the prefix **extra-** has main stress assigned to it (as in the word **ex'trapo,late**) its first syllable behaves just like unstressed **ex-**, giving [,ek'stræpə,leɪt] for northern English speakers and [ɪk'stræpə,leɪt] for others.

4   As stated above (Section 3.3 and Section 6.3), when stress-shift occurs in the noun of a noun-verb pair, the root syllable normally does not reduce, but maintains its full vowel quality, e.g. **'im,port** by comparison with **'cömfort** (without stress shift).

5   The last type of unstressed syllable which regularly escapes reduction contains a short vowel followed by a consonant or consonant cluster of a particular type. We can illustrate this with the pair of words **syllabus** and **syllabub**, which differ only in their final consonants; these words are pronounced ['sɪləbəs] and ['sɪlə,bʌb] respectively. The final and penultimate syllables of each are weak, and so main stress falls on the initial syllable in each word. The retention of the full quality [ʌ] for the **u** of **syllabub**, as opposed to the reduction of the **u** of **syllabus**, will be attributed to the difference in final consonant: the final **b** of **syllabub** blocks reduction of the preceding vowel whereas the final **s** of **syllabus** permits it.

Table 7.2　*Reduction of Vowels before Reduction-Permitting Consonants*

Before	Word-finally	Word-medially
zero	**America** [əˈmerɪkə]	**dislo.cate** [ˈdɪslə‚keɪt]
d	**learned** (adj.) [ˈlɜːnɪd]	
l	**naval** [ˈneɪvl̩]	*****incul.cate** [ˈɪnkəl‚keɪt]
m	**kingdom** [ˈkɪŋdəm]	*****contem.plate** [ˈkɒntəm‚pleɪt]
n	**milkman** [ˈmɪlkmən]	**concen.trate** [ˈkɒnsən‚treɪt]
r	**boiler** [ˈbɔɪlə]	**infor.mation** [ˈɪnfəˈmeɪʃn]
s	**syllabus** [ˈsɪləbəs]	**neuras.thenia** [ˈnjʊərəsˈθiːnɪə]
t	**pilot** [ˈpaɪlət]	
th [θ]	**Elizabeth** [ɪˈlɪzəbəθ]	
ld	**emerald** [ˈemərəld]	
lt	*****difficult** [ˈdɪfɪklt]	
mph [mf]	*****triumph** [ˈtraɪəmf]	
nce [ns]	**science** [ˈsaɪəns]	
nd	**husband** [ˈhʌzbənd]	
nt	**elephant** [ˈelɪfənt]	
rd	**Oxford** [ˈɒksfəd]	
rt	**culvert** [ˈkʌlvət]	
st	**earnest** [ˈɜːnəst]	

* Sometimes pronounced with a full vowel in the syllable in question.

In general, unstressed short vowels *reduce* in open syllables and in syllables that end in dental or alveolar consonants or **m**, or in certain (almost all alveolar) consonant clusters; Table 7.2 gives examples. In other types of syllables, unstressed short vowels maintain their full quality *except where the preceding syllable is stressed and weak*. Thus -**b** does not allow reduction of the **u** of **syllabub** (where the preceding syllable, although weak, is unstressed), whereas it *does* allow reduction of the **u** of ʹ**che.rŭb** [ˈtʃerəb] (where the preceding syllable [tʃe] is both weak and stressed). Similarly, the **o** of **hemlock** is not reduced (since the preceding syllable is stressed but strong), whereas the **o** of **hammock** (which is followed by the same consonant as the **o** of **hemlock**) *is* reduced (the preceding syllable being of the form [ˈhæ.], i.e. stressed and weak).[2] Table 7.3 shows words with reduction-blocking consonants occurring in both types of context.

The simplest way of accounting for this rather complicated situation is to distinguish two processes: (1) the blocking of reduction when the vowel is followed by a consonant or cluster of the appropriate type (this could be achieved by counting the syllable as 'stressed' in the broad sense introduced in 7.1 above), and (2) the overriding of this

Table 7.3 · *Treatment of Vowels before Reduction-Blocking Consonants*

Before	Reduction blocked in final syllable	Reduction blocked in medial syllable	Reduction occurring after a stressed weak syllable
b	syllabub [ˈsɪləˌbʌb]		Arab [ˈæ.rəb]
c [k]	almanac [ˈɔːlməˌnæk]	pernoctate [ˈpɜːˌnɒkˌteɪt]	stalactite [ˈstæ.ləkˌtaɪt]
ck [k]	hemlock [ˈhemˌlɒk]		hammock [ˈhæ.mək]
ff	fisticuff [ˈfɪstɪˌkʌf]		
g	gollywog [ˈgɒlɪˌwɒg]	impregnate [ˈɪmˌpregˌneɪt]	stalagmite [ˈstæ.ləgˌmaɪt]
k	anorak [ˈænəˌræk]		dibbuk [ˈdɪ.bək]
ng [ŋ]	boomerang [ˈbuːməˌræŋ]	elongate [ˈiːˌlɒŋˌgeɪt]	shilling [ˈʃɪ.lɪŋ]
p	handicap [ˈhændɪˌkæp]	acceptation [ˈækˌsepˈteɪʃn]	gallop [gæ.ləp]
ph [f]	epitaph [ˈepɪˌtæf] or [ˈepɪˌtɑːf]		seraph [ˈse.rəf]
v [f]	Molotov [ˈmɒləˌtɒf]		
rch=r[k]	oligarch [ˈɒlɪˌgɑːk]		monarch [ˈmɒ.nək]
rg	Brandenburg [ˈbrændənˌbɜːg]		
rk	aardvark [ˈɑːdˌvɑːk]		
sc [sk]			mollusc [ˈmɒ.ləsk]
sk	abelmosk [ˈeɪblˌmɒsk]		damask [ˈdæ.məsk]
x [ks] or [k.s]	equinox [ˈekwɪˌnɒks] or [ˈiː-]	relaxation [ˈriːˌlækˈseɪʃn]	flummox [ˈflʌ.məks]

blocking if the preceding syllable is stressed and weak (this could be achieved by removing the 'stress' assigned to the syllable by process (1), hence the name 'destressing' often applied to process (2)). For examples illustrating this see Figures 7.8, 7.9 and 7.10.

There are exceptions of several kinds:

(a) Cases where vowels do not reduce before a reduction-permitting consonant or cluster, e.g. **caravan** [ˈkærəˌvæn], **exorcise** [ˈekˌsɔːˌsaɪz];

(b) Cases where vowels do not reduce even though they occur in the right context for destressing to apply, e.g. **hiccup** [ˈhɪˌkʌp];

(c) Cases where vowels reduce even though they occur before a reduction-blocking consonant and are not in a destressing context, e.g. **Jacob** [ˈdʒeɪkəb].

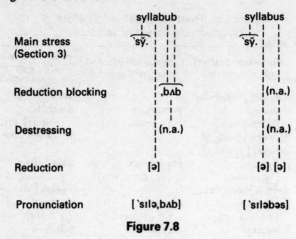

Figure 7.8

There are a number of words in which reduction fails to occur in some varieties but occurs in others. **Amazon**, for instance, is ['æmə‚zɑ:n] for most American English speakers, but ['æməzən] for most British speakers. In almost all these exceptional cases, whether or not they are variable, there is no substitute for noting each individual word as an exception; a fairly complete list of such anomalies is given in Appendix 7.1. However, one or two classes of exceptions are more systematic, and are worth noting:

(i)   Scientific words ending in -on, e.g. **electron** [ɪ'lek‚trɒn], **neon**

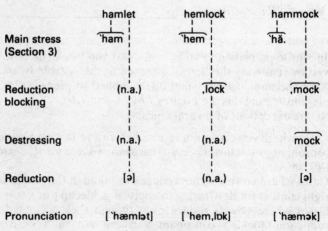

Figure 7.9

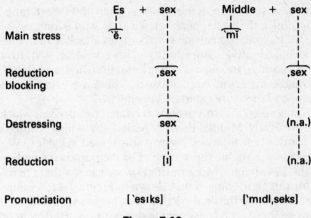

Figure 7.10

['ni:,ɒn] (though not the more common **carbon** ['kɑ:bən]); or in **-ol**, e.g. **phenol** ['fi:,nɒl]; or a few other combinations;

(ii)   Many nouns derived from verbs by stress-shift, e.g. the second syllable of **convert** ['kɒn,vɜ:t] from the verb **convert** [kən'vɜ:t] (this should be contrasted with the second syllable of the noun **culvert** ['kʌlvət] not derived from a verb); see also Section 6.3 above. This type of exception is so regular that it is not specially noted in Appendix 7.1.

7.3   Vowel Shortening Rules

We now come to a consideration of the relationship exemplified by the pair **explain-explanatory** cited in the introduction to this section. Most of the pairs of this kind show exactly the correspondences between vowels which are incorporated in the system of notation used in this book (vowel letter plus macron compared with the same letter without macron or with a breve mark). There are, however, one or two sporadic correspondences which are worth noting:

(a)   [aʊ]/[ʌ]:   pro'found/pro'fundity, pro'nounce/pro'nunci'ation;
(b)   [ju:]/[ʌ]:   'pūnitive/'pŭnish (even though the 'short' vowel corresponding to [ju:] is normally [ju:] itself);
(c)   [ɔɪ]/[ʌ]:   'join/'junction;
(d)   [a:]/[æ]:   'drāma/'drămatist;
(e)   [i:]/[æ]:   'clear/'clărify, ap'pear/ap'părent;
(f)   [i:]/[ɪ]:   'imbe,cïle/'imbe'cïlity.

1   The easiest way of remembering when this shortening takes place is to notice that it happens when a stem with a long vowel in its final syllable has one of a certain set of suffixes attached to it; this set of suffixes includes: **-ative, -atory, -(e)fy, -(i)fy, -ic, -ical, -ics, -itive, -ity, -tude, -ual, -uant, -uate, -uous**. Full information on shortening is given under all these affixes in Appendix 4.1. There are exceptions to the shortening, and these are listed in Appendix 7.2.

Historically speaking, this process is related to a process which took place in the Early Middle English period, by which a long vowel became short when followed by two unstressed syllables. We shall refer to this as 'trisyllabic shortening'. For the purpose of understanding how this has affected Modern English, we can say that the relevant context for this shortening is that shown in Figure 7.11; an important point to notice is that the final syllable must begin with at least one consonant (when there is no consonant in this position, a different process is likely to take place – cf. Figure 7.13 below, and also Section 7.4). The penult must also begin with at least one consonant, since otherwise the long vowel would come immediately before the vowel of the penult – a position in which vowels are always long (see 7.4 below).

It can be seen that many, though not all, of the suffixes listed above are of such a structure that, when added to a stem whose final syllable contains a long vowel, they produce exactly the context needed for 'trisyllabic shortening', and the change might just as easily be regarded as being brought about by this rather than by the properties

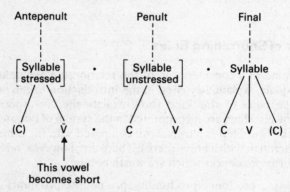

C represents one or more consonants
(C) represents zero, one or more consonants.

'Antepenult', 'Penult' and 'Final' refer to the corresponding syllables of the *stressable portion* of the word in question.

Figure 7.11

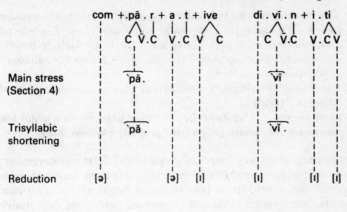

Pronunciation [kəmˈpærətɪv]   [dɪˈvɪnɪtɪ]

The vowel of the second syllable of each of the above examples is marked *long* because it is long when the stem occurs without the suffix. We are thus regarding **compărative** as being formed by adding the suffix **-ative** to the free form **compāre** and then letting the relevant rules apply.

Figure 7.12

of the suffixes (see Figure 7.12). However, for **-ic, -ics, -ual, -uant, -uate** and **-uous**, the accentual properties will need to be brought in, as the context for 'trisyllabic shortening' will not be set up by adding these suffixes.

2   Do we then need a rule of 'trisyllabic shortening' as well as a rule for shortening vowels before certain suffixes? The fact is that English words demonstrate an overwhelming tendency to have short vowels in this position, even when they are not derived from a form containing a long vowel. Thus words like ˈcăbinet, ˈĕmerald, ˈrĕtina and ˈvăgaˌbond are very much more numerous than words like ˈāpriˌcot, ˈdȳnamo, ˈīvory, ˈōmega. In fact, 'trisyllabic shortening' is a useful, largely productive rule enabling the learner to predict that the vowel of a stressed open antepenult will be short.

Exceptions to 'trisyllabic shortening' usually fall into one of the following types:

(a)   The short version of ū [juː] is also pronounced [juː]: thus ˈcūpola, ˈmūtiˌlāte, ˈūniˌcorn are only apparent exceptions. The same holds for ü after those consonants where ū does not occur (see note to Table 1.6 in Section 1 above, p. 8): adˈjüdiˌcate, ˈlüdicrous, ˈrübicund.

(b) Vowels written with two letters regularly remain long: `ˈcausative ['kɔ:-], `ˈOedipus ['i:-] (though note American English pronunciation with ['e-]), `ˈsouveˌnïr ['su:-]. If such a vowel is shortened, the spelling is usually changed: ex`ˈplain – ex`ˈplănatory

(c) Stress-neutral suffixes do not normally cause shortening: `ˈfīnally, `ˈlāziness, `ˈvōcalist.

(d) Compounds: `ˈmōtorˌbīke,   `ˈōverˌpäss,   ˌtor`ˈpēdō-ˌboat, `ˈmīcroˌphōne, `ˈphōtoˌgräph (or -ˌgrăph), `ˈchrōmoˌsōme.

Other exceptions are listed in Appendix 7.2. It is interesting to observe that a large number of these true exceptions are words whose antepenult has a zero onset (i.e. does not begin with a consonant): alongside the regular `ˈĂbiˌgail, `ˈĕmerald, etc., are a relatively numerous set of words like `ˈāpriˌcot, `ˈīvory, `ˈōmega, etc. Perhaps there is a need for such antepenultimate syllables without onsets to be strengthened in some way. One way of achieving this would be to have shortening blocked.

3   Shortening also takes place in the contexts represented by Figure 7.13, which is similar to Figure 7.11, but with no initial consonant in the

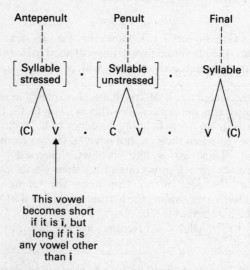

C and (C) are as for Figure 7.11.
'Antepenult', 'Penult' and 'Final' refer to the corresponding syllables of the *stressable portion* of the word in question.

Figure 7.13

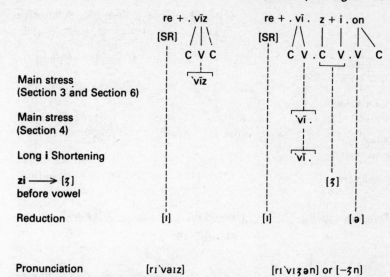

Figure 7.14

The vowel of the second syllable of **revision** is marked long because it is long in **revise**. We are regarding **revision** as being formed by adding the suffix **-ion** to the free form **revise** and then letting the relevant rules apply.

final syllable; it is restricted in such cases to the vowel **ī** (and occasionally **ȳ**) – for examples see Figure 7.14. We shall refer to this process as 'long **i** shortening'. Note that when any vowel other than **i** or **y** occurs in this context it is almost invariably *long* (if short, it is *lengthened* – see 7.4.2 below).

7.4 Vowel Lengthening Rules

1   A stressed vowel preceding another vowel is always long in English ˈchaos [ˈkeɪˌɒs], soˈciety [səˈsaɪɪtɪ]. This applies to many unstressed vowels as well: preˈamble [priːˈæmbl], chaˈotic [ˌkeɪˈɒtɪk].

If any stem ending in a short vowel is followed immediately by a suffix beginning with a vowel, one of three things may happen:

(a)   The short vowel is deleted: **Canada** plus **-ian** becomes **Canad+ian** (and eventually **Caˈnād+ian** – see 7.4.2 below), **vertigo** plus **-inous** becomes **vertig+in+ous**, **tympani** plus **-ist** becomes **tympan+ist**.

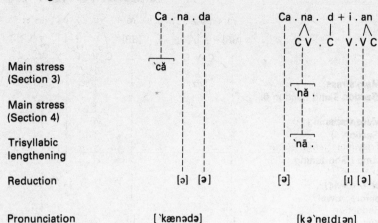

Figure 7.15

(b) The short vowel remains, but is not stressed – it does not lengthen: **soci** plus **-al** becomes ˋsoci+al (and eventually ˋsōci+al – see 7.4.2 below).

(c) The short vowel is stressed, and then becomes lengthened: **algebra** plus **-ic** becomes 'algeˋbra+ic and then 'algeˋbrā+ic ['æ1dʒɪ'breɪk], **soci** plus **-ety** becomes soˋci+ety and then soˋcī+ety [sə'saɪɪtɪ]. We shall refer to this as 'VV lengthening'.

2　In the contexts represented by Figure 7.13, all vowels other than **i** and **y** lengthen (if they are not already long); this is the process which applies to **Canad+ian** and **soci+al** (see 7.4.1 above, and also Figures 7.15 and 7.16). It should be borne in mind that the 'shortening' affixes **-ual**, **-uant**, **-uate**, and **-uous** do not participate in this 'trisyllabic lengthening' (cf. 7.3 above). Interestingly, just as 'trisyllabic shortening' turned out to be a general process governing the length pattern of the large majority of the relevant antepenultimate-stressed words, so 'trisyllabic lengthening' governs the length pattern of most of the words which have (i) stressed open antepenults, and (ii) final syllables without initial consonants. Again there are exceptions, such as ˋspĕcial, ˋvăliant, with *short* open antepenults: these are listed in Appendix 7.3.

3　The vowels **o** and **u** are always long when word-final (see Section 2.2): ˋhēro ['hɪərəu], ˋcargo ['kɑ:gəu], ˋrādio ['reɪdɪəu], ˋmĕnu ['menju:]. The final syllables may be given rhythmic prominence: ['hɪə,rəu], ['kɑ:,gəu], ['reɪdɪ,əu], ['me,nju:].

4　Word-final short **i**, as in **taxi**, and short **y**, as in **city** may be heard

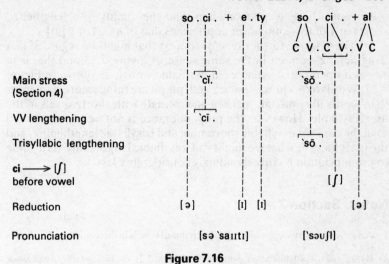

Figure 7.16

in a wide range of pronunciations depending on regional and social factors; in some varieties they may be as close phonetically as the vowel [i] and in others as open as [e]. Some speakers may physically lengthen this sound, and in some cases it may be as long as a genuinely long vowel; however, such lengthening does not form part of the *system* of lengthening which we have denoted by the use of the macron

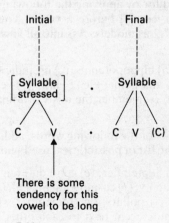

C and (C) are as for Figure 7.11.
'Initial' and 'Final' refer to the corresponding syllables of the *stressable portion* of the word in question.

Figure 7.17

– it is not a 'yes/no' phenomenon, and the quality of a lengthened short i or y of this kind never approaches that of long ī or ȳ [aɪ].

5   There is one further type of context that might be regarded as a 'lengthening' context in the same sense as Figure 7.13 and that is in stressed open initial syllables in disyllabic words, as shown in Figure 7.17. Words like 'chī.na, 'mē.tre and 'pū.pil are rather more numerous than words like 'mĕ.tal, 'prĭ.son and 'sĕ.nate with short vowels in the initial syllable. However, the preponderance is not nearly so marked as in the cases of trisyllabic shortening and trisyllabic lengthening, and the usefulness of what we might call 'disyllabic lengthening' as a guide to pronunciation is correspondingly considerably less.

Notes: Section 7

1   Actually not every variety of English has reduced vowels in these prefixes. For details see 7.2.3.
2   By the rules of syllabification given above (Section 2.2), the first syllable of **hammock** would have the form **ham**, which is a strong syllable. However, the process we are discussing at the present moment deals with the *pronounced* form rather than the *written* form, and from this point of view the division is /hă.mok/.

Exercises

1   Show how, in the words given below, stress- and vowel-patterns can be accounted for by applying the following rules: main stress, secondary stress, ci→[ʃ] before a vowel, vowel reduction. Use Figures 7.1 and 7.2 as models. Assume all vowels are short unless marked long.

(*a*) matern+al, (*b*) hippopotamus, (*c*) prejudic+i+al, (*d*) gramin+i+fer+ous, (*e*) mathemat+ic+i+an, (*f*) epistolo+graph+ic, (*g*) generalissimo (remember the **o** is word-final), (*h*) valetūdin+āri+an.

2   The same exercise for the following words, adding the strong initial syllable rule to the list of possibilities (use Figure 7.5 as a model).

(*a*) artichōke, (*b*) September, (*c*) con+dit+ion+al, (*d*) magnific+ent, (*e*) cosmo+log+y, (*f*) cosmo+log+ic+al, (*g*) re+pet+it+ive, (*h*) lōc+āt+ion, (*j*) pollūt+ion (remember what happens when identical consonants occur next to each other within the SP; see Section 2, p. 21).

3   The same exercise, adding reduction blocking and destressing to the list of rules (model of Figures 7.8, 7.9 and 7.10).

(*a*) Alec, (*b*) almanac, (*c*) Aztec, (*d*) canvas, (*e*) carob, (*f*) de+velop, (*g*) handicap, (*h*) Lilliput, (*j*) maximum, (*k*) nābob, (*l*) re+cogn+īse, (*m*) scallywag, (*n*) sentinel, (*o*) Slōvak, (*p*) Tagälog.

4 The same exercise, adding the three shortening rules (suffix, tri-syllabic, and long **i**) to the list of rules (model of Figures 7.12 and 7.14).

(*a*) de+cīs+ion (long **i**, cf. de'cīsive, and the verb stem de'cīde), (*b*) de+clār+at+ive (long **a**, cf. de'clāre), (*c*) ex+trēm+ity (long **e**, cf. ex'trēme), (*d*) fāc+i+al (long **a**, cf. 'fāce), (*e*) in+flāt+ion (long **a**, cf. in'flāte), (*f*) tele+phōn+ic (long **o**, cf. 'tele,phōne).

5 The same exercise, adding the two lengthening rules (trisyllabic, and VV) to the list (model of Figures 7.15 and 7.16).

(*a*) barŏn+i+al (short **o**, cf. baron ['bærən]), (*b*) electr+ĭc+i+an (short **i**, cf. e'lectr[ɪ]c, 'elec'tr[ɪ]city), (*c*) formulă+ic (short **a**, cf. 'formul[ə]), (*d*) ignomĭn+i+ous (short **i**, cf. 'ignom[ɪ]ny), (*e*) mamm+ăl+i+an (short **a**, cf. 'mamm[ə]l), (*f*) manag+ĕr+i+al (short **e**, cf. 'manag[ə]r).

6 In the following pairs of words, both members of each pair are clearly derived from the same root; taking as given the rules in the preceding section, say whether the form of the root with the *long* vowel or the form with the *short* vowel ought to be taken as basic, and state the rules which must apply in order to account for the other form. (Note: you may need to bring in other words with the same root before you can make a decision; even then, there may be cases where no final decision is possible.)

(*a*) 'grain (/grān/), 'grănū,lāte
(*b*) fe'lōn+i+ous, 'felŏn+y
(*c*) ar'thr+īt+is, ar'thr+ĭt+ic
(*d*) bar'bār+i+an, bar'băr+ic
(*e*) fe'rōc+i+ous, fe'rŏc+ity
(*f*) hys'tēria, hys'tĕr+ic+al
(*g*) di'vīs+or, di'vĭs+ion

7 All the following words are exceptions to at least one rule given in Section 7. State which rule or rules each one violates.

(*a*) annexation ['æ,nek'seɪʃn], (*b*) Atlantic [ət'læntɪk], (*c*) Joseph ['dʒəuzəf], (*d*) Negev ['ne,gev], (*e*) obesity [ə'bi:sɪtɪ], (*f*) wombat ['wɒm,bæt].

8 Each of the following words has two pronunciations as shown; state which pronunciation is irregular, and which of the rules of Section 7 it violates.

		(i)	(ii)
(a)	dandruff	[ˈdæn,drʌf]	[ˈdændrəf]
(b)	hedonist	[ˈhiːdə,nɪst]	[ˈhedə,nɪst]
(c)	patriot	[ˈpeɪtrɪət]	[ˈpætrɪət]
(d)	perfect (adj.)	[ˈpɜːˌfekt]	[ˈpɜːfɪkt]
(e)	record (noun)	[ˈre,kɔːd]	[ˈrekəd]
(f)	vitamin	[ˈvaɪtəmɪn]	[ˈvɪtəmɪn]

Further Reading

(Where full bibliographical details of a work are not given, they may be found in the 'Further Reading' for Section 1. See pp. 14–16 above).

7.1   Vowel Reduction in Relation to Secondary Stress

On vowel reduction see Jespersen, *Modern English Grammar*, Part I, pp. 248–79, and on its relation to secondary stress see Chomsky and Halle, *Sound Pattern*, pp. 110–26; Hill and Nessly's review of *Sound Pattern* (Goyvaerts and Pullum, *Essays*, pp. 93–100, 110–11); and Guierre, *Essai*, pp. 137–57, 187–97.

7.2   Syllable Types Protected from Reducing

On the strong initial syllable rule see Chomsky and Halle, *Sound Pattern*, p. 118 and Guierre, *Essai*, pp. 244–5. For the **syllabus/syllabub** difference consult Ross, 'Reanalysis', pp. 241–58.

7.3   Vowel Shortening Rules

Chomsky and Halle use the term 'laxing' for our 'shortening' in their detailed treatment (*Sound Pattern*, pp. 50–5, 178–87). Jespersen, *Modern English Grammar*, Part I, pp. 139–45, and Guierre, *Essai*, pp. 86–95, 233–310, are also worth reading.

7.4   Vowel Lengthening Rules

The Chomsky and Halle reference (see preceding section) is also relevant for lengthening (their 'tensing'); again, Guierre, *Essai*, pp. 69–85, 172–232, 522–31, 557–9, is useful.

Appendix 7.1   Anomalies in Vowel-Reduction

There are six lists:

(a)   Expected reduction not applied: final syllables ending in a reduction-permitting consonant or cluster preceded by a short vowel;

(b) Expected reduction not applied: rule of 'de-stressing' suspended in final syllables;
(c) Expected reduction not applied: non-final syllables;
(d) Reduction applied unexpectedly: strong initial syllable rule suspended in prefixes;
(e) Reduction applied unexpectedly: strong initial syllable rule suspended other than in prefixes;
(f) Reduction applied unexpectedly: reduction-blocking consonants not blocking reduction.

(a) Reduction Suspended before Reduction-Permitting Elements

Note: The following types of words are not shown:

(i) Words with suffixes which have non-reduction as one of their accentual properties: 'nē‚on, 'trī‚ad.
(ii) Compounds: 'sail‚cloth.
(iii) Prefixed words showing stress-shift: 'com‚bat.
(iv) Reduplicated words: 'can‚can, 'tom‚tom.

On the other hand, we have included French loan-words ending in a consonant (usually **t**) which is not pronounced (this leads to the vowel of the final syllable becoming long).
The following signs are used:

* Final syllable reduction takes place for some speakers.
† Some speakers have final stress (and *ipso facto* no vowel reduction) in these words.
§ Reduction blocked in order to ensure pronunciation of **h**.

Words ending in **-d**: 'cō‚ed, 'drȳ‚ad, 'ē‚phod, §'Gāla‚had, 'gŏ‚nad, 'Ïcha‚bod ['ɪkə-], *'Ïli‚ad, 'mŏ‚nad (or 'mō-), 'näi‚ad, 'Nim‚rod, 'nō‚mad (or 'nōmad with vowel reduction), O'lympi‚ad, *'sȳ‚nod.

-l: §'alco‚hol, 'Anna‚bel, 'an‚vil, 'ă‚toll, 'bĕcha‚mel [-ʃə-], 'călo‚mel, 'căra‚cal, 'căra‚col, *'căra‚mel, 'căra‚vel, 'căsca‚bel, 'daffo‚dil, 'dē‚cal, *'ē‚vil, 'Ïsa‚bel, *'Jĕze‚bel, 'men‚thol, *'mis‚tral (or -‚träl), 'păral‚lel, 'păra‚sol, 'phē‚nol, 'phĭlo‚mel, 'pimper‚nel, 'prōto‚col, 'tormen‚til, *'wee‚vil.

-m: §'Ābra‚ham, §'Bethlë‚hem, 'dīa‚dem, *'dīa‚tom, §ë'lō‚him, 'ïbi‚dem, 'Is‚lam (or -‚läm), §'may‚hem, 'quon‚dam, 'wig‚wam (or [-‚wɒm]).

-n: *'Āma‚zon, 'ănaco'lü‚thon, *'Băby‚lon, 'ban‚yan, †'ba‚ton, 'bouil‚lon ['buɪ‚jɒn], *'caf‚tan, 'Căli‚ban, †'căra‚van, 'căril‚lon [-‚jɒn], †'cătama‚ran, 'chif‚fon ['ʃɪ‚fɒn], 'chi‚gnon ['ʃiː‚njɒn], *'cō‚lon, 'cŏlo‚phon, 'cor‚don (in the phrase **cordon bleu** only: the noun meaning 'police or soldiers surrounding an area' and its derived verb are both pronounced ['kɔː‚dn]). 'coü‚pon, 'cram‚pon, 'croü‚ton, 'ĕche‚lon ['eʃə-], 'ĕty‚mon, *'gnō‚mon ['nəʊ-], 'ï‚con, *'lĕxi‚con, li'ai‚son, 'mă‚cron, *'măra‚thon, †'marzi‚pan, *'măsto‚don, 'mō‚ron, 'neu‚ron, 'nȳ‚lon, *'Ŏrë‚gon, 'ŏxy'mō‚ron, *'păra‚gon, 'pē‚on, *'plank‚ton,

*ˈpȳ͵lon, *ˈRübi͵con, ˈsă͵lon, ˈsam͵pan, *ˈsïli͵con, ˈsoüp͵çon [ˈsu:p͵sɒn], ˈtam͵pon, ˈtar͵pon.

-r: ˈăva͵tar, *ˈcan͵tor, ˈcăvi͵ar, ˈcinna͵bar, ˈcon͵dor, ͵conˈquista͵dor, corˈrĕgi͵dor, *ˈcŏrri͵dor, ˈcŭspi͵dor, ˈDă͵kar, ˈdĕ͵cor (or [ˈdeɪ-]), ˈdēo͵dar, ˈdī͵nar, ëxˈcelsi͵or, †ˈguăran͵tor [ˈgæ-], ˈhūmi͵dor, ˈin͵star, *ˈjăgū͵ar, ˈLăbra͵dor, ˈLas͵car, ˈlec͵tor, ˈMag͵yar, ˈMăla͵bar, ˈmăta͵dor, *ˈmĕta͵phor, *ˈmētë͵or, ͵monˈsï͵gnor [-͵njɔ:], ˈNes͵tor, ˈpïca͵dor, *ˈreal͵tor, ˈsămo͵var, ˈsĕmi͵nar, ˈsir͵dar, ˈsï͵tar, ˈtŏrëa͵dor.

-s: ˈalba͵tross, ˈbā͵thos, ˈblunder͵buss, ˈbū͵gloss, ˈchă͵os [ˈkeɪ-], ˈcos͵mos, ˈē͵ros, ˈē͵thos (or ˈĕ-), ˈfră͵cas [-͵kɑ:], ˈgrăvi͵tas, ˈkū͵dos, ˈlŏ͵gos, ˈpalli͵asse, ˈpā͵thos, ˈrere͵dos [ˈrɪə-], ˈsassa͵fras, ˈtrī͵pos.

-t: ˈăcro͵bat, ˈaegro͵tat [ˈaɪ-] or [ˈi:-], *ˈalpha͵bet, ˈāpri͵cot, ˈar͵got [-gəʊ], ˈas͵set, ˈăvo͵cet, †ˈbal͵let [-͵leɪ], ˈbĕ͵ret [-͵reɪ], ˈberga͵mot, ˈbuf͵fet [-͵feɪ] (meaning 'light meal or place where such meals are served'; the verb buffet 'to knock about' is regular – [ˈbʌfɪt]), ˈcăba͵ret [-͵reɪ], ˈcăbrio͵let [-͵leɪ], ˈcăcha͵lot [ˈkæʃə-], ˈcă͵chet [-͵ʃeɪ], ˈcălū͵met, ˈCăme͵lot, ˈcăvë͵at, ˈchă͵let [ˈʃæ͵leɪ], conˈcor͵dat, ˈcrō͵chet [-͵ʃeɪ], ˈcrō͵quet [-͵keɪ], ˈde͵but [ˈdeɪ͵bju:], ˈdïplo͵mat, †ˈĕpau͵let, ˈĕpi͵thet, *ˈëxë͵at, ˈfor͵mat, ˈgoür͵met [-͵meɪ], ˈhăbi͵tat, ˈhări͵cot [-͵kəʊ], ˈHotten͵tot, ˈHügue͵not [-gə͵nəʊ], ˈlā͵bret (or ˈlă-), ͵magˈnïfi͵cat, *ˈnou͵gat [-͵ga:] (or [-͵gət] when reduction takes place), ˈŏce͵lot, *ˈpăra͵pet, ˈpar͵quet [-͵keɪ], ˈpier͵rot [ˈpjɛə͵rəʊ], ˈrïco͵chet [-͵ʃeɪ], ˈsă͵bot [-͵bəʊ], ˈsă͵chet [-͵ʃeɪ], ˈsor͵bet [-͵beɪ], ˈsoübri͵quet [-͵keɪ], ˈtă͵rot [-͵rəʊ], ˈtoürni͵quet [-͵keɪ], *ˈvă͵let [-͵leɪ] (or [ˈvælət] when reduction takes place), *ˈwain͵scot, ˈwom͵bat.

-th: ˈă͵zoth, Bëˈhē͵moth, ˈSă͵bā͵oth, *ˈshibbo͵leth, ˈSuc͵coth.

-z: ˈAlca͵traz, ˈDï͵az, Ferˈnan͵dez (and other Spanish names ending in **-ez**), *†ˈSü͵ez, ˈtō͵paz.

-ld: ˈpie͵bald [-͵bɔ:ld], ˈskew͵bald [-͵bɔ:ld].

-lt: †ˈă͵dult, ˈas͵phalt, ˈbā͵salt [-͵sɔ:lt] (or ˈbă-), *ˈcăta͵pult, ˈcō͵balt [-͵bɔ:lt], *ˈdiffi͵cult, ˈpĕ͵nult, *ˈtū͵mult.

-nd: ˈamper͵sand, ˈcontra͵band, ˈcummer͵bund, ˈdachs͵hund [ˈdæks͵hʊnd], ˈdïvi͵dend, ˈgoür͵mand [-͵mɒŋ], ˈmultipli͵cand, ˈŏpe͵rand, ˈordi͵nand, ˈŏro͵tund, ˈsăra͵band, ˈstī͵pend, ˈsubtra͵hend, ˈvăga͵bond, ˈvïli͵pend.

-nt: *ˈad͵vent, ˈcomman͵dant, ˈcom͵ment, ˈconfi͵dant, *ˈcon͵vent, ˈcrois͵sant [ˈkrwæ͵sɒŋ], ˈdes͵cant, ˈgalli͵vant, ˈHellës͵pont, ˈmalcon͵tent, ˈpen͵chant [ˈpɒŋ͵ʃɒŋ], ˈpï͵quant [-͵kɒŋ], ˈsă͵vant [-͵vɒŋ], ˈsȳco͵phant. (Note also ˈdēbū͵tănte or -͵tänte, in which the final **-e** is not pronounced, thus putting the word in the [nt] class as far as pronunciation is concerned.)

-nth: ˈăma͵ranth, ˈcoela͵canth [ˈsi:-], ˈtrăga͵canth.

-rd: ˈĂbe͵lard, ˈBal͵lard, ˈblack͵guard [ˈblæ͵gɑ:d], ˈboüle͵vard, caˈmëlo͵pard (or ˈcămelo͵pard), ˈcă͵nard, ˈdul͵lard, ˈfoü͵lard, ˈHan͵sard, ˈLol͵lard, ˈLom͵bard, *ˈman͵sard, ˈplă͵card, ˈpol͵lard, ˈRey͵nard, ˈRic͵kard, ˈspïke͵nard, *ˈtă͵bard.

-rn: ˈă͵corn, ˈCăpri͵corn, ˈcŏmin͵tern, ˈtăci͵turn, ˈūni͵corn.

-rs: There are no relevant words whose spelling ends in **-rs**, but note the following words ending in **-rse** where **e** is not pronounced: 'ad,verse (or ad've̦rse), 'con,course [-,kɔ:s], 'dī,verse (or ,dī've̦rse), 'inter,course [,kɔ:s], 'ob,verse, 'ūni,verse.

-rt: 'ad,ve̦rt, 'Bō,gart, §'cō,hort, 'ex,pert, 'măla,pert, 'Mō,zart ['məut,sa:t], 'ram,part.

-st: 'arba,lest, 'bom,bast, 'com,post, 'flabber,gast, 'in,cest, 'in,quest, *'inte,rest, 'măni,fest, 'pălimp,sest, 'Pentë,cost, †'rō,bust.

(b) 'De-stressing' Suspended in Final Syllables

Note: The following types of words are not shown:
    (i) Compounds: 'set-,up.
    (ii) Prefixed words showing stress-shift: 'an,nex (noun, from verb an'nex).

The following signs are used:
*   Final syllable reduction takes place for some speakers.
†   Some speakers have final stress (and *ipso facto* no vowel reduction) in these words.
‡   Some speakers have a long vowel in the penultimate syllable; 'de-stressing' cannot apply in this context.

†'ă,dult, *'ă,rak, 'as,set, 'ă,toll, 'ă,zoth.

'Bal,lard, ‡'bă,salt, †'bă,ton.

'că,nard, 'chif,fon, 'com,ment, 'Cos,sack.

'Dă,kar, 'dĕ,lūge, 'dul,lard.

‡'ĕ,thos.

'fen,nec, 'fră,cas [-,ka:].

'gŏ,nad.

'hic,cup ['hɪ,kʌp], 'Hic,kok, 'Hil,lel, 'hub,bub.

'ĭ,dyll.

'Kel,logg.

‡'lă,bret, 'lŏ,gos, 'Luc,kock.

'mă,cron, ‡'mŏ,nad.

'Nĕ,gev.

'Pă,nov, 'pĕ,nult, 'phă,lanx, 'phy̆,sog, 'plă,card, 'pol,lex, *'Pol,lux, 'pŏ,tash, *'prŏ,duct.

*'rĕ,cord, 'Ric,kard.

'să,lon, 'să,trap, 'să,vant [-,vɒŋ], 'sĭ,tar, 'Suc,coth, *'sy̆,nod.

*'tă,bard, 'tĕ,trad.

‡'Xĕ,rox ['ze-].

(c) Unexpectedly Unreduced Non-Final Syllables

Note: There are two main types of these:

(i) Syllables ending in reduction-permitting consonants;
(ii) Syllables where 'de-stressing' might be expected to apply.

The following signs are used:

*   Some speakers have a pronunciation with a reduced vowel.
†   Expected 'de-stressing' does not apply.

†'ā,dap'tātion, †'af,fec'tātion, †'an,nĕ'xātion, †'at,tes'tātion, *'aug,men'tā-tion, *'aus,cul,tāte, *'aus,cul'tātion.

†'Că,mem,bert   ['kæ,mɒm,bɛə],   †'col,lec'tĭvity,   †'com,men'dātion, 'com,part'mental, *'com,pen,sāte, *'com,pen'sātion, 'comple,men'tātion, *'con,dem'nātion, *'con,den'sātion, *'con,for'mātion, †'con,nec'tĭvity, *'con,tem,plāte, *'con,tem'plātion.

'dē,fal,cāte, 'dē,fal'cātion, 'dē,mar,cāte, 'dē,mar'cātion, 'dē,part'mental, 'dē,por'tātion, 'dē,tes'tātion, *'dis'ōri,en,tāte, *'dis,ōri,en'tātion, *'dis,pen-'sātion, *'dŏcū,men'tātion.

'ē,lon,gāte, 'ē,lon'gātion, 'em,bar'kātion, 'ē,men'dātion, 'ĕ,xal'tātion ['eg,zɔ:l-], 'ex,cul,pāte, 'ex,cul'pātion, 'ex,hor'tātion ['eg,zɔ:-], 'ĕ,xor,cīse, 'ĕ,xor,cist, 'ĕ,xul'tātion.

*'fer,men'tātion, *'frag,men'tātion.

*'implë,men'tātion, 'in,can'tātion, 'in,car'nātion, *'in,crus'tātion, *'in,cul-,cāte, 'in,cul,pāte, 'in,cul'pātion, 'in,cur'vātion, 'in,den'tātion, *'in,fes'tātion, *†'in,ner'vātion, *'instru,men'tātion, *†'ĭ,nun,dāte, *†'ĭ,nun'dātion.

*†'lă,men'tātion.

*'măni,fes'tātion, †'mŏ,les'tātion.

*'ōri,en,tāte, *'ōri,en'tātion, *'os,ten'tātion, *'os,ten'tatious.

'prŏ,lon'gātion (or †'prŏ-), *†'prŏ,tes'tātion.

'rĕcom,men'dātion, *'rĕpre,sen'tātion, 'rē,tar'dātion, 'rē,ten'tĭvity.

*'seg,men'tātion, †'sŭ,bor'nātion, *'supplë,men'tātion.

*'trans,por'tātion (or *'träns-).

'ū,sur'pātion.

(d) Unexpectedly Reduced Strong Initial Syllables in Prefixes

Note: In all these prefixes (except those ending in **r**, i.e. **for₁**, **per-** and **sur-**), speakers from northern England will normally *not* reduce the vowel.

The following signs are used:

* These exceptions to the general principle have an alternative pronunciation in which the vowel of the initial syllable reduces.

A, B, C, 1 These subscripts refer to the relevant sub-type of the particular prefix (as set out in Appendix 6.1). The sub-type is stress-repellent in all cases.

ab-

Examples: ab'duct [əb'dʌkt]
ab'scond [əb'skɒnd]

Exceptions: *,ab'dōminal (not a prefix here)
,ab'jection (to contrast with **objection**)
*,ab'normal

ac- Forms a strong syllable before stems beginning with **c** pronounced [s]; when the **c** of the stem is pronounced [k], the **c** of the prefix coalesces with it, giving a weak syllable (e.g. ac'claim [ə'kleɪm]).

Examples: ac'cept [ək'sept]
ac'cessible [ək'sesɪbl]

Exceptions: *,ac'centūal
*,ac'centū,āte
*,ac'centū'ātion

ad-

Examples: ad'just [əd'dʒʌst]
ad'mit [əd'mɪt]

Exceptions: *,ad'mixtūre
,ad'nōminal
,ad'verbial

com-

Examples: com'bīne [kəm'baɪn] (verb)
com'press [kəm'pres] (verb)

con-

Examples: con'dition [kən'dɪʃn]
con'tain [kən'teɪn]

Exceptions: ,con'cave (also pronounced 'con,cāve)
,con'căvity
,con'cūbinage
*,con'gressional
,con'grüity
,con'vex (also pronounced 'con,vex)
,con'vĕxity

ec-   Forms a strong syllable before stems beginning with **c** pronounced [s].

Example: ĕc'centric [ɪk'sentrɪk]

em_A-

Examples: ĕm'balm [ɪm'bɑːm]
ĕm'power [ɪm'paʊə]

en_A-

Examples: ĕn'dūre [ɪn'djʊə]
ĕn'joy [ɪn'dʒɔɪ]

ex_B-

Examples: ĕx'plain [ɪk'spleɪn]
ĕx'trēme [ɪk'striːm]

for₁-

Examples: for'get [fə'get]
for'lorn [fə'lɔːn]

im_B-

Examples: im'port [ɪm'pɔːt] (verb)
im'print [ɪm'prɪnt] (verb)

in_C-

Examples: in'crease [ɪn'kriːs] (verb)
in'hĭbit [ɪn'hɪbɪt]

ob-

Examples: ob'ject [əb'dʒekt]
ob'struct [əb'strʌkt]

per-

Examples: per'form [pə'fɔːm]
per'mit [pə'mɪt] (verb)
per'suāde [pə'sweɪd]

pur-

Examples: pur'port [pə'pɔːt] (verb)
pur'sue [pə'sjuː]
pur'vey [pə'veɪ]

Exception: *ˌpur'loin

sub_B-

Examples: sub'due [səb'djuː]
sub'sīde [səb'saɪd]

suc- Forms a strong syllable before stems beginning with **c** pronounced [s].

Example: suc'ceed [sək'si:d]

sug- Forms a strong syllable before stems beginning with **g** pronounced [dʒ] (American English only).

Example: sug'gest [səg'dʒest] (Amer., ctr. Brit [sə'dʒest])

sur$_B$-

Examples: sur'pass [sə'pɑ:s]
sur'vey [sə'veɪ] (verb)

trans$_B$- Undergoes reduction in the speech of *certain speakers only*; thus not only speakers from northern England have full vowels in the examples given here.

Examples: trans'fer [trəns'fɜ:] (verb)
tran'scrībe [trən'skraɪb]

(e) Unexpectedly Reduced Strong Initial Syllables other than in Prefixes

Note: In the majority of cases the syllable concerned ends in **r** (and the vowel is most likely to be **e**, **i**, or **u**).

The sign * indicates that the pronunciation with a full vowel in the initial syllable may also occur.

At'lanta, At'lantic, At'lantis (in these three words, speakers from northern England may have a full vowel).

Bar'nar,dō, *Ber'mūda, ber'serk.

Caer'narfon, *Caer'philly, Car'marthen, cer'tĭficate, *cer'vīcal, *Cir'cassian, *cir'cūitous, cir'cumference, cur'tail.

fer'ment (verb), *fer'tĭlity, *for'maldĕ,hȳde.

*ger'māne, *Ger'mănic.

*her'măphro,dīte.

Mac- or Mc- in names when unstressed, e.g. McDonald [mək'dɒnld]; *mer'cūrial.

par'tĭcūlar, *por'tray.

*ser'vĭlity, sul'täna.

ther'mŏmeter.

*ver'bātim, *ver'bōse, *ver'bŏsity, ver'mĭlion, ver'năcūlar, *ves'tĭgial, *Vir'gĭlian, Vir'gĭnia, vir'gĭnity.

(f)   Reduction-blocking Consonants Not Blocking Reduction

Note: This list does not include words in which the syllable before the reduced one is weak (these would be accounted for by 'de-stressing').

The sign * indicates that the pronunciation with a full vowel (e.g. ['dæn‚drʌf]) may occur.

> *dandruff ['dændrəf]
> diagnose ['daɪəg‚nəʊz]
> diagnosis ['daɪəg'nəʊsɪs]
> diagnostic ['daɪəg'nɒstɪk]
> eunuch ['juːnək]
> Isaac ['aɪzək]
> Jacob ['dʒeɪkəb]
> Joseph ['dʒəʊzəf]
> julep ['dʒuːləp]
> *object (noun) ['ɒbdʒɪkt]
> *objectivity ['ɒbdʒɪk'tɪvɪtɪ]
> *perfect (adjective) ['pɜːfɪkt]
> *subject (noun, adjective) ['sʌbdʒɪkt]
> *subjectivity ['sʌbdʒɪk'tɪvɪtɪ]

Appendix 7.2   Anomalies in Vowel-Shortening

There are two lists:

(a)   Exceptions to shortening before suffixes.
(b)   Exceptions to trisyllabic shortening other than before suffixes.

Note: Examples with ū or ü have not been included, as these vowels are normally left unchanged by the shortening process.

*   indicates that there is an alternative pronunciation with shortening.

(a)   Exceptions to Shortening before Suffixes

-ative	dë'nōtative
	*rë'stōrative
	'vībrative (or ‚vī'brātive)
-atory	'mīgratory (Amer. -‚tōry)
	'vībratory (Amer. -‚tōry)
-fy	'cōdi‚fȳ
	'glōri‚fȳ
	'nōti‚fȳ
-ic	a'cētic
	'ănal'gēsic
	a'phāsic
	'bāsic
	'chrōmic

'claustro'phōbic
*'cȳclic
ēn'cȳclo'pēdic (note alternative spelling -**paedic** with two vowel
letters)
'ĕpi'cȳclic
'ĕpi'stēmic
*'gēo'dēsic
*'gnōmic ['nəʊ-]
'hĕmi'plēgic
'hȳdric
'hȳdro'phōbic
'nītric
'ortho'pēdic (note alternative spelling -**paedic** with two vowel
letters)
*'ōtic
'păra'plēgic
*pë'lāgic
pho'nēmic
'phthīsic ['taɪ-] or ['θaɪ-]
'psȳchic ['saɪkɪk]
'quadri'plēgic ['kwɒdrɪ-]
*ra'cēmic
'rhōtic
*'scēnic
stra'tēgic
*sy'stēmic

-**ical**   *'āpical
*'cȳclical
*'nōdical
'psȳchical ['saɪkɪkl]

-**ity**   *a'mēnity
o'bēsity
'prōbity

-**ual, -uant**   In 'ēqual, 'pĭ,quant ['pi:,kɒŋ] the **u** belongs with the consonant **q**
and does not form a separate syllable. These words are therefore
only apparent exceptions.

(b)   Exceptions to Trisyllabic Shortening Other than before Suffixes

Note: The following types of words are not included in this list:

(i)   Compounds: 'mīcro,scōpe
(ii)   Words with long vowels spelt with two letters: 'caute,rīze
(iii) Words with stress-neutral prefixes or suffixes: 'fīnery, 'rē-con'nect

*   indicates that there is an alternative pronunciation with a short vowel in the
relevant position.

'āpri,cot, 'artë'mïsia.
'bāke,līte ['beɪkə-], 'bīnary.
'chlōri,nāte, *'cōdi,cil, 'cōma,tōse, 'cȳno,sūre.
'dȳna,mīte, 'dȳna,mō.
*'ēqui,nox, 'ēvo,lute.
'fāvourite, ,for'sȳthia.
*'hēdo,nism, *'hēdo,nist.
'ïrony, 'ïvory.
'kātydid.
'lïbrary.
'nōtary.
'ōmëga, 'ōpa,līne, 'ōvary.
'pāpacy, 'pīracy, 'plēnary, 'prīmacy, 'prīmary, *'prīvacy, 'prōto,col.
'rhōta,cīse, 'Rōmany, 'rōsary, 'rōtary.
'sāvo(u)ry, 'sōda,līte, 'sōle,noid, 'sȳba,rīte, *'sȳco,phant.
'vāgary (or va'gāry), 'vēhement (**h** is unpronounced in an unstressed syllable, and the first and second **es** therefore come together so that the first is lengthened by 'VV lengthening'), *'vēnery, *'vïtamin, 'vōtary.

Appendix 7.3   Anomalies in Vowel Lengthening

The sign * indicates that there is an alternative pronunciation with a long vowel as expected.

*'ăquëous.
bat'tălion, 'bŭnion.
'chăriot, 'clărion, com'pănion, com'pătriot.
dis'crĕtion.
*'ëx'pătriate, *'ëx'pătri,āte.
'fănion, *'fërial.
*'gäli'mătias ([-'mætɪəs] or [-'meɪʃəs]), *'gäsëous.
'Hĕriot.
'indis'crĕtion, Is'căriot, I'tălian.
'lăriat, 'lŏgia ['lɒgɪə] (and its singular 'lŏgion).
'măfia, 'măni,oc.
'ŏnion.
*'pătriot, 'prĕcious.
'rătion, ,rē'pătri,āte, rë'tăli,āte.
'săcri'legious [-'lɪdʒəs], 'Spăniard, 'spĕcial, *'stërë,ō.
'tălion.
'văliant.

Solutions to Exercises

Section 1

1 (a) let, (b) θɪk, (c) bɔːl, (d) greɪs, (e) həum, (f) wɒʃ, (g) raɪt, (h) raɪt, (j) θruː, (k) ðəu, (l) θɔːt, (m) pauə, (n) tʃiːz, (o) dʒɪndʒə, (p) fɪŋgə.

2 (a) ˈărˌrōw   (g) ˌLoüˈïse
   (b) ˈbörŏugh   (h) ˈöven
   (c) ˈbrĕakfast   (j) rëˈfrĭgeˌrātor
   (d) ˌcăˈshiēr   (k) ˈstäff
   (e) dëˈfȳ   (l) ˈsüitable
   (f) ˈgrănūlar   (m) ˈsūitable

3 (a) (i) bleak, (ix) growl, (xii) make, (xix) rush, (xx) sour, (xxiii) trail.
   (b) (ii) bōth, (iii) ˈcalcūˌlāte, (iv) ˈcămoˌmīle, (vi) ëˈnormöus, (vii) ˈfreezing, (viii) greăt, (xiii) ˈnītric, (xxi) ˈsüët, (xxiv) trĕad, (xxvi) ˌvolˈcănic.
   (c) (v) /dɔː/ or /dor/   (xvi) /ˈsūdŏnim/
      (x) /onest/   (xvii) /sūˈdŏnimos/
     (xi) /lam/   (xviii) /puʃ/
     (iv) /plau/   (xxii) /θruː/
     (xv) /pruːv/   (xxv) /trof/

Section 2

1 (a) crowd, (b) possible, (c) detrimental, (d) fortunate, (e) care, (f) splinter, (g) other, (h) invert, (in- is not the negative prefix in-, and so is part of the SP).

2 (a) 1, (b) 2, (c) 2, (d) 2, (e) 1, (f) 3, (g) 3, (h) 4.

3 (a) lo.cal,
   (b) hack.ney ([kn] is not possible word-initially or word-finally, so the syllable boundary has to fall between them),
   (c) win.ter (or possibly wint.er, though the phonetic characteristics of the [n] and the [t] favour the division with the boundary between the n and the t),
   (d) vint.ner (and no other possibility since [tn] is not possible word-initially, and [ntn] is not possible word-initially or word-finally),

(e) /eks.pla.na.ʃon/ (ek.spla.na.ʃon is also possible),

(f) /sub.stan.ʃal/ ([bs] and [bst] are not possible word-initially or word-finally),

(g) frame.work ([mw] is not possible word-initially or word-finally),

(h) /mŏ.to/ (or perhaps mot.to with the double t pronounced as a single consonant),

(j) /pur.pel/ (since [rp] is not possible word-initially).

4 (a) **lō** open, **cal** weak

(b) **ney** both open and weak

(c) **ter** weak

(d) **ner** weak

(e) **pla**, **nā** open; **pla**, /ʃon/ weak

(f) /ʃal/ weak

(g) no open or weak syllables

(h) /mo/ open and weak (the alternative /mot/ is closed and strong), **tō** open and weak (the vowel is underlyingly short, but becomes lengthened in word-final position (see page 23)).

(j) /pel/ weak.

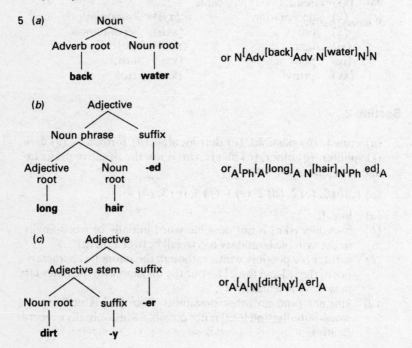

5 (a)

    Noun
    ┌──────┴──────┐
Adverb root   Noun root
    │   │
   back   water

or N[Adv[back]Adv N[water]N]N

(b)

         Adjective
    ┌────────┴────────┐
Noun phrase   suffix
┌──────┴──────┐
Adjective   Noun   -ed
root   root
 │   │
long   hair

orA[Ph[A[long]A N[hair]N]Ph ed]A

(c)

          Adjective
    ┌──────────┴──────────┐
Adjective stem   suffix
┌──────┴──────┐
Noun root   suffix   -er
 │   │
dirt   -y

orA[A[N[dirt]Ny]A er]A

(*d*)

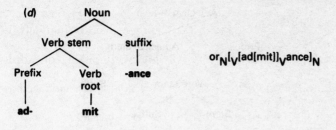

$$or _N[_V[ad[mit]]]_Vance]_N$$

(*e*)

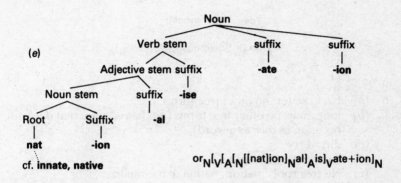

cf. **innate, native**

$$or _N[_V[_A[_N[[nat]ion]_Nal]_Ais]_Vate+ion]_N$$

(*f*)

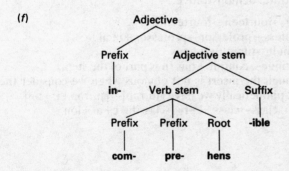

$$_A[in _A[_V[com + pre [hens]]_Vible]_A]_A$$
-hens- is another form of **hend** (cf. the verb **comprehend**.)

(g)

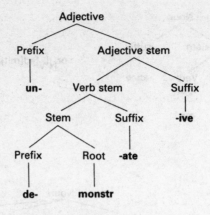

$_A[un_A[_V[[de[monstr]]ate]_Vive]_A]_A$

6 (a) back, water; no other free forms.
   (b) long, hair; no other free forms (not **haired** since that does not occur *on its own* as a word).
   (c) dirt; dirty.
   (d) No free roots; admit.
   (e) No free roots; nation, national, nationalize.
   (f) No free roots; comprehend (with change to last consonant of root), comprehensible.
   (g) ?monster (possibly related to root of **demonstrate**); demonstrate, demonstrative.

7 (a) No: four→fourteen→fourteenth
   (b) Yes: profess→professor→professor +i+al
   (c) Yes: tumult→tumult+u+ous
   (d) No: continue→continu+ous (**u** is part of the stem)
   (e) Yes, though the insert is not obvious when we consider the spelling: phonetically we have [ju:rəp]→[ju:rəp+i:+ən]
   (f) Yes, two: class→class+i+fy→classifi+c+at+ion

Section 3

1 (a) 2, (b) 1, (c) 1 (**im-** is not part of the SP), (d) 3(b)(ii), (e) 1 (-**less** and -**ness** are not part of the SP), (f) 3(b)(i), (g) 2 (**im-** is not part of the SP), (h) 3(b)(i) (-**dō** is weak in spite of the phonetically long vowel), (j) 3(b)(ii) (**in-** is not the negative prefix and is part of the SP), (k) 3(a).

2 (*a*) 5: 'audi`tōrium, (*b*) 4: ë`mĕritus, (*c*) 4: rë`gatta, (*d*) none: `cāre-
lessness, (*e*) 5: 'innū`endō, (*f*) 6(ii): 'sarsăpa`rilla, (*g*) 6(i): a'mon-
til`lädō.

3 (*a*) 6(ii): 'cătama`ran, (*b*) 6(ii): per'sŏnifi`cation, (*c*) 6(i): con'tem-
po`raneous, (*d*) 5: 'gĕron`tocracy, (*e*) 6(i): ëc'clēsi`astical,
(*f*) 6(ii): 'trĭgono`metric, (*g*) 6(i): ë'lectro`static.

Section 4

1 (*a*)

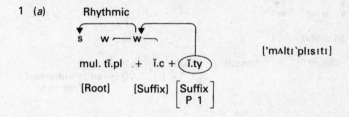

2 (*b*)

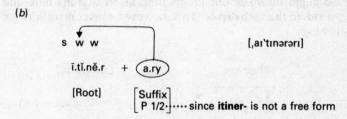

(*c*)

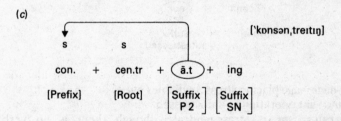

(*d*)

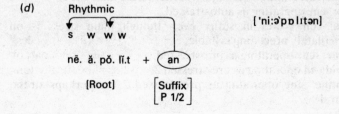

(e)

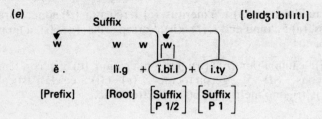

(f)

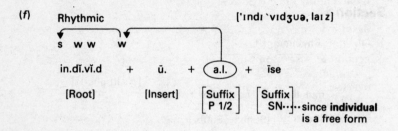

Some case might be made out for treating **in-** as a prefix here and relating **-divid-** to the verb **divide**. This, however, makes no difference to the stressing.

(g)

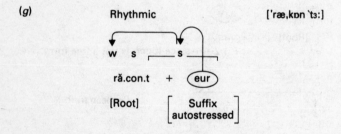

2 **espionage**: -age placing stress 3 syllables back.

gallant: -ant operating as autostressed.

numerator: -or is stress-neutral although there is no verb 'nŭme‚rāte (though the adjective 'nŭmerate does exist).

serene: -ene operating as autostressed.

hostess: full vowel in suffix even though main stress is on immediately preceding syllable.

amateur: -eur operating as pre-stressed.

pyramid: -id operating as pre-stressed 2.

serpentine: -ine operating as pre-stressed 2 (or perhaps stress-neutral).

impoverish: -**ish** operating as pre-stressed 2.

isomorphism: -**ism** operating as pre-stressed 1.

obscurantist: -**ist** operating as pre-stressed 1 or 1/2.

exquisite: -**ite** operating as pre-stressed 1.

systematize: -**ize** operating as pre-stressed 3, or SN with insert -**at**-.

flageolet: -**let** operating as autostressed.

comment: -**ment** operating as pre-stressed and retaining a full vowel although unstressed.

igloo: ending -**oo** not autostressed as it normally is.

alligator: as if derived from a verb 'alli,gāte with stress-neutral -**or**.

desultory: -**ory** operating as pre-stressed 2 (since -**sul**- is a strong syllable and would therefore be expected to take stress).

grandiose: -**ose** operating as autostressed although the word is not a disyllable.

overture; -**ure** operating as pre-stressed 2 (-**ver**- is a strong syllable).

attribute: -**ute** operating as pre-stressed 1 (since -**trĭ**- is a weak syllable).

Section 5

1   (*a*)   finally-stressed: category (d).

     (*b*)   initially-stressed: exception type (i) to category (b).

     (*c*)   initially-stressed: exception to category (c).

     (*d*)   initially-stressed: regular.

     (*e*)   finally-stressed: category (e).

     (*f*)   initially-stressed: regular.

     (*g*)   finally-stressed: category (b).

     (*h*)   initially-stressed: regular (note that **lawn** is the object of the action, not the location, so that this is not an exception of category (a), unlike **lawn tennis**).

     (*j*)   initially-stressed: regular

     (*k*)   finally-stressed: category (c).

     (*l*)   finally-stressed: category (c).

     (*m*)   finally-stressed: category (a).

     (*n*)   initially-stressed: exception type (ii) to category (a).

     (*o*)   initially-stressed: regular.

     (*p*)   finally-stressed: category (d).

     (*q*)   finally-stressed: category (b).

2   (*a*)   initially-stressed: structure 2 (adj.+noun), category (a).

     (*b*)   initially-stressed: structure 19 (verb+particle).

     (*c*)   initially-stressed: structure 7 (verb+noun).

     (*d*)   finally-stressed: structure 5 (numeral+noun+-**er**).

    (*e*)   finally-stressed: structure 6 (adj.+noun+-**er**), cf. noun phrase '**hard** '**line**.
    (*f*)   initially-stressed: structure 2 (adj.+noun), category (b).
    (*g*)   initially-stressed: structure 7 (verb+noun).
    (*h*)   initially-stressed: structure 4 (noun+-'s+noun).
    (*j*)   initially-stressed: structure 2 (adj.+noun), category (a).
    (*k*)   initially-stressed: structure 19 (verb+particle).
    (*l*)   initially-stressed: structure 7 (verb+noun).
    (*m*) finally-stressed: structure 5 (numeral+noun+-**er**).
    (*n*)   initially-stressed: structure 8 (noun+verb).

3   (*a*)   finally-stressed: structure 9 (noun+noun+-**ed**).
    (*b*)   initially-stressed: structure 13 (noun+verb+-**ed**).
    (*c*)   finally-stressed: structure 11 (adj.+noun+-**ed**).
    (*d*)   finally-stressed: exception to structure 13.
    (*e*)   initially-stressed: structure 12 (noun+adj.) category (b).
    (*f*)   initially-stressed: structure 13 (noun+verb+-**ed**).
    (*g*)   finally-stressed: structure 12 (noun+adj.) category (a).
    (*h*)   finally-stressed: structure 10 (numeral+noun+-**ed**).
    (*j*)   finally-stressed: structure 11 (adj.+noun+-**ed**).
    (*k*)   initially-stressed: exception to structure 9.
    (*l*)   finally-stressed: exception to structure 12 category (b).
    (*m*) initially-stressed: structure 12 (noun+adj.) category (b).

4   (*a*)   finally-stressed: category 16 (adv.+verb).
    (*b*)   finally-stressed: category 15 (noun+noun).
    (*c*)   finally-stressed: category 16 (adv.+verb).
    (*d*)   initially-stressed: category 15 (noun+noun).
    (*e*)   initially-stressed: category 14 (noun+verb).
    (*f*)   finally-stressed: category 16 (adv.+verb).

Section 6

		Main stress (Section 3 rules)	Stress repellence	Resulting pattern
(*a*)	accuse (vb)	'accuse (rule 2)	⌒ac̅'cuse	ac'cūse
(*b*)	advent (n.)	'advent (rule 2)	no effect in a noun	'advent
(*c*)	appertain (vb)	'appertain (rule 3a)	⌒ap⌒per'tain	apper'tain
(*d*)	bemoan (vb) (**be**- not in SP)	'moan (rule 1)	not applicable	be'moan
(*e*)	collapse (vb)	'collapse (rule 2)	⌒col̅'lapse	col'lăpse
(*f*)	collapse (n.)	'collapse (rule 2)	⌒col̅'lapse	col'lăpse
(*g*)	compress (vb)	'compress (rule 2)	⌒com̅'press	com'press
(*h*)	compress (n.)	'compress (rule 2)	no effect in a noun	'compress
(*j*)	dethrone (vb) (**de**- not in SP)	'throne	not applicable	dē'thrōne

(*k*)	delay (vb)	'delay (rule 2)	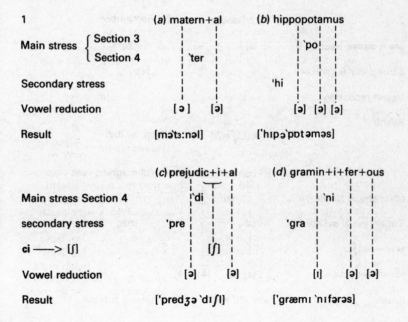de̍'lay	dë'lay
(*l*)	delay (n.)	'delay (rule 2)	de̍'lay	dë'lay
(*m*)	exchequer (n.)	'exchequer (rule 3biii)	ex̍'chequer	ëx'chĕquer
(*n*)	interplay (n.)	'interplay (rule 3a)	no effect in a noun	'interplay
(*o*)	persist (vb)	'persist (rule 2)	per̍'sist	per'sist
(*p*)	prejudge (vb) (**pre**- not in SP)	'judge (rule 1)	not applicable	prē'judge
(*q*)	prefect (n.)	'prefect (rule 2)	no effect in a noun	'prēfect
(*r*)	sublime (adj.)	'sublime (rule 2)	sub̍'lime	sub'līme

2   (*a*)   'concen,trāte, 'confla,grāte, 'conju,gāte, 'conse,crāte, 'consti,pāte, 'consti,tūte, 'consum,māte, 'contem,plāte, 'contri,būte.

    (*b*)   'incre,ment, 'incū,bāte, 'incul,pāte, 'indi,cāte, 'influence, 'inner,vāte, 'inno,vāte, 'insti,gāte, 'insti,tūte, 'insū,lāte, 'inte,grāte, 'inti,māte, 'inun,dāte.

    (*c*)   'perco,lāte, 'pĕro,rāte, 'perpe,trāte, 'perse,cūte, 'perso,nāte.

    (*d*)   'rĕcog,nīze, 'rĕle,gāte, 'rĕno,vāte, 'rĕpli,cāte (and perhaps 'rĕgi,ment, 'rĕgu,lāte, though it seems likely that these have **re**- as part of the root rather than a prefix).

Section 7

1

		(*a*) matern+al		(*b*) hippopotamus			
Main stress	Section 3				'po		
	Section 4	'ter					
Secondary stress				'hi			
Vowel reduction		[ə]	[ə]		[ə]	[ə]	[ə]
Result		[mə'tɜ:nəl]		['hɪpə'pɒtəməs]			

	(*c*) prejudic+i+al			(*d*) gramin+i+fer+ous			
Main stress Section 4	'di				'ni		
secondary stress	'pre			'gra			
ci ——> [ʃ]		[ʃ]					
Vowel reduction	[ə]		[ə]		[ɪ]	[ə]	[ə]
Result	['predʒə 'dɪʃl]			['græmɪ 'nɪfərəs]			

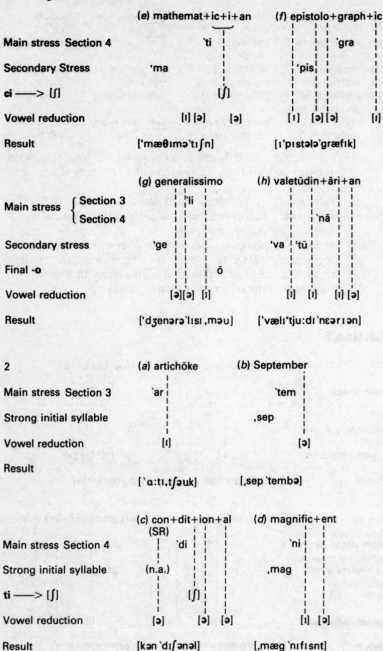

	(e) mathemat+ic+i+an	(f) epistolo+graph+ic
Main stress Section 4	`ti	`gra
Secondary Stress	'ma	'pis
ci ——> [ʃ]	[ʃ]	
Vowel reduction	[ɪ] [ə] [ə]	[ɪ] [ə] [ə] [ɪ]
Result	['mæθɪmə`tɪʃn]	[ɪ'pɪstələ`græfɪk]

	(g) generalissimo	(h) valetūdin+āri+an
Main stress { Section 3	`li	
Section 4		`nā
Secondary stress	'ge	'va 'tū
Final -o		ō
Vowel reduction	[ə][ə] [ɪ]	[ɪ] [ɪ] [ɪ] [ə]
Result	['dʒenərə`lɪsɪ,məu]	['vælɪ'tju:dɪ`nɛərɪən]

2

	(a) artichōke	(b) September
Main stress Section 3	`ar	`tem
Strong initial syllable		,sep
Vowel reduction	[ɪ]	[ə]
Result	[`ɑːtɪ,tʃəuk]	[,sep`tembə]

	(c) con+dit+ion+al (SR)	(d) magnific+ent
Main stress Section 4	`di	`ni
Strong initial syllable	(n.a.)	,mag
ti ——> [ʃ]	[ʃ]	
Vowel reduction	[ə] [ə] [ə]	[ɪ] [ə]
Result	[kən`dɪʃənəl]	[,mæg`nɪfɪsnt]

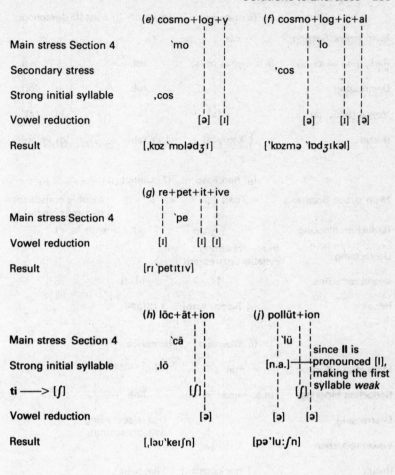

	(e) cosmo+log+y	(f) cosmo+log+ic+al
Main stress Section 4	`mo	`lo
Secondary stress		'cos
Strong initial syllable	,cos	
Vowel reduction	[ə] [ɪ]	[ə] [ɪ] [ə]
Result	[,kɒz`mɒlədʒɪ]	[`kɒzmə`lɒdʒɪkəl]

	(g) re+pet+it+ive
Main stress Section 4	`pe
Vowel reduction	[ɪ] [ɪ] [ɪ]
Result	[rɪ`petɪtɪv]

	(h) lōc+āt+ion	(j) pollüt+ion
Main stress Section 4	`cā	`lü
Strong initial syllable	,lō	[n.a.] — since ll is pronounced [l], making the first syllable *weak*
ti ──> [ʃ]	[ʃ]	[ʃ]
Vowel reduction	[ə]	[ə] [ə]
Result	[,ləʊ`keɪʃn]	[pə`lu:ʃn]

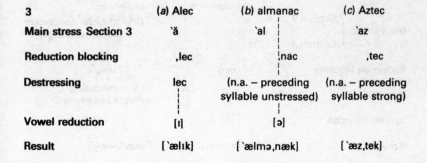

3	(a) Alec	(b) almanac	(c) Aztec
Main stress Section 3	`ă	`al	`az
Reduction blocking	,lec	nac	,tec
Destressing	lec	(n.a. – preceding syllable unstressed)	(n.a. – preceding syllable strong)
Vowel reduction	[ɪ]	[ə]	
Result	[`ælɪk]	[`ælmə,næk]	[`æz,tek]

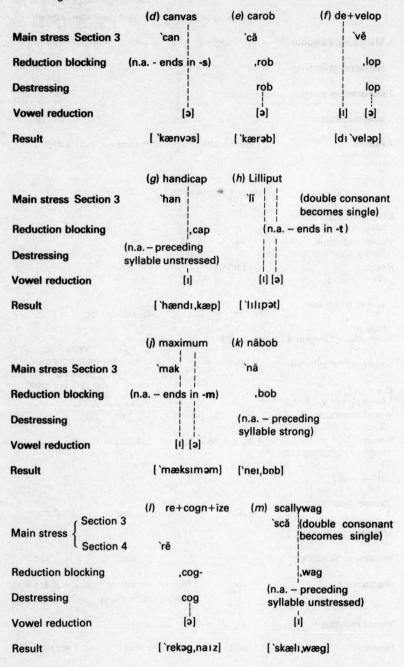

	(*d*) canvas	(*e*) carob	(*f*) de+velop
Main stress Section 3	ˈcan	ˈcă	ˈvĕ
Reduction blocking	(n.a. - ends in -s)	ˌrob	ˌlop
Destressing		rob	lop
Vowel reduction	[ə]	[ə]	[ɪ] [ə]
Result	[ˈkænvəs]	[ˈkærəb]	[dɪ ˈveləp]

	(*g*) handicap	(*h*) Lilliput
Main stress Section 3	ˈhan	ˈlĭ (double consonant becomes single)
Reduction blocking	ˌcap	(n.a. – ends in -t)
Destressing	(n.a. – preceding syllable unstressed)	
Vowel reduction	[ɪ]	[ɪ] [ə]
Result	[ˈhændɪˌkæp]	[ˈlɪlɪpət]

	(*j*) maximum	(*k*) nābob
Main stress Section 3	ˈmak	ˈnā
Reduction blocking	(n.a. – ends in -m)	ˌbob
Destressing		(n.a. – preceding syllable strong)
Vowel reduction	[ɪ] [ə]	
Result	[ˈmæksɪməm]	[ˈneɪˌbɒb]

		(*l*) re+cogn+īze	(*m*) scallywag
Main stress	Section 3		ˈscă (double consonant becomes single)
	Section 4	ˈrĕ	
Reduction blocking		ˌcog-	ˌwag
Destressing		cog	(n.a. – preceding syllable unstressed)
Vowel reduction		[ə]	[ɪ]
Result		[ˈrekəgˌnaɪz]	[ˈskælɪˌwæg]

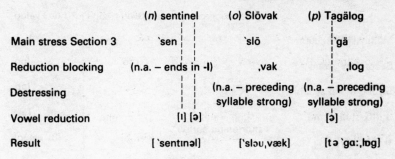

	(n) sentinel	(o) Slōvak	(p) Tagälog
Main stress Section 3	`sen	`slō	`gä
Reduction blocking	(n.a. – ends in -l)	,vak	,log
Destressing		(n.a. – preceding syllable strong)	(n.a. – preceding syllable strong)
Vowel reduction	[ɪ] [ə]		[ə]
Result	[`sentɪnəl]	[`slɔu,væk]	[tə `gɑː,lɒg]

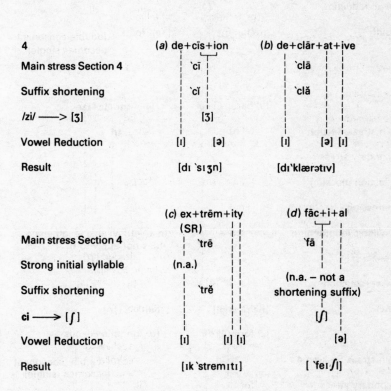

4	(a) de+cīs+ion	(b) de+clār+at+ive
Main stress Section 4	`cī	`clā
Suffix shortening	`cĭ	`clă
/zi/ —> [ʒ]	[ʒ]	
Vowel Reduction	[ɪ] [ə]	[ɪ] [ə] [ɪ]
Result	[dɪ `sɪʒn]	[dɪ`klærətɪv]

	(c) ex+trēm+ity (SR)	(d) fāc+i+al
Main stress Section 4	`trē	`fā
Strong initial syllable	(n.a.)	
Suffix shortening	`trĕ	(n.a. – not a shortening suffix)
ci —> [ʃ]		[ʃ]
Vowel Reduction	[ɪ] [ɪ] [ɪ]	[ə]
Result	[ɪk `stremɪtɪ]	[`feɪʃl]

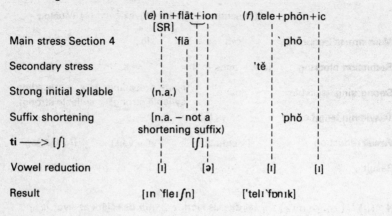

	(e) in+flăt+ion [SR]	(f) tele+phōn+ic
Main stress Section 4	`flā	` phō
Secondary stress		'tĕ
Strong initial syllable	(n.a.)	
Suffix shortening	[n.a. – not a	`phŏ
	shortening suffix)	
ti ——> [ʃ]	[ʃ]	
Vowel reduction	[ɪ] [ə]	[ɪ] [ɪ]
Result	[ɪn `fleɪʃn]	['telɪ `fɒnɪk]

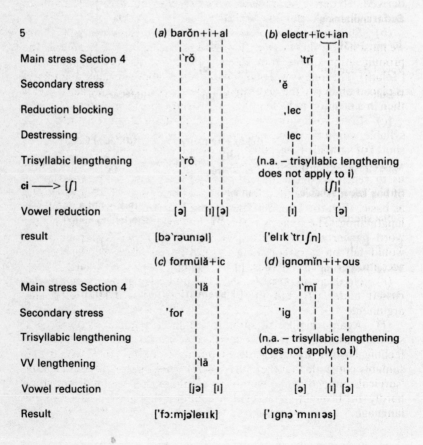

5	(a) barŏn+i+al	(b) electr+ĭc+ian
Main stress Section 4	`rŏ	`trĭ
Secondary stress		'ĕ
Reduction blocking		,lec
Destressing		lec
Trisyllabic lengthening	`rō	(n.a. – trisyllabic lengthening does not apply to i)
ci ——> [ʃ]		[ʃ]
Vowel reduction	[ə] [ɪ] [ə]	[ɪ] [ə]
result	[bə`rəunɪəl]	['elɪk `trɪʃn]

	(c) formūlă+ic	(d) ignomĭn+i+ous
Main stress Section 4	`lă	`mĭ
Secondary stress	'for	'ig
Trisyllabic lengthening		(n.a. – trisyllabic lengthening does not apply to i)
VV lengthening	`lā	
Vowel reduction	[jə] [ɪ]	[ə] [ɪ] [ə]
Result	['fɔːmjə`leɪɪk]	['ɪgnə `mɪnɪəs]

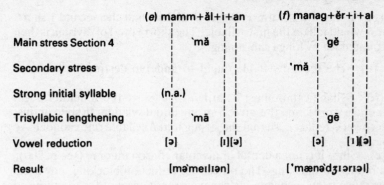

	(e) mamm+ăl+i+an		(f) manag+ĕr+i+al	
Main stress Section 4	ˋmă		ˋgĕ	
Secondary stress			ˈmă	
Strong initial syllable	(n.a.)			
Trisyllabic lengthening	ˋmā		ˋgē	
Vowel reduction	[ə]	[ɪ][ə]	[ə]	[ɪ][ə]
Result	[məˋmeɪlɪən]		[ˈmænəˋdʒɪərɪəl]	

6 (a) Long-vowel form is basic; if the short-vowel form is taken to be basic there is no rule by which the long vowel of **grain** can be derived. To derive ˋ**grănū,lāte**, we must apply main stress (Section 4) and trisyllabic shortening.

(b) Short-vowel form is basic; to get a reduced vowel in [ˈfelənɪ] we must have a short vowel there (this is backed up by considering the pronunciation of the root when it occurs as a word on its own – [ˈfelən]). The long vowel of **feˋlōnious** comes about because main stress is placed on **lo** (by the accentual properties of -**ous**), and the vowel is then in a position to be lengthened by trisyllabic lengthening.

(c) Long-vowel form is basic; if **arthritis** had short **i**, the second syllable would be weak, and main stress would pass over to **ar**-. The short **i** of **arthritic** is accounted for by suffix shortening.

(d) Short-vowel form is basic. The two words given do not allow us to reach a conclusion. If we take long **a** as basic, the short **a** of **barˋbăric** is accounted for by suffix shortening – if we take short **a** as basic, then the long **a** of **barˋbārian** is accounted for by trisyllabic lengthening. The issue is resolved, however, when we consider the word ˋ**barbarous**: if the second syllable of the root were strong, stress would fall on it rather than on the first syllable, because of the accentual properties of -**ous**.

(e) No decision possible; this is a similar situation to the one discussed under (d), but there are no related words to settle the argument.

(f) Again a similar situation to (d) and (e), and the only English speakers who could reach a decision would be those who knew the technical word ˈ**hysteroˋgenic**, 'inducing hysteria' (they would presumably conclude that the short-vowel form is basic). ˈ**Hysterˋectomy**, 'surgical removal of the womb', is etymologically related, but could hardly be brought in as evidence about the present state of the language.

(*g*)   Long-vowel form is basic; if **divisor** had the second **i** short, stress would fall on the first syllable. The short vowel of **divĭsion** is then accounted for by long **i** shortening.

7   (*a*)   The second syllable ought to undergo destressing but does not.

(*b*)   Syllabification must be at.lan.t+ic (since **tl** can neither begin nor end a word), and this gives a strong initial syllable. In spite of this, the vowel is reduced, so that the strong initial syllable rule cannot have operated.

(*c*)   Since it is not a dental or alveolar consonant or **m** (see p. 200), **f** is reduction-blocking. The process of reduction blocking, however, must have been suspended, since we cannot account for the reduced vowel by destressing (the first syllable is strong).

(*d*)   Again, the second syllable should undergo destressing, but does not.

(*e*)   Suffix shortening should apply to give [əˈbesɪtɪ].

(*f*)   Reduction blocking must have applied in the final syllable, although -**t** is not a reduction-blocking consonant.

8   (*a*)   (i) is regular; (ii) involves not applying reduction blocking before a reduction-blocking consonant.

(*b*)   (ii) is regular; (i) fails to undergo trisyllabic shortening.

(*c*)   (i) is regular; (ii) fails to undergo trisyllabic lengthening.

(*d*)   (i) is regular; (ii) fails to undergo reduction blocking (or alternatively, it undergoes destressing, although the conditions for the application of this rule are not fulfilled).

(*e*)   (ii) is regular; (i) fails to undergo destressing (and -**rd** is not a reduction-blocking combination anyway).

(*f*)   (ii) is regular; (i) fails to undergo trisyllabic shortening.

Index

Entries in **bold type** refer to **definitions** of the terms concerned. Entries in *italics* refer to **lists** of the elements designated by the term.